THREE CLASSICAL POETS

Three Classical Poets

Sappho, Catullus, and Juvenal

Richard Jenkyns

Harvard University Press
Cambridge, Massachusetts
1982

Library of Congress Cataloging in Publication Data

Jenkyns, Richard.
    Three classical poets—Sappho, Catullus, and
Juvenal.

    Bibliography: p.
    Includes index.
    1. Classical poetry—History and criticism.
2. Sappho—Criticism and interpretation. 3. Catullus,
Gaius Valerius—Criticism and interpretation. 4. Juvenal
—Criticism and interpretation. I. Title. II. Title:
3 classical poets—Sappho, Catullus, and Juvenal.
PA3019.J4   881'.01'09   82–1011
ISBN 0–674–88895–2   .   AACR2

CONTENTS

PREFACE

This book has both general and particular purposes. On the particular plane it seeks to contribute to the understanding of three individual poets, selected for no more complex reason than that I thought myself to have something worth saying about them. The general purpose is to maintain that no single theory, method or system will suffice for the understanding and appreciation of all ancient poetry, still less for all poetry whatsoever. If this seems to any reader an obvious truth, I can only reply that I wish all scholars thought so.

My general purpose is most explicit in the second section of the book, on the sixty-fourth poem of Catullus, but it is also, by implication, pervasive throughout. None the less, the book contains no sustained or exhaustive assault upon those positions with which I disagree, and this for three reasons. The first is that polemic is never attractive, though sometimes inevitable. The second is that although I do not hold with Blake that 'To Generalise is to be an Idiot. To Particularise is the Alone Distinction of Merit', I think that we are most likely to come to some understanding of the nature of poetry not by arguing about first principles but through an empirical study of individual poems and poets, and a recognition of their diversity. The third reason is that I am not eager to condemn any method of approach, but rather to encourage an awareness of its limitations. What we need is to combine a readiness to exploit any method that may be able to enlighten us with the flexibility that will allow us to abandon it in places where it no longer seems to be useful. The rejection of dogmatism is the one dogma that is advocated by this book.

Thus, though critical of the lengths to which 'generic studies' have been carried, I would not want to deny that they have their place. Equally, while I do not believe that there is necessarily a single 'right' interpretation of a poem or that complete objectivity is attainable in literary judgments, the view that 'there are as many valid readings of a poem as there are readers', though apparently espoused by a good many intelligent people, seems to me sentimental, unevidenced and upon the briefest reflection manifestly false. I believe that we should approach each poem on the poet's own terms, but not that we are thereby prevented from making judgments of quality. Two critics may agree about what Virgil, for example, was trying to do in the *Aeneid* and yet differ profoundly over how far he succeeded. Moreover, we need not, and indeed should not, place an equal value upon every type

of poetry; we may well conclude that an imperfect *Aeneid* is worth
more than a faultless Horatian ode. We shall certainly not understand
Catullus' *Peleus and Thetis* unless we realise what kind of poem it is;
but it may still remain an open question how far that kind is to be
admired.

Though a historical understanding of poetry may be very desirable,
we are not utterly crippled where this is not attainable. I have tried
to suggest that although we know almost nothing useful about the
background against which Sappho lived and composed, we are not
seriously hindered in our aesthetic appreciation by this limitation
(most of the many vexing problems with which her poetry presents us
spring from the fragmentary nature of what has survived, not from
historical ignorance). Where historical information is more abundant,
it too should be used flexibly, not just to reveal patterns, but to show
when the pattern fails to fit. We appreciate Juvenal better when we
see him as a child of his time, but also when we see in what ways he
was unique among his contemporaries.

I have referred freely to renaissance and later literature for comparison, contrast or analogy whenever it has seemed to me enlightening to do so. But here too I have had a more general purpose as well.
How far the poetry of antiquity is like or unlike that of moore recent
times is a very interesting question, but I have noticed that those who
are most absolute upon this topic usually display no interest in any
literature much later than the fourth century A.D. Unless we are
willing to set ancient and modern side by side, claims about the
peculiar character of classical poetry are likely to remain assertiOn
merely.

I am aware of my indebtedness to many scholars, and there must be
other debts of which I am unconscious. In the case of Sappho I have
gained above all from the work of Sir Denys Page, but I should also
make explicit mention of the books of Schadewaldt, Bowra and Kirkwood and the monumental edition of Sappho and Alcaeus by E.-M.
Voigt. I have also learnt from more individual articles than can be
mentioned here; I think it best not to try to single out a few names for
especial tribute. For Catullus 64 I have found Klingner a wise guide;
Fordyce's commentary was a reliable support; and though I now disagree with much of it, J. C. Bramble's important article first stimulated my interest in the poem. In the case of Juvenal I have perhaps
profited most from Duff, de Decker, Mason and Kenney. Throughout
the book I realise that I have been trampling on other people's special
fields; I hope for indulgence, but I am prepared to face the
consequences.

With one exception I have cited Catullus and Juvenal from the
Oxford texts of Mynors and Clausen. In the case of Sappho, no such
simple solution seemed possible; I have based myself on Page's *Lyrica*

Graeca Selecta (or, where a fragment was not included in that volume, on Lobel and Page's *Poetarum Lesbiorum Fragmenta*), but I have sometimes followed other scholars, and for the sake of readability I have allowed in a few plausible supplements, indicating them only when I thought a point of interpretation might be affected. I have translated what I quote; it will be obvious that these translations have no pretensions to literary merit whatever. I am grateful to Dr Richard Buxton, Mr Jasper Griffin and Professor Niall Rudd for reading drafts of various parts of this book and giving me their advice; there has been plenty of time for me to add in the mistakes and misjudgements since.

R.H.A.J.

Part One

The Poetry of Sappho and its Reputation

1

In 1895 Pierre Louÿs, minor poet and highbrow pornographer, published a small, plump volume entitled *Les Chansons de Bilitis*. It contained a series of fairly short passages in prose, composed by Louÿs himself but purporting to be translations of Greek poems found in an Egyptian tomb. They were, apparently, the intimate musings of a Pamphylian girl – Bilitis – who had come to Lesbos in her youth, met Sappho, fallen passionately in love with another woman, and finally made her way to Amathus, where she set up as a temple prostitute. As one would expect, the work is a somewhat prurient mixture of aestheticism and titillation. It has been preserved from oblivion principally because Debussy set three of the poems to music, but classical scholars remember them for another reason also: for exciting the wrath of Wilamowitz. The great man was enraged by the slur that they cast upon the morality of Sappho and her circle, and in a long and devastating review, buried in the pages of a learned journal, he exposed the impudent forgery. It is difficult to believe that Louÿs can seriously have expected to deceive anybody – one French reviewer spoke of 'une pastiche délicieuse' – but Wilamowitz was undeterred,[1] and the Parisian butterfly was sentenced to be broken upon the Prussian wheel. After the article had appeared, Louÿs responded gaily with a new edition of the poems, now augmented by a bogus bibliography, which began with a German edition of the 'original' Greek text ('Leipzig, 1894', he added helpfully) and included Wilamowitz's review, with the author's name misspelled; however, so small a sense of the ridiculous did the great scholar have that as late as 1913 he reprinted his piece as part of his book *Sappho und Simonides*, adding

[1] But he was evidently puzzled. Near the beginning of his review he spoke of Louÿs's 'strange pedantry, almost as if he wanted to mystify' (*Sappho und Simonides*, p. 63), but then took laborious care to 'expose' his victim.

further expostulations. When Sappho's name came up nowadays, he protested, more people thought of perversion than of a great poetess, but they were scandalously wrong: Sappho was an excellent woman, wife and mother, a paragon of the domestic virtues.

Now for every person who can appreciate what makes a scholar outstanding there must be a dozen who can see the joke when he slips on a banana-skin, and as Bentley is chiefly remembered today for his disastrous edition of Milton, so Wilamowitz is perhaps best known for the silly things he said about Sappho. It may therefore seem tasteless to draw attention, yet again, to an eminent man's lapse of judgment; however, it is so extraordinary that it deserves consideration by any-one who is interested in the history of taste. It is not as if it were an isolated phenomenon. Wilamowitz saw himself as carrying on the torch handed to him by Welcker, in whose *Minor Writings* the virtue of Sappho is something of a leitmotiv, and K. O. Müller spoke with fervour of her 'unimpeached honour' and 'moral worth'.[2] In 1897 Gil-bert Murray, then a young professor at Glasgow, wrote in his *Ancient Greek Literature* (ch. 4), 'It is clear that Sappho was a respectable person in Lesbos; and there is no good early evidence to show that the Lesbian standard was low.' It is probable, none the less, that the moral codes of archaic Mytilene and late Victorian Kelvinside were discern-ibly different. In France Sappho's character was ardently defended by Théodore Reinach, who compared her to Mme de Sévigné. That was in 1911; around the same time appeared *La chaste Sappho . . . ,* by a doctor named Bascoul, who found himself remodelling his heroine's verses to fit the high opinion that he had imbibed, from that same poetry, of her moral excellence (Mora, p. 203). As late as 1935 Gennaro Perrotta could write (p. 52), 'Sappho felt profoundly not only sisterly affection, but also maternal love: no delicate or kindly sentiment was a stranger to her soul.' It is the word 'profoundly' ('profondamente') that gives him away; we may (perhaps) be able to conclude that Sappho had these amiable feelings, but how can we gauge their depth? Eighty years earlier William Mure, whose *Critical History of the Language and Literature of Antient Greece* (1850–7) was a standard work in the mid-Victorian age, described Sappho as 'a woman of gen-erous disposition, affectionate heart, and independent spirit'. 'Her in-dulgence of the passion of love,' he wrote (vol. 3, p. 29), 'as of every other appetite, sensual or intellectual, while setting at nought all moral restraints, was marked by her own peculiar refinement of taste, exclusive of every approach to low excess or profligacy.' This was an enthusiastic, yet essentially a moderate view. Mure attacked the 'popular authorities of the present day' who presented Sappho as 'a

---

[2] Welcker, *Kleine Schriften*, esp. vol. 2, p. 80ff.; Müller, *A History of the Literature of Ancient Greece* (London, 1858), vol. 1, p. 229.

dazzling extreme of beauty and brilliancy, exhibiting a model of perfection physical and moral, such as was never probably exemplified in
woman . . .' And to show what he meant he cited a German scholar
named Richter: 'In Sappho a warm and profound sensibility, a virgin
purity, feminine softness, and delicacy of sentiment and feeling, were
combined with the native probity and simplicity of the Aeolian character: and although imbued with a fine perception of the beautiful and
brilliant, she preferred genuine conscious rectitude to every other
source of human enjoyment.'

The silliness was by no means all on one side: Louÿs was no more
an isolated phenomenon than Wilamowitz. John Addington Symonds,
Swinburne, and other heroes of the Victorian counter-culture exhibi-
ted a wild enthusiasm for a Sappho very different from the lady
described by Mure and Murray. Swinburne's Sappho overflows with a
lurid eroticism which reads rather like a cross between *The Song of
Solomon* and *Pale hands I loved beside the Shalimar*. Here is an
extract from *Anactoria*, a poem which Harold Acton is said to have
declaimed through his megaphone from the Meadow Building of Christ
Church to undergraduates coming back from Eights:

> Ah that my mouth for Muses' milk were fed
> On the sweet blood thy sweet small wounds had bled!
> That with my tongue I felt them, and could taste
> The faint flakes from thy bosom to the waist!
> That I could drink thy veins as wine, and eat
> Thy breasts like honey! that from face to feet
> Thy body were abolished and consumed,
> And in my flesh thy very flesh entombed!
> Ah, ah, thy beauty! like a beast it bites,
> Stings like an adder, like an arrow smites.

This is really rather comic stuff: brevity and restraint are two Hellenic
qualities which Swinburne, passionate Hellenist though he was, never
thought of acquiring. The painful truth is that Swinburne's Sappho,
despite her rather jolly masochism, has one very Victorian quality:
she is pompous. It is sad that he made her so absurd, for his adoration
was almost boundless: 'Aeschylus,' he once said, 'is the greatest poet
who ever was also a prophet, Shakespeare is the greatest dramatist
who ever was also a poet; but Sappho is simply nothing less – as she
is certainly nothing more – than the greatest poet who ever was at
all.'[3] Symonds's admiration was almost as great: he described her work
as 'the most exquisite lyrical poetry that the world has known', con-

---

[3] Cecil Y. Lang (ed.), *The Swinburne Letters* (New Haven, 1959–62), vol. 4, p. 124. By
way of compensation some words from Sappho's fr. 2 were perhaps the inspiration for
a famous line in the first chorus of *Atalanta in Calydon*: 'With lisp of leaves and ripple
of rain.'

cluding that 'the world has suffered no greater literary loss than the loss of Sappho's poems . . . of all the poets of the world, of all the illustrious artists of all literatures, Sappho is the one whose every word has a peculiar and unmistakable perfume, a seal of absolute perfection and inimitable grace.'[4]

Why did Sappho's poetry and way of life arouse such intense passions? The phenomenon is so very odd that it demands some explanation. Of course, the Victorians were vigorous hero-worshippers; nowadays we positively prefer our heroes to have feet of clay, but our ancestors demanded that the objects of their admiration should be more or less above reproach. Many Victorians, too, had an exalted not to say fantastic picture of womanhood; to question the orthodoxy of Sappho's morality was to cast a slur upon the whole sex. It is perhaps no coincidence that some of the silliest examples of Sappho-worship come from Germany; in Wilamowitz's lifetime there was a widespread belief among his countrymen that the ancient Greeks were really Germans dressed up in chitons, and it may not be too far-fetched to suppose that he was subconsciously defending German womanhood against the assaults of a decadent Frenchman. A glance down the very first page of the section on Sappho in his book (p. 17) is sufficiently revealing: already during the French *grand siècle* . . . frivolity of the eighteenth century . . . Sappho to share the fate of Joan of Arc . . . Sappho and Lesbos obscene words in French . . . Welcker to the rescue. The names and phrases in his original review tell the same story: '*fin de siècle*' . . . 'a piece of Parisian life' . . . ; and to complete the picture those exemplars of Gallic wickedness, Huysmans and the brothers Goncourt (pp. 68, 71, 77). These bogeys of the night are scattered, in the final sentence of the article (p. 78) by the last radiant words of the central masterpiece of German literature, *Faust*: 'The eternal feminine draws us on.'[5] To Sappho herself Wilamowitz adopted an attitude of romantic chivalry,[6] touching in so formidable a scholar; his purpose, he said (p. 63), was 'to speak of things that have long lain upon my heart. I have to do with the purity of a great woman.' 'My bile overflowed,' he later admitted impenitently (p. 18), and that bile may have been exceptional; but surveying England and Germany generally, we must also remember a nagging worry that plagued dons, clergymen, schoolmasters and the other pillars of traditional classical education in the nineteenth century: the fear that Greek literature and philo-

---

[4] *Studies of the Greek Poets* (3rd edn., London, 1902), vol. 1, p. 292f.

[5] The same wildly inappropriate quotation had occurred in 1871 to T. W. Higginson, when defending Sappho's reputation to the American public (Robinson, p. 238).

[6] One catches the same atmosphere when Wilamowitz's pupil Robinson describes Welcker as 'the bachelor who loved Sappho's genius and who by his chivalrous vindication made himself her knight'. Welcker and Wilamowitz, he adds, were two of the three 'great defenders' who 'rescued' her from 'disgrace' (p. 129).

sophy could be used to defend adultery, homosexuality, atheism, and so on. It was important that the Greeks should be on the side of the angels.

But these are only partial explanations. After all, who cares a fig about Anyte or Nossis, or any other poetess of ancient Greece? There is one belief which Symonds, Wilamowitz and the rest of them have in common, and that is a fervent conviction of Sappho's greatness. My purpose is to ask whether this belief is justified, indeed whether it is even tenable. Sappho was a prolific writer, but since only a few fragments have survived, are we in any position to say that she was a major poet, let alone to rank her among the greatest in the world? In one of his essays T. S. Eliot took as the test of a major poet, 'Whether a knowledge of the whole, or at least of a very large part, of a poet's work, makes one enjoy more, because it makes one understand better, any one of his poems. That implies a significant unity in his whole work.'[7] This is a test which manifestly cannot be applied to Sappho. In somewhat similar vein, W. H. Auden asserted that a poet must satisfy 'about three and a half' of five conditions to qualify as major: 'He must write a lot. His poems must show a wide range in subject matter and treatment. He must exhibit an unmistakable originality of vision and style. He must be a master of verse technique.' Lastly, 'In the case of the major poet, the process of maturing continues until he dies.'[8] These conditions seem designed to deposit Auden himself neatly on the right side of the divide; none the less, they would be widely accepted by modern critics. Sappho narrowly avoids automatic disqualification because we know that she 'wrote a lot', but it cannot honestly be said that this is something which we can deduce from the nature of her surviving poetry. It is simply a piece of evidence which we happen, by chance, to possess. Besides, we know little of value about Sappho's background and way of life, about possible literary antecedents, or even about her purpose in composing her poems. In her case so many of the techniques which the literary critic expects to be able to use are simply not available. We are compelled to study the individual fragments of her poetry in almost total isolation; we have to handle them like pieces of treasure trove lifted from the sands of the desert (which is literally what some of them are). We can pick them up like bibelots, so to speak, and turn them to the light, assessing their value as aesthetically pleasing objects. There is little else we can do. Yet these poor fragments, as we have seen, have excited the passionate admiration of a remarkable diversity of people. However incomplete our critical armoury may be, Sappho's remains deserve a close examination.

---

[7] *On Poetry and Poets* (London, 1957), p. 49f. ('What is Minor Poetry?').
[8] *Nineteenth-Century Minor Poets* (London, 1967), p. 17.

But this examination should not be conducted without some pre-
liminary thought about method. One approach which is unlikely to
get us far with Sappho is what might be called the Theory of Poetic
Productivity. For instance, a recent writer on fr.16 has striven to find
in the myth of Helen as many points of correspondence with the rest
of the poem as he can: 'For the simpler a comparison is, the less it can
express; and if Sappho deserves her reputation we should not expect
her to indulge in mere superfluities' (Macleod, p. 217). The *consequences* of analysis based upon this argument may often be satisfactory: Virgil, it is clear, composed similes containing many points of
correspondence, with results that are sometimes brilliant, sometimes
of a rather dead efficiency; and the complexity of Aeschylus' imagery
is one of the greatest achievements of Greek art. But the argument
itself is false. When Angus says of Macbeth (act 5, sc. 2, line 17f.),

> Now does he feel
> His secret murders sticking on his hands

he utters a metaphor of unsurpassed power. Much could be written,
no doubt, on why these words are so perfectly expressive of trapped
and furtive guilt (if it is not obvious); but the explanation would not
consist in multiplying correspondences. The metaphor grips the imagination with such force precisely because of its simplicity, because
it instantly persuades us that it is *right*: we should not know Macbeth's
fear and shame as we do if the image were not so plain and immediately apprehensible. Few lyric poems have been more admired (in
Germany at least) than Gretchen's song at the spinning-wheel, and
that admiration has been largely for its very simplicity. If we were to
discover ingenuity or elaboration in this song, we should have destroyed the very means by which it affects its audience. I do not claim
that Sappho is never elaborate or ingenious, but I do suspect that
those who assume that multiplicity or density must be found in her
work if her reputation is to be salvaged are likely to be led either to
disappointment or to fantasy. The latter consequence is obvious, and
common enough; the former is more rarely found, but Page's rather
cool assessment seems to derive from a notion that a poet whose work
is not complex or profound (at least in the usual sense) cannot be of
really high worth.

If it were not a matter of necessity to approach Sappho by first
looking at her fragments in isolation, it should in any case be a matter
of choice. The wrong approach is to start from some general presupposition about the nature of ancient or archaic poetry and force her
poems to fit it. This principle may seem a truism, but it has been
continually ignored. Wilamowitz's preposterous theory that fr.31 was

designed to be sung at a marriage ceremony derives from a general presupposition – archaic poetry was always composed for a particular occasion, and what other occasion but a wedding can we imagine here? – and it persuaded such notable scholars as Schadewaldt, Bowra and Snell. Nor is the danger now safely in the past. Another recent writer on fr.16 purports to demonstrate from the rhetorical structure of Greek poetry, manifested in Pindar, that the poem is 'a negative moral exemplum set in an encomium' (Howie (1977), p. 209). The parallels with Pindar lead him to discover 'two remarkable omissions' that have not bothered previous readers: 'the wider ill consequences of Helen's action and the identity of her beloved, Paris' (p. 218). How are we to solve this problem? The former omission, we learn, has a delicate effect: 'It ensures that Sappho's love for Anactoria is not given an exaggerated importance' (p. 222). Now the fifth stanza of this fragment has stamped itself upon the memory of countless readers; it is perhaps the most radiant declaration of love in all Greek poetry. What has got into the scholar who, arriving at the conclusion that Sappho wishes not to emphasise her love, does not deduce that he has been arguing from false premisses? Of course it is proper to consider whether external evidence can help us to guess the significance of fragmentary verses, of course we need in the study of all poetry to consider the social and literary context taken for granted by the writer and his audience; but the former process should always be regarded as a *pis-aller*, and the latter should be carefully tested against the poems themselves. If Sappho fits the pattern that we have predicted for her, well and good; if not, we must think again. But why indeed should we be disappointed if conventions and parallels do not enable us to dispense with the individual voice?

2

Ποικιλόθρον᾽ ἀθανάτ᾽Ἀφρόδιτα,
παῖ Δίος δολόπλοκε, λίσσομαί σε·
μή μ᾽ἄσαισι μηδ᾽ ὀνίαισι δάμνα,
πότνια, θῦμον,

ἀλλὰ τυίδ᾽ ἔλθ᾽, αἴ ποτα κἀτέρωτα   5
τὰς ἔμας αὔδας ἀίοισα πήλοι
ἔκλυες, πάτρος δὲ δόμον λίποισα
χρύσιον ἦλθες

ἄρμ᾽ ὑπασδεύξαισα· κάλοι δέ σ᾽ἆγον
ὤκεες στροῦθοι περὶ γᾶς μελαίνας   10
πύκνα δίννεντες πτέρ᾽ ἀπ᾽ ὠράνωἴθε-
ρος διὰ μέσσω·

αἶψα δ᾽ ἐξίκοντο, σὺ δ᾽ ὦ μάκαιρα
μειδιαίσαισ᾽ ἀθανάτωι προσώπωι
ἦρε᾽ ὄττι δηὖτε πέπονθα κὤττι   15
δηὖτε κάλημμι

κὤττι μοι μάλιστα θέλω γένεσθαι
μαινόλαι θύμωι· τίνα δηὖτε πείθω
ἄψ ἄγην ἐς σὰν φιλότατα; τίς σ᾽ ὦ
Ψάπφ᾽ ἀδικήει;   20

καὶ γὰρ αἰ φεύγει, ταχέως διώξει,
αἰ δὲ δῶρα μὴ δέκετ᾽, ἀλλὰ δώσει,
αἰ δὲ μὴ φίλει, ταχέως φιλήσει
κοὐκ ἐθέλοισα.

ἔλθε μοι καὶ νῦν, χαλέπαν δὲ λῦσον   25
ἐκ μερίμναν, ὄσσα δέ μοι τέλεσσαι
θῦμος ἰμέρρει, τέλεσον, σὺ δ᾽ αὔτα
σύμμαχος ἔσσο.

[Elaborate-throned immortal Aphrodite, child of Zeus, weaver of wiles, I
entreat you, do not overpower my spirit, lady, with pain and anguish; but
come hither, if ever before you heard my voice from afar and hearkened
to it, and came, leaving your father's house, yoking your golden chariot.
Fair swift sparrows brought you over the black earth, with rapid fluttering of wings, from heaven through the middle air. Swiftly they came; and
you, blessed one, smiling with immortal face, asked me what had happened to me now, why now again I was calling, what in my frenzied spirit
I most wanted for myself: 'Whom now am I to persuade back (?) into
friendship with you? who wrongs you, Sappho? For if she flees, she shall
soon pursue; if she does not accept gifts, yet shall she give them; if she
does not love, she shall soon love even against her will.' Come to me now
also, free me from harsh anxiety, accomplish what my spirit desires to
accomplish, and be yourself my ally.]

Fr.1 is almost certainly the only complete poem of Sappho to survive.[9] Formally it is a cletic or 'summoning' hymn containing a prayer
for aid. These prayers follow a regular pattern. The suppliant begins
by addressing the god whose help he desires. The god may have numerous names or cult-titles; so the suppliant will probably use several
of these, often adding for safety's sake a blanket clause: 'or by whatever name you prefer to be called.' The god may also need to be fetched
from a particular place: 'Come to me from Olympus,' the suppliant
may say, or 'from Cyprus,' or again he may use a blanket clause: 'from
wherever you may now be.' There may follow a story illustrating the
god's power before the suppliant states his request. Sappho's poem has

[9] Few scholars, if any, now think that fr. 31 ends at line 16. I do not believe that fr.
168b Voigt (= fr. 94D) is by Sappho, least of all if it is complete in four lines (see below,
p. 79).

a private and personal quality which makes it unlike the hymns written by any other early Greek poet; none the less, it adopts the conventional form.

The opening words set the tone of the whole poem and conjure up an atmosphere that is at once splendid, intimate and gently humorous. Every word counts. *poikilothrone* immediately presents us with a vivid visual picture: Aphrodite in this poem is opulently and delightfully ornamental, as we shall see again in lines 7–12 and 14. But there is another facet to the word. *poikilothron'* sounds remarkably like *poiki-lophron* ('cunning-minded'), which occurs, indeed, in some of the manuscripts. Whether or not Sappho's original audience sensed a *double entendre*, *poikilos* and its compounds are inherently ambivalent. The very first word of the poem suggests Aphrodite's dual character: on the one hand she is an Olympian deity, on the other she is Sappho's subtle and teasing friend. *athanata* ('immortal') amplifies the one side of her personality, *doloploke* ('weaver of wiles') the other. *athanata* is an important word: not only does it counteract the gentle touches of humour in *poikilothrone* and *doloploke*, but the word is also to recur with stunning effect in line 14. Even *pai Dios* ('child of Zeus') is significant, for Aphrodite must leave her father's house (line 7) and the throne upon which she is seated (*poikilothrone* again) in order to come to Sappho's aid. The poem does not simply begin with a pile of epithets; every word is carefully chosen and peculiarly apt for its place in this particular poem. There is also a nice ambivalence of tone, which is brought out by the succeeding words, *lissomai se* ('I entreat you'). The opening lines are in the form of a solemn address to a deity, but the epithets are not cult titles; indeed both *poikilothronos* and *doloplokos* seem to be of Sappho's own coinage. Is there rather not something wheedling, cajoling in the string of laudatory adjectives that Sappho heaps upon her patroness, followed by the coaxing *lissomai se*? Yet *formally* this is a cletic hymn; the intimacy within the traditional structure is a part of the charm.

'Not with *asai* nor yet with *oniai*'; the structure of the sentence demands a difference of nuance between these two nouns. Our understanding is limited, but it is at least clear that these are forceful words: *asē* is found in the medical writers with the sense of 'surfeit' or 'nausea'. And even with an imperfect understanding, we can still appreciate the verse technique. The Sapphic stanza might seem to be a rigid verse form, but Sappho handles it with fluency and grace; it is worth observing that Horace, who so powerfully transformed the Alcaic stanza, never managed to use the Sapphic stanza with quite Sappho's elegance and ease. Essentially it is a three-line unit, the third line being extended for a further five syllables. Here the extended third line seems exactly to fit the pleading, supplicatory tone of Sappho's address. This is matched by the lingering, coaxing effect of *mē* picked up by *mēde*, the three-syllabled word *asaisi* answered by the four-syllabled *oniaisi* and the predicate interrupted, in a tone of appeal, by *potnia*. The sound of these lines, too, with their delicate blend of *m*'s, *n*'s and *s*'s is very euphonious; it is to Dionysius' admiration of the poem's euphony that we owe its preservation.

In the second stanza Sappho resumes (or assumes) a tone of formal invocation; but her imagination remains vivid. *pēloi* is a significant word: Aphrodite has to come *from afar*. Page renders *aïoisa* 'catch hearing of'; perhaps this word too helps to suggest Aphrodite's physical and emotional remoteness from Sappho in her father's house. So the description of Aphrodite's journey which occupies lines 7–12 is not merely an opportunity for Sappho to exhibit her descriptive powers, or even to glorify the goddess, though this in a hymn is important. However, even as pure description, these are splendid lines. Page has drawn attention to some of their qualities: the gorgeous image of the golden chariot passing over the black earth,[10] and the sparrows, 'notorious for wantonness and fecundity'. Now sparrows are also notorious for noise and chatter, and the mere mention of them drawing a chariot creates a picture of vigorous bustle, reinforced by *pukna dinnentes*. The metrical 'fussiness' of the following words – the elisions, the synecphonesis, the word *aitheros* spilling over from line 11 into line 12 – sustains the atmosphere of energetic agitation. Then in line 13 the chariot comes to a sudden halt, and Aphrodite steps into the foreground of the scene. The tempo slows. Line 14 is entrancing; it consists of just three large words which sprawl luxuriously across it; the repeated *ai* sounds in the first word, the repeated *o*'s in the third enhance its peculiar character of lingering languorousness.[11] But it is not only the sound of these words that seems so miraculous, it is also what they say; lines 13–14 form the culminating expression of Aphrodite's dual character. She is *makaira* ('blessed one'), a felicitous word that expresses the vast distance between the eternal calm of the Olympian goddess and Sappho's intense but transient passions. 'Smiling with immortal face' – on one level this is the perfect realisation of Aphrodite's divine serenity (and of course she is traditionally *philommeidēs*, a lover of smiles); and yet the goddess's smile, as Sappho describes it, is so radiant, so entrancing, that paradoxically it seems to be entirely 'human'. Aphrodite's enquiries display this same combination of intimacy and distance. Page compares her to a mother with a troublesome child, and the comparison is apt, for no one can be more lovingly solicitous than a mother, and yet her experiences are

[10] Unless *chrusion* ('golden') should be taken with *domon* ('house').

[11] I am supposing that the *ō* element in the dipthong *ōi* is distinctly audible before the 'glide' to a different sound quality begins.

enormously far removed from those of her child.[12] The word *dēute* occurs three times in the next four lines, and sets the tone of Aphrodite's questions. Her smile implied amusement (among other things), and *dēute* picks up the hint. However, tone is a delicate matter, and we must be careful not to exaggerate. The goddess's questions illustrate what modern jargon might call a personal relationship: tenderness and reproach, affection and amusement are inextricably blended. We are meant to be touched by Sappho's portrayal of her patroness's teasing sympathy. Under the pressure of emotion her account breaks from indirect into direct speech, while the vocative 'O Sappho' at once reveals Aphrodite's closeness to the poet and forces our attention away from generalities to the experience of one individual human being. *dēute* was to become a catch-phrase in Anacreon's poetry, but we must try to forget about Anacreon when reading Sappho; his later practice does not entitle us to regard this part of her poem as a display of frivolous elegance. One will seek in vain for any other place in the surviving fragments where she suggests that love is not to be taken seriously. She has been in trouble before with her affairs and she will be in trouble again, but these are not just cases of light-hearted lechery, as Anacreon's often are; she falls in love too much, maybe, but her loves are passionate and intense.

The sixth stanza charms everybody. The series of balanced clauses, the repetitions of words, the rhymes at the ends of lines 21 to 23 have almost an incantatory quality. They enforce a sense that the rhythm of change is inevitable, the power of the goddess resistless. Yet the second line slightly varies the proportion of its clauses, and the word *tacheōs* drops out; these small variations within the overall symmetry make all the difference, and give the stanza its peculiar grace. The sentence is in the form of a tricolon, with two balanced pairs of clauses followed by a third pair that is a little longer; it is a pattern that suits the extended third line of the Sapphic stanza to perfection. Yet the rhyming of lines 21 to 23 has the effect of detaching line 24 from what precedes it; we can hardly help marking just a hint of a pause after *philēsei*, so that the words *kouk etheloisa* slip in at the end of the speech with a touch of slyness suitable to a goddess who has been called *doloplokos*.

The last lines bring the poem to a neat conclusion, *elthe moi kai nun* referring back to *alla tuid'elthe* in line 5, while the stanza as a whole amplifies the appeal in lines 2 to 4; but we are also conscious of having advanced a long way from the beginning. Gone are the suggestively

---

[12] Krischer has since pointed out the similarity of this scene to that between Achilles and his mother Thetis in *Iliad* 1. Achilles, of course, is not a child, but the combination of intimacy and distance in the interview between mortal son and immortal mother is what gives the passage its poignancy. Virgil was to exploit this idea to the full in depicting the encounter of Venus and Aeneas in *Aen.* 1.

elaborate epithets and the picturesque scene-painting; gone equally is the gracefulness of Aphrodite's epiphany and speech. The languge is now bare and simple; there is no adjective except for the plain *chalepos*. The stanza is simple and unaffected. These are the closing words of the poem, the final summing up, and I do not see that they can be read as anything other than an earnest appeal for help. *summachos* ('ally') is a happily chosen word; Aphrodite is Sappho's friend, and she is also her protectress. There is a genuine battle to be fought, and the goddess will help Sappho to fight it. In the final analysis Aphrodite, however gracious she may be to her votary, is a great and mighty goddess, and as the poem ends we are reminded that it has been, in part at least, a hymn to her glory.

From time to time the poem has been misunderstood through being approached with unexamined assumptions. The most natural of these is the belief that the importance of any section of a poem to the work as a whole is in proportion to its length. Such a belief will commonly be justified, but not necessarily so; we shall find evidence in other fragments suggesting that Sappho liked to use areas of stillness or slackened tension to set off the emotional high points of her poem. In a literal sense such passages may be 'irrelevant' while remaining poetically 'relevant' as part of a total structure. In this poem the words *mainolai thumōi* in line 18 pierce through the elegance that surrounds them; their brevity in relation to the whole does not detract from their eloquence and significance but enhances them.

M. L. West (p. 310) has written, 'What is individual in fr.1 is the description of the confrontation: it constitutes the body of the song and, we may say, its *raison d'être*. The groans of love serve as a neat symmetrical frame for that ornately pretty centrepiece.'[13] The spatial metaphor concealed here is almost impossible to avoid, but it is none the less liable to mislead. When we look at a painting or an architectural facade we commonly expect the weight of expression to be concentrated in the centre. It is quite otherwise with a piece of music: in a minuet or scherzo, for example, it is rare for the central trio section to dominate the sections before and after it. In music the beginning and end of a movement will tend to impress themselves more forcefully upon the listener, and this is because a piece of music is an experience in time, which cannot be perceived as a whole at any one moment. A poem acquires spatial dimensions when it is written down or printed, but has only a temporal dimension as it is read or sung. We shall discover in due course that Theocritus and Catullus write poems in which the centre, on the analogy of visual art, is the most dramatically arresting part; but we shall also find that this type of composition is

---

[13] There is, incidentally, some special pleading here; the 'ornately pretty' part of the poem is in stanzas 2 and 3, before the central lines are reached.

essentially self-conscious and artificial. We should not expect to find
it in Sappho who lived in what was to a large extent still an oral
culture and whose verses were composed, in the first instance, to be
performed. In fr.1 the ornamental account of Aphrodite's journey prepares for the moment of her epiphany and is in a sense subordinate to
it; what follows cannot have the same preparatory function, and we
should hardly wish it to be one long anticlimax. Nor is it: the poem
has a continuous forward movement, from the goddess's appearance
to her questions, to her promise of help, and lastly to Sappho's own
appeal for aid.

Another mistaken assumption is that the tone of a lyric poem is
uniform: if we have found that one part of the poem is humorous, we
have shown that it is humorous throughout. A subtler variation of
this rather obvious error is the notion that the tone of a passage is
identified by labelling it with the appropriate adjective; more specifically, that it can be located somewhere along a spectrum ranging from
comic to serious. And yet no one, surely, imagines that Shakespeare's
heartbroken little joke,

Golden lads and girls all must,
As chimney-sweepers, come to dust

diminishes the grief of his dirge. Page was always an acute reader,
even where his conclusions have least commended themselves to other
scholars, and his great service to this poem was to recognise its smiling
element. Where he went astray was in his apparent assumption that
every ounce of humour discovered in the piece was an ounce of
earnestness lost to it.

His interpretation of the poem as detached and light-hearted rests
upon two arguments. One of these concerns the verb *diōkein* ('pursue'), which, he claims, can only mean to run after somebody who is
running away; so when Aphrodite says in line 21 that the girl will
soon be pursuing Sappho, she indicates that Sappho will soon have
lost interest in the girl and be actively shunning her. As a statement
about the usage of *diōkein* in later Greek Page's claim would be false
(as he seems himself to have recognised); as a statement about archaic
usage it is arbitrary; as a statement about 'pursue' and its equivalents
in any language it is implausibly rigid. We may regard it as well
established by now that Aphrodite's epiphany fulfils the role taken in
more conventional hymns by a myth illustrating the power of the god;
the sixth stanza asserts the power of love, and contains an implicit
promise of success.[14]

Page's other argument (1955, pp. 13, 15f.) concerns Aphrodite's at-

---

[14] The important articles here are Cameron (1964), Koniaris (1964) and Krischer.

titude. The repeated *dēute* shows her tone to be 'one of reproof and impatience'. Furthermore, 'we must not forget that the smile and speech of Aphrodite are given to her by Sappho: it is Sappho herself who is speaking, and the smile must be Sappho's too, laughing at herself even in the hour of her suffering. This everlasting sequence of pursuit, triumph, and ennui is not to be taken so very seriously.' This argument fails from the viewpoint of natural psychology. It is not in the least frivolous for a woman in love to hope for a friend and helper who might smile, sympathise, console, perhaps tease a little, and above all grant her what she most desires. In fact, it is the humane warmth of Sappho's reminiscences that give them their authenticity. We may compare the eloquent charm of the real Sappho with the ranting that Swinburne puts into her mouth. Which is the more genuine and earnest? which is – in the best sense – 'serious'?

Page's argument also fails in terms of Sappho's own beliefs. The *Iliad* reveals the superiority of gods to men by means of two great contrasts: the gods are immortal, while human life is brief and uncertain; human life is full of sorrow, but the gods are free from care. On one level, the gods are passionately involved in the Trojan War; Ares and Aphrodite are even wounded; Zeus rains tears of blood. But in a deeper sense, or on a longer view, they do not know or share the griefs of mankind; Achilles' famous words sum up one of the central themes of the poem (*Iliad* 24. 525f.):

ὣς γὰρ ἐπεκλώσαντο θεοὶ δειλοῖσι βροτοῖσι
ζώειν ἀχνυμένοις· αὐτοὶ δέ τ᾽ἀκηδέες εἰσί.

[This fate have the gods woven for poor mortals, to live in sorrow; but themselves are free from care.]

Nor is this only a Homeric view: Euripides' Hippolytus comes to recognise that the goddess to whom he has been so devoted can see his passing without a pang (see below, p. 65), and the indifferent gods of Epicurus are best understood as a philosophical development of an old and durable idea. The epic poet and the materialist thinker are at one in regarding the divine indifference as an essential part of the divine blessedness; the gods would seem less godlike if they cared more for men. This attitude implies no resentment, but rather an acceptance which is the antithesis of that fist-shaking at the deity enjoyed by romantic Hellenists like Swinburne and Shelley. Still less does it mean that the woes of men are unimportant; to draw such a moral from the *Iliad* would be manifestly absurd. For an Achilles or a Sappho a man's present life is everything to him; he cannot, like St Paul, reckon the sufferings of the present time as nothing to the glory that is to be revealed. To say that Aphrodite's smile must be Sappho's as well is exactly wrong: the goddess's smile and speech reveal the divine beneficence and even friendliness, but in the very act they expose the great gulf between her votary and herself. Aphrodite smiles with immortal face because she is serenely happy and always happy; there is a contrast between her immutability and the violence and transience of Sappho's own passions, a contrast which is more not less poignant for being so sweetly expressed. Sappho's self-knowledge shows her that her frustrated love is no great tragedy to the goddess; but just because she can externalise this 'knowing' attitude by giving it to an onlooker she can let her own feelings stand forth in opposition. Many other poets – Catullus, for example, or Virgil in his second Eclogue – show us a fluctuation of emotions within the lover, towards detachment and away from it again. That is not Sappho's method here: whatever the variations in the *surface* of the poem, the emotions of the poet herself, as lover, are uniform and undeviating.

mainolai thumōi – chalepan . . . ek merimnan – mē m'asaisi mēd' oniaisi damna . . . thumon – these phrases all insist that the anguish is real, even if it is not dwelt upon. Sappho burns, and we feel the heat; but at a distance. Her method is very different, however, from the kind of distancing that we shall find in Catullus, where a romantic remoteness is created for the sake of its own nostalgic charm. Fr.1 fits Coleridge's demand for more than usual emotion combined with more than usual order; we feel it to be the intensity of emotion that demands some separation of the passion itself from the words that give it expression. Similarly, we should not suppose that the poems of gentle memory, like fr.94, give love a lower importance. Rather, by continuing to dwell upon love even when it is over or can no longer attain fulfilment, such poems give it a degree of significance that it has not had before in Greek poetry.

Whatever we make of fr.1, we must beware of generalising from it about the nature of Sappho's oeuvre; one may suspect that it was placed at the head of her works partly because it had qualities that particularly appealed to Hellenistic taste. The picturesque quaintness of the golden chariot drawn by sparrows (a little like the *putti* who flutter around Aphrodite in later Greek poetry), the goddess's teasing charm, the obvious prettiness of the sixth stanza – none of these things is insipid in Sappho's poem, but they might well hold an especial attraction for an age which relished the insipidities of the earlier Anacreontea. Fr.31, therefore, must be examined like fr.1 in isolation and without preconceptions.

Φαίνεταί μοι κῆνος ἴσος θέοισιν
ἔμμεν᾽ ὤνηρ, ὄττις ἐνάντιός τοι
ἰσδάνει καὶ πλάσιον ἆδυ φωνεί-
σας ὑπακούει

καὶ γελαίσας ἰμέροεν, τό μ᾽ ἦ μὰν   5
καρδίαν ἐν στήθεσιν ἐπτόαισεν·
ὡς γὰρ ἔς σ᾽ ἴδω βρόχε᾽, ὥς με φώναι-
σ᾽ οὐδ᾽ ἒν ἔτ᾽ εἴκει,

ἀλλὰ κὰμ μὲν γλῶσσα ἔαγε, λέπτον
δ᾽αὔτικα χρῶι πῦρ ὑπαδεδρόμηκεν,   10
ὀππάτεσσι δ᾽οὐδ᾽ ἒν ὄρημμ᾽, ἐπιρρόμ-
βεισι δ᾽ἄκουαι,

κὰδ δέ μ᾽ ἴδρως κακχέεται, τρόμος δὲ
παῖσαν ἄγρει, χλωροτέρα δὲ ποίας
ἔμμι, τεθνάκην δ᾽ὀλίγω ᾽πιδεύης   15
φαίνομ᾽ ἔμ᾽ αὔται·

ἀλλὰ πὰν τόλματον ἐπεὶ †καὶ πένητα†

[He seems to me to be equal to the gods, that man who is sitting opposite
to you and listening close by you, to your sweet voice and charming
laughter; this in truth has fluttered my heart in my breast. For when I
look at you for a moment, I no longer have the power of speech, but my
tongue is broken, straightway a thin flame has run under my skin, I can
see nothing with my eyes, my ears roar, sweat pours down me, trembling
seizes me all over, I am greener than grass, and I seem to myself only a
little short of death. But all can be endured since . . . even a poor man . . .]

We owe the preservation of these lines to the so-called Longinus, who
praises Sappho for her skill in selecting and combining contradictory
emotions (10.3). For this judgment he has been sharply rapped over
the knuckles by Page (1955), who continues (p. 27), 'More justice might
be done to Sappho's art by recognition of qualities of a different kind
– the uncommon objectivity of her demeanour towards her own extremity of passion; the accurate definition of its physical symptoms
. . . Despite the fact that everything possible is packed into a few lines
. . . the description is free from exaggeration and self-pity. There is
certainly no lack of self-control in the expression . . . The symptoms
. . . are delineated with exactitude and simplicity.' There is shrewd
observation here; and yet Page's overall picture is so radically mistaken that we must consider what has gone wrong.

Ruskin once declared 'objective' and 'subjective' to be 'two of the
most objectionable words that were ever coined by the troublesomeness
of metaphysicians' (*Modern Painters* 3.12.1). This was a characteristically violent exaggeration, but we may agree that the use of these
terms often befogs the issues that it was designed to clarify. Let us
therefore begin by asking what 'objectivity' means. In a literal sense
any description that anyone gives of his own emotions or sensations
is necessarily 'objective'. My feelings may be foolish or irrational or
exaggerated, but they *are* my feelings none the less: if I cry out in the

utmost extremity of despair, 'I hate everything! I want to die!' my cry is strictly 'objective' (unless I am lying): it is a fact that I hate everything; it is a fact that I want to die. So if what Page is saying when he draws attention to Sappho's objectivity is that she gives a true account of her sensations, then his statement is possibly true but certainly vacuous. In fact Page seems to be making a more substantial claim than this: Sappho displays not just objectivity but *uncommon* objectivity of demeanour. This claim is mistaken; it is hard to see how Sappho could possibly, by any means whatever, have made the poem more intensely subjective than it is. The 'objective' descriptions in which so many love poems delight – the cherry lips, the rosy cheeks, the sparkling eyes – all these are totally banished. We do not know who the girl is, who the man is, or where or when the incident took place. All Sappho's energy and all our attention are focused on her own violent sensations, and the background is left obscure. The aberrations of modern scholarship, admirably refuted by Page, bear witness to the extent of this obscurity; it seems highly unlikely that the missing lines of the poem (if we may assume that it continued after line 16) would have made the context any clearer, and equally improbable that a poet of Sappho's skill would have created so vague a context unintentionally. On the contrary, the vagueness is deliberate. The poem begins, 'He *seems* to me', and the long recital of the poet's agonised sensations ends, 'I *seem* to myself.' Sappho could hardly have made her subjective intention plainer: we are not to know what really happened but how she felt. She does not so much as say, 'I felt love', or, 'I felt jealousy'; even that amount of analysis is excluded. Nothing comes between us and the immediate mental and physical experience.

Even in the opening stanza Sappho, with brilliant economy, describes not so much the girl and her man friend as the relation that exists between them. The girl chatters, the man is all attention – not just *akouei* but *upakouei*. The verb means to 'hearken' or 'pay attention', but the *hupo-* compound also suggests privacy or secrecy. We seem to see the man straining closer to the girl to catch each intimate remark; with just two letters Sappho puts before our eyes a world of private and exclusive delight. It is the confidences passing from the one to the other which, like an electrical charge leaping a gap, create the spark that kindles the blaze of Sappho's jealous and passionate avowal. We do not know what the man looks like, we only know that he seems to Sappho, in the height of his good fortune, to be like a god; we do not see where he is sitting, merely that he is sitting opposite the girl whom Sappho loves; we do not hear what the pair are saying to each other, we simply hear the girl's sweet voice and delicious laughter, and observe the lucky man hanging upon her words. Here at least Sappho's 'skill in selection' is superb. It is the girl's laughter that Sappho emphasises above all, isolating it at the beginning of the second stanza, immediately before she plunges into the impassioned recital of her emotional and physical collapse. This is profound and subtle: there are few things more desolating than to hear the laughter of other people and to be excluded from a share in their merriment. And besides, it is not just any laughter that Sappho is overhearing, but the voice and laughter of her beloved. It is often small but special things, those minor but distinctive traits of individual personality, that enslave a lover most. Just as in fr.16 Sappho especially praises Anactoria's way of walking and the bright mobility of her expression, so here she makes us feel that it was the voice and laughter of the girl which entranced her above all things.

Nor is there objectivity in Sappho's actual description of her sensations. Let us take line 15 first: 'I am greener than grass.' In what useful sense is this objective? Are we seriously to suppose that Sappho in the height of her agony turned to look into a mirror to check whether she were objectively greener than grass or not? That idea is self-evidently absurd. The words only make sense if we take them as an expression of subjective experiences: 'I *feel* paler than grass (but heaven only knows whether I really am).' The only way of saving the 'objective' hypothesis is to insist (with extreme perversity) that Sappho is so fantastically dispassionate that she is considering what she must look like to other people. We need not attempt to refute this view, though it is worth observing incidentally, as one of the marks of Sappho's subjectivity, that we are given no clue as to whether her breakdown is seen by the man and the girl. Perhaps they break off in confusion, perhaps they do not even notice: Sappho is in no state to know, and we too, entering into her experience, cannot know either.

At line 14 it is particularly clear that Sappho is not being objective, but there is no reason to suppose that her other sensations are any more objectively described. Page refers to the 'accurate definition' of 'physical symptoms', rather as though she were discussing her little problem with the doctor. Medical men, one imagines, would find talk of hearts startled in the breast and then fires running beneath the skin more poetical than helpful, and yet Page can say that 'Sappho speaks of her sensations as dispassionately as if she were an interested bystander.' When we suffer really violent emotions, we experience them physically as well as mentally, but at the same time we lose the capacity to analyse our experiences, so that we can hardly tell whether they belong to the mind or the body. It is Sappho's achievement to have found words which vividly convey this experience of confusion. Her first sensation? A flutter of the heart – a familiar physical symptom of excitement, and at the same time a metaphor of mental tension. The verb *ptoeō* has connotations of both fear and erotic excitement; Sappho's use of it suggests an unanalysable blend of anxiety or jealousy with an awe or wonderment inspired by love. Then she says that she can no longer speak. Mental confusion surely. Well, perhaps; but then in the next line Sappho tells us that she feels a physical constraint upon her tongue. Next, a thin flame running – one could hardly hope for a more expressive description of that bright tingling sensation which seems to shoot along the limbs. Yet the phrase is also suggestive of metaphor, and of mental experience. 'The flame leaped up him, under his skin' – the words come from D. H. Lawrence (*The Rainbow*, ch. 1, sect. 2), but Sappho had said it, and said it much better, more than two and a half thousand years before. *pur*, fire or flame, is bound to suggest Sappho's burning, consuming passion. It is *lepton*, not only thin but fine, subtle. The metaphor of penetrative subtlety is continued with *chrōi*: the flame has made its way beneath Sappho's skin. *upadedromēken* is a brilliantly apt word: the sound of it, so long and with so many light syllables, perfectly suggests rapid secret movement; 'running' expresses the speed with which the spark of jealousy has so quickly kindled the blaze of Sappho's passion; the *hupo*- compound suggests stealth – the metaphor of subtle penetration yet again. We may notice too the perfect tense: straightway (*autika*) the fine flame *has already* stolen beneath the flesh, so swift and furtive is its movement.

In the lines that follow Sappho's experiences become more plainly physical, and yet simultaneously more and more wildly 'unrealistic', as though they were simply the projections of acute mental stress: she can no longer see, her ears are buzzing (*epirrombeisi*, a good onomatopoeic word), she trembles, she feels paler than grass (Sappho's adjective *chlōros*, besides its associations with fear, implies both greenness and dampness and very well describes the complexion and sensation of one about to faint);[15] finally she seems to be practically on the point of death. The whole passage is a telling realisation of dizziness, faintness and mental anguish. In a curious way Page's claim that the poem is free from exaggeration turns out to be justified, for Sappho's artistry and directness are such that she manages to persuade us, as she does Page, that her extravagant reactions to what is after all a pretty common human experience are realistic and untheatrical. But even so we can hardly accept that Sappho was literally struck dumb, literally blinded, literally greener than grass, and anyway Sappho's reactions to the sight of the man and the girl are, by normal standards, so exaggerated that to say that a description of them is not exaggerated is to say very little. Page claims that there is no lack of control in the expression; but he seems to be referring to something that is common to almost all poetry. To be sure, the sentences are grammatical and the lines scan, but apart from that there

---

[15] Irwin discusses Sappho's use of this adjective at p. 63ff. She is perhaps too absolute in ruling out an implication of pallor also.

could hardly be a more direct emotional outpouring: all sixteen lines
are virtually a single sentence, and from line 7 onwards, at any rate,
the clauses spill out one after another in apparently irrepressible
profusion, end stoppings become less and less frequent, clauses start
close to the beginnings and ends of lines, so that the violence of
emotion seems to be straining against the straitjacket of the metre.

And all this is in forceful contrast with the opening lines, when the
leisurely movement of the sentence corresponds to the 'divine' happiness described in it. After the economical scene-setting of line 1, the
words *emmen' ōnēr*, virtually redundant, slow the pace. The long
loose relative clause beginning with *ottis* appears still more unhurried;
twice when the sense seems complete, a *kai* casually attaches new
material, while the lingering effect natural at the end of the Sapphic
stanza is further reinforced as the clause sprawls over into line 5. At
this point the mood quickly changes, though the second stanza continues to use subordinate clauses. As the emotion increases, the construction becomes purely paratactic, and lines 9–16 are a succession of
short, independent clauses linked by *de*, a connective more unobtrus-
ive than *kai*. The language, too, is straightforward and almost colloquial, that the minimum of artifice may seem to be interposed between
the experience and its expression. Elaborate similes or magniloquent
apostrophes might in a sense be more 'exaggerated', but their effect
would certainly be to make the poem more cool and more controlled;
real people in real distress do not turn to metaphor or declamation.

However uncertain the ending of the poem may be, we can at least
be confident that there is a heavy stop at the end of line 16, by far the
weightiest pause in the surviving part of the poem. Here the apparently ungovernable torrent of words ceases for a while to flow: 'I feel
on the point of death,' Sappho says, and for a moment at least she
collapses, exhausted, into quietness. It is perverse to deny that *phai-
nom' em' autai* echoes *phainetai moi*, the very first words of the piece;
in a sense the theme of the poem – Sappho's jealous passion – comes
to an end at line 16, and though any theory must be speculative, it
seems likely that such lines as followed had the character of a coda,
a quiet conclusion to a storm of passion. In any case, the sixteen lines
that we possess are sufficiently self-contained for us to be able to judge
their quality and purpose. Moreover, we can gain illumination by
comparing the first twelve lines of the poem with Catullus' paraphrase
of them in his Poem 51. The comparison is entirely to the lady's
advantage. She begins with a very plain, direct statement: 'That man
seems to me to be equal to the gods.' The old Homeric cliché of the
isotheos phōs, the godlike man, springs suddenly into new life: the
gods, so handsome, so serene, so maddeningly self-controlled and irresistible – as an image of the envious lover's sense of reluctant
admiration and impotent frustration what could be more simple or

more perfect? Catullus begins similarly – 'That man seems to me to be equal to a god' – but then spoils the effect by adding a weak piece of conventional piety: 'He seems to excel the gods, if that is not blasphemy.' At lines 5–6 Catullus writes '. . . which has snatched all my senses from me . . .' – a flabby substitute for Sappho's '. . . which has fluttered my heart in my breast . . .'. Catullus also adds a self-pitying 'misero' ('wretch that I am'). At lines 11–12 Catullus tells us that his 'eyes are covered by a twin night'. The word he has used for eyes is 'lumina', which of course means 'lights' as well as 'eyes'; he has two eyes (or lights), and so it needs two nights to cover them.[16] This is an ingenious and cool conceit, a far cry from Sappho's passionate directness. It is interesting to see that in the parallel passage she has used the most 'unphysical' words possible for eyes and ears. The ears are *akouai*, 'instruments of hearing', and the eyes are *oppata* (*ommata* in more familiar dialects), 'things you see with', rather than *korai, augai*, or *blephara*. True to her consistent subjectivity, she is only interested in eyes and ears as organs of sensation, and she chooses her words accordingly.[17] Every departure that Catullus has made from his model is a change for the worse, and we shall look in vain for the equivalents of the verbal subtlety and virtuosity which we found in the Greek poem. The point of the comparison is not to belittle Catullus but to stress Sappho's merits. Catullus is enormously admired today, and his Poem 51, if the fragment of Sappho had not by chance survived, would surely be highly valued as a characteristic example of his powerful and imaginative love poetry; yet it seems weak compared with its Greek model. This is no small tribute to Sappho's art.

We have now examined two of Sappho's poems, both quite short, both about love, but remarkably different in mood and style; the one, addressed to a goddess, poignant, humorous and sophisticated, the other addressed nominally to an unnamed girl but in reality to the poet herself, ferociously and uncompromisingly direct. But there are certain qualities which we have found in both: not only verbal virtuosity but what for want of a better word I will call truth – a true and vivid realisation of the quirks and complexities of human experience. Yet it cannot be said that these are difficult or complicated poems; Sappho has no 'message' to get across, nor has literary artifice woven elaborate webs of symbolical allusion. Swinburne's distinction be-

---

[16] 'Gemina' has been suspected; Schrader, for instance, read 'geminae' (i.e. 'my twin ears'); But (*a*) it is not plausible that casual scribal error should have produced an idea as neat and pointed as that presented by the text as transmitted to us (for a witty variation on the same conceit, cf. Ov. *Met.* 1.721: Argus has a hundred eyes, but one night comes over them all); (*b*) the last clause, 'teguntur lumina nocte', becomes disagreeably flat after the more powerful clauses that have preceded it.

[17] Compare *kardia* in line 6 in place of (say) *thumos*. This is the only occurrence of *kardia* in Sappho's extant verse.

tween Aeschylus, the great poet who was also a prophet, and Sappho, the great poet who was a poet and nothing more, may prove to be a shrewd one. Few modern scholars would care to describe Aeschylus as a prophet, but nonetheless it remains true that he has something to say about god and man and life and destiny that seems to spill out beyond the confines of his dramas, whereas with Sappho there is nothing beyond the poem itself. Her poems state; they do not examine. I have suggested that we are compelled to study them rather as though they were *objets d'art*; these two at least seem sufficiently self-contained and complete in themselves to answer well to this approach. But from now on the ground will be less solid beneath our feet; the rest of Sappho's fragments survive in a much more battered condition.

3

Fragment 2:[18]

δεῦρύ μ᾿ἐκ Κρήτας ἐπὶ τόνδε ναῦον
ἄγνον, ὄππαι τοι χάριεν μὲν ἄλσος
μαλίαν, βῶμοι δὲ τεθυμιάμε-
νοι λιβανώτωι,

ἐν δ᾿ὕδωρ ψῦχρον κελάδει δι᾿ ὔσδων   5
μαλίνων, βρόδοισι δὲ παῖς ὀ χῶρος
ἐσκίαστ᾿, αἰθυσσομένων δὲ φύλλων
κῶμα κατέρρει,

ἐν δὲ λείμων ἰππόβοτος τέθαλεν
ἠρίνοισιν ἄνθεσιν, αἰ δ᾿ἄηται   10
μέλλιχα πνέοισιν . . .

ἔνθα δὴ σὺ στέμματ᾿ ἔλοισα Κύπρι
χρυσίαισιν ἐν κυλίκεσσιν ἄβρως
ὀμμεμείχμενον θαλίαισι νέκταρ   15
οἰνοχόαισον

[Come hither, pray, from Crete to this holy temple, where is your pleasant grove of apple-trees, and altars fuming with frankincense. Here cold water babbles through apple boughs, the whole place is shadowed with roses, and from the flickering leaves slumber comes down. Here a meadow, pasture for horses, blooms with spring flowers, the breezes blow graciously . . . Here, Cyprian, take garlands and pour gracefully in golden cups nectar mingled with our festivities.]

[18] The sherd on which this fragment is scratched precedes the first line quoted here with some puzzling letters which may represent the end of the previous stanza. Athenaeus quotes the fourth stanza together with what may be a paraphrase of its continuation. But the poem may have been complete in four stanzas. The text of the sherd is very corrupt; I refer to textual problems only where they affect my argument.

The first stanza (to call it that for convenience) shows us at once that Aphrodite is not a fleshless symbol or flimsy abstraction. She is to come *deuru*, 'hither', to the grove where Sappho is here and now awaiting her; and she is apparently to leave another real place, Crete.[19] Then in the second line Sappho begins to describe the place and its ambience. 'Holy', 'pleasant', 'apple trees'; with a minimum of very simple words she conveys the idea of a spot which combines the 'specialness' of a sacred place with the simple natural beauty of an orchard. Then she adds a perfect touch, the 'altars fuming with frank-incense'. No detail could have been better chosen to sustain and enrich the atmosphere of mingled sanctity and scenic charm. The incense and altars are, on one level, part of the apparatus of religious ritual, but they also appeal directly to our sense of sight and smell. No one English word can give the savour of *tethumiamenoi*. Liddell and Scott render *thumiaō* 'burn so as to produce smoke'; instantly it brings to mind both the fragrance of burning and the sight of rising smoke, and the religious colouring of the word (it was particularly associated with the burning of incense) is more evocative still. We all know that smoke rises slowly and lazily; we know also that the smell of incense is heavy, heady and somniferous. It seems to be, too, a smell in which there is an inexpungeable hint of the exotic even to those most familiar with it, and in Sappho's poetry it does, incidentally, make its first appearance in surviving Greek literature. There is, literally, a whiff of sensuous languor in the air; we are in a world of slumberous pleasure faintly tinged with the hues of the strange and the super-natural. The mood is enhanced by the sound of *bōmoi de tethumia-menoi libanōtōi*. A few cold statistics reveal that Sappho has created a harmony of subdued coloration. If we take the nine long vowels in lines 3 and 4, we find that they comprise only five vowel sounds and that these are predominantly low and dove-like: *a, ō* and *u*. An *ōi*, perhaps very close in sound to *ō*, and two *oi*'s complete the tally. *ē* (the sound of bleating, as we know from Aristophanes)[20] and the harsher diphthongs, *ai, au, ei* and so on, are all equally absent. Turning to consonants, we discover that Sappho's tonal range is still more subdued. There are fifteen in all. No less than four are *m*'s and three *n*'s – a predominance of murmurous sound. There are two *b*'s and a *d*, letters related to *m* and *n*, as anyone can tell who has ever suffered from the common cold, and two *l*'s, liquid sounds as the name of their phonetic category suggests. Lastly, there are two *t*'s and a *th* (sounds which are much more closely related to each other than English t and

[19] *ek Krētas* seems the simplest way of mending the text. This reading has been considerably suspected, but I know no other conjecture that appears plausible.
[20] However, Dionysius of Halicarnassus says that *ē* is the most euphonious vowel after long *a* (*Comp.* 14).

th; the difference between the two is said to be equivalent to that between French t and English t, a distinction of which most Anglophones are unaware). There are no gutterals at all, and no sibilants. The last two words are strangely splendid; the effect is produced by a marriage of content with form, the length of the two words conveying a feeling of sleepy opulence enhanced by the overflowing of *tethumia-menoi* from the third line into the fourth and by the faintly oriental tinge of the Asiatic word *libanōtos*. But there is also a fifth essence that evades definition, the 'mysterious perfume' of which Symonds spoke.

The next four lines are exceptionally beautiful, and here, more than ever, form and content are indivisible, even though we may have to examine them separately. In this stanza the powers of selection which Longinus rather unconvincingly claimed to find in fr.31 are admirably displayed, each detail being designed to seduce our senses into drowsy and voluptuous ease. Almost everything that is mentioned appeals, like the smoky altars in the previous lines, to more than one of the senses, and together they convey an overall impression of pleasantly sensuous indolence. The first of the natural delights to be mentioned is cold water. In the context – a welcoming invitation to an agreeable outdoor festivity – this at once suggests that it is a hot day, but at the instant that the idea of heat is introduced, the coolness of the water refreshes it.[21] And it is running water: *keladei*. This delectably onomatopoeic word means 'splash' or 'babble'; it is strictly speaking used to describe sounds, but here it carries irresistibly, like its English equivalents, a visual image too. The water babbles *through* the apple boughs, says Sappho in a phrase which used to mislead commentators considerably.[22] This is a richly evocative idea: in the drowsy atmosphere of the sacred grove the various perceptions of the several senses are blended into one hazy overall impression; the shade of the apple branches and the cool trickle of the water mingle to make a single indistinct consciousness of relaxation. At the end of the stanza we shall learn that Sappho is drifting into sleep; I think that we can imagine her here lying on the ground snoozing with half-shut eyes (a scene rather like the outdoor siesta described in the battered fr. 94). Logically, the sound of the water should come along the ground, not down from the branches, but as Sappho looks up through the canopy of foliage with half-closed eyes, her senses are dimmed, and the soo-

---

[21] I do not know why Schadewaldt (p. 78) supposes the scene to be set at night or why Fränkel (p. 179) puts it in the evening. The action of a poem will naturally be in the daytime unless the author indicates otherwise.

[22] In the *Oxford Book of Greek Verse* the stanza appears under the heading *Rain*. Now that we have so much more of the poem, the misapprehension is obvious; no one will suppose that Sappho invited Aphrodite to join her in mackintosh and sou'wester.

thing sounds that lull her towards sleep seem to drop gently from above.

'The whole place is shadowed with roses.' This is another enticing phrase, even in translation; besides, there is something of a paradox in the thought of flowers, the brightest features of the natural scene, being a source of shade, a paradox which conveys a slightly uncanny sense of dimly glowing opulence. *aithussomenōn* is an elusively many-sided word. Liddell and Scott translate *aithussō* 'set in rapid motion, stir up, kindle', and the passive form 'quiver'; it seems to be primarily a visual verb. Here, however, it is used as a participle qualifying *phullōn*, and we cannot escape remembering the rustle of leaves in motion; even the sound of the word suggests the whispering of foliage. Yet once again the impressions of two different senses are blended together; and moreover, the word is particularly subtle as a visual description. In the first place, it describes the quivering motion of leaves themselves, but it goes further than that. *aithussō* is akin to *aithō*, to light or kindle, or in the passive to burn or blaze; so the word suggests not only the moving leaves, but the effects of sparkling light that they produce. Now the leaves of apple trees are glossy on their upper surfaces, and when a breeze stirs the trees, it turns the leaves half over from time to time, so that bright points of light are reflected off the surfaces. Besides, an apple tree will not provide completely solid and uniform shade on a bright sunny day;[23] the sunlight will penetrate through interstices between leaves and branches, and whenever a breath of wind stirs them, the sharp fragments of scattered light will dance and flicker, like flames;[24] the movement, too, of dappled shade over the ground resembles the shadows cast by a fire upon a wall. This dancing, fluctuating light has a dazzling, almost hypnotic effect, as Sappho herself implies. Her word for 'sleep' is *kōma*, which is explained by Page (1955, p. 37): 'In each of the few places where it occurs in early poetry, it means not simply "sleep" or "deep sleep" but *sleep (or deep sleep) induced by enchantment or other special or supernatural means*. It is not natural sleep, but a kind of trance or coma artificially induced.' Is the *kōma* literal or metaphorical? In our dreamy, trance-like state we can hardly tell. There is a numinous quality about the slumberous atmosphere of the sacred grove; surely some god is in this place. Yet perhaps the numinousness is nothing

[23] Despite Kilvert; see below, p. 37.

[24] It is worth comparing W. B. Stanford's commentary on *Od.* 7, 106: ' "Like the leaves of a tall poplar-tree": the comparison is between the continuous movement of the lightly hung leaves ... and the busy hands of the women. Sophocles ... imitated this lovely simile in his *Aigeus* ... A similar appreciation of the beauty of quivering, flickering leaves is implied in the epithet *einosiphullos* for a mountain ... and in Sappho's *aithussomenōn* ... *phullōn*. The Greeks loved the play of light on bright moving surfaces.'

but an illusion induced by muted light and whispering sound, for Aphrodite has yet to make her visitation. At all events, slumber seems to descend from above (*katerrei*) like a divine benison, just as the trickling sound of the water seemed to flow down through the branches.

And so the whole stanza is about mood, and the mood is a pervasive sense of sensuous beauty and numinous trance. Once again, the sheer euphony of Sappho's language plays no small part in bringing off the trick. The trickling sound of *keladei* and the rustle of *aithussomenōn* have already been mentioned; we should notice too the cool *u*'s and *r*'s of *udōr psuchron* and throughout this stanza a patterning of sounds which, without conveying any special effect, is simply melodious for melody's own sake: *r*'s and *s*'s in the phrase about the roses, *u*'s and *ō*'s in the words that follow it, and the two *k*'s beginning the final words. The last clause seems to have a wave-like motion of flowing descent that matches the flowing of sleep down from the leaves. If the double consonants, *ss*, *ll* and *rr*, are pronounced in the Italian way, with a slight pause in the middle, the full effect can be appreciated.[25] A five-syllable word is placed plumb in the centre of the line; any hint of caesura is smoothed away as part of the effect of mesmeric restfulness. The fourth syllable of the Sapphic stanza may be either long or short, a licence which allows the rhythm of the verse to be slightly speeded up or slowed down. In this case Sappho slows it down. Two long syllables, the very slightest pause at the double consonants, and then a couple of light short syllables make up the word *aithussome-nōn*; like a wave, it seems to rise slowly to a crest, hang for a moment, and then plunge downwards, and like a wave, it seems to sweep irresistibly right across the middle of the line.[26] Then another wave sweeps across into the next line. *phullōn kōma* . . .; again the line is slowed down by the lengthening of the second syllable, by the double consonants between the vowels, by the repeated *ō*'s; and again there follows a pair of rapid short syllables before the wave finally flattens out into the two long syllables that end the stanza. We are dealing with something more than 'word music' in the conventional sense. Such famous lines as

> The moan of doves in immemorial elms,
> And murmuring of innumerable bees

or for that matter,

---

[25] *katerrei* is Sitzler's emendation; Hermogenes quotes the lines with the verb *katarrei* ('flows down'), which is not Lesbian dialect; the sherd has *katagrion* or *kataìrion*. Bergk's *katagrei* ('seizes') produces doubtful grammar and poor sense.

[26] The sense of climax in *aithussomenōn* is not a matter of sound merely: after so much simple language this rare word, paradoxically employed, stands forth prominently.

nec tamen interea raucae, tua cura, palumbes
nec gemere aëria cessabit turtur ab ulmo

[Meanwhile neither shall the hoarse pigeons, your delight, nor the turtle-dove cease to moan from the lofty elm]

delightful as they are, add nothing to their meaning by their sound.[27] Ah, doves, says the poet – let us coo; ah, bees – let us hum. We enjoy this technique, but we *know* nothing more than we would know from a prose paraphrase. Sappho's sound creates her meaning; the peculiar beauty and atmosphere of the grove cannot be experienced apart from it.

In the next stanza there appears to be a slight but perceptible change of tone. The previous lines have mesmerised us into stillness and sleep; in what direction is the poem to go next? Sappho's answer is, literally, to let in a little fresh air. We move out from the shadows of the grove into a field that lies beside it. The scene is still idyllic, but just a little more lively, now that we are out in the open. There is more activity; horses are mentioned indirectly by means of the epithet *ippobotos*, and we think perhaps of their lissom movements as they graze. The roses in the previous stanza were described as providing shade within the grove; the meadow, on the other hand, 'blooms with the flowers of spring', a phrase instantly suggestive of bright young vegetation to an audience familiar with the brilliance of the Greek countryside in April and May.[28] In the earlier stanza the leaves rustled; the poet implied that there was a breeze about, but it did not penetrate the sacred orchard. Now, however, in the more open surroundings of the meadow, we are directly told that the breezes are blowing. Sappho's word for 'gently' is from *mellichos*, an Aeolic dialect form of Homer's *meilichos*. In the *Iliad* this word so far retains its original signification as to be used only of persons (men or gods), though the similar *meilichios* is freely used of speech: it was originally connected with the idea of appeasement, and there was a cult of Zeus Meilichios, the god who can be moved to pity. We can perhaps catch the flavour of the word in Sappho's poem if we translate, 'the breezes blow graciously'; we have the feeling of a personal, benevolent intervention by some numinous power. And *mellicha* seems to carry with it still other associations. *meilichios* and its cognates were thought by the Greeks to be etymologically connected with *meli*, 'honey'.[29] In Homer eloquence can be described, with little apparent distinction of meaning, as either gentle or honeyed: *meilichiois epeessi* ('with gentle

---

[27] Tennyson, *The Princess*, sect. 7, line 206f.; Virgil, *Ecl.* 1. 57f.

[28] *ērinoisin* is conjectural; but that the scene is laid in the springtime is sufficiently plain without it.

[29] Wrongly, it seems. See Chantraine.

words') is a common formula for persuasive speech, but when Homer is describing Nestor's eloquence, he calls him *hēduepēs*, 'sweet-speaking', and says that his voice flowed more sweetly than honey, *melitos glukiōn rheen audē* (*Iliad* 1.249). Sappho's dialect, by turning *meil-* into *mell-*, brings it particularly close to *meli*; among her epithets can be found both *meliphōnos* ('honey-voiced') and *mellichophōnos* ('gentle-voiced'),[30] the latter word occurring, it is interesting to note, almost next to an adjective meaning sweet. The two compound adjectives are not identical in meaning, but it would seem perverse to deny that their meanings are very close. Similarly, in fr. 2, when we have just been told that the meadow is full of spring flowers, and then that the breezes blow *mellicha*, we not only feel their breath, we also scent their honeyed fragrance. Here, as so often, Sappho's choice of words is very simple, so simple that it seems natural and even inevitable, and yet it is very skilful. Soft words, honeyed words – these are mere clichés; but a single word suggesting both the softness and fragrance of a breeze is distinctive and evocative.

Sappho displays the elegance of her composition by the way in which the fourth stanza at once reflects the first lines and moves on to a new theme.[31] The appeal to Aphrodite is renewed, and the words *entha dē su* correspond to *deuru moi*. The vocative *Kupri* may look back to a similar vocative in a missing first stanza, but it is also possible that the goddess's name was held back until this moment, to enter the verse for the first time at the point where the excitement quickens as the epiphany itself is imagined. In making her new appeal to Aphrodite, Sappho imagines the goddess actually coming among them and pouring their wine into golden cups. This must be some sort of metaphor, dream or vision, and it presents the poet with a problem that only a delicate literary tact can solve. She must not shatter the mood of voluptuous solemnity which she has so brilliantly developed; yet she must modify her tone in such a way that the poem may drift serenely from the 'realistic' evocation of the Lesbian grove and meadow into a more immaterial realm of reverent but gorgeous imagination. She is equal to the occasion. In the first line of the new stanza she invites Aphrodite to come bringing garlands; this request, combining a reminiscence of the flowery meadow in the previous stanza with the new theme of joyous festivity, makes the transition of tone smooth and almost imperceptible. The expected coming of the goddess is described in language of almost Pindaric resplendence. 'Pour out the wine,' Sappho says in a single grandiose verb, *oinochoai-*

---

[30] Frs. 185 and 71.6. Lobel-Page suggest that *meliphōnos* ought perhaps to be corrected to *mellichophōnos*; but why should Sappho not have used both words?

[31] There is a similar technique in the fifth stanza of fr. 16. It need not follow that fr. 16 ends with the fifth stanza or fr. 2 with the fourth, or indeed that fr. 2 begins with *deuru m'ek Krētas*.

son. But the object of the verb is not wine or some synonym for wine; it is *nektar*. This word is not used as a mere poetical synonym for wine until the third century, and we must not play down the boldness of what Sappho is saying: when she and her friends drink in the presence of Aphrodite, they will consume not some man-made brew but the ambrosial liquid of the gods. Or is it a metaphor? Is it simply that in the magical surroundings of the sacred grove and meadow the wine will seem to acquire a more than earthly fragrance? Sappho leaves the answer uncertain, for we have now passed into a cloudy realm of numinous unclarity. It is in keeping with this mood of hazy exaltation that the poet should mix abstract and actual, speaking of 'nectar mingled with festivities'. The divine charm passes from the wine cup into the conversation and companionship of Sappho and her circle. Or is it again purely metaphorical? Is *nektar* a symbol of the mixture of delicacy and splendour that seems to constitute Aphrodite's peculiar charm? Delicacy and splendour are certainly blended in line 14. The golden chalices (the dative plurals lend sonority) express the opulence and joyousness of the festivities, but they are juxtaposed with *abrōs*, a favourite word of Sappho's, something between 'gracefully', 'charmingly' and 'tastefully'. Aphrodite will display a natural *savoir faire*, if it is not absurd to say so; we may be reminded of her epiphany in fr. 1, and her dual role in that poem as Olympian goddess and sophisticated woman of the world. Pindar, too, was later to describe the radiance of aristocratic life and the glories of poetry with imagery of good drink, good cheer and the bright beauty of nature. 'Greetings, my friend!' he calls to Aristoclides of Aegina. 'I send you this honey, mixed with white milk, and mingling dew is spread about it, a drink of song on the breath of Aeolian pipes' (*Nem.* 3.76–9, tr. Bowra); and elsewhere (*Ol.* 1.97f.) he declares that a victor in the games 'has honey-sweet clear weather for the rest of his life'. In Sappho's fourth stanza there is just a hint of the grandiose, something we rarely find in Sappho; but whereas Pindar writes in the complex and elaborate choral tradition, Sappho thickens her texture by no more than minimal adjustments to her simple style. The three previous stanzas have followed a very similar pattern, each beginning with an adverb of place and containing three units, indicated by the commas in modern texts. In each case the first unit flows over from the first line into the second, and the second unit from the second line into the third; the avoidance of end-stopping is a vital counterbalance to the symmetry with which the clauses and stanzas are constructed. The chain of descriptive phrases advances gently and paratactically; after the *men* of line 2 every line has a *de* (until line 11 at least, where the sherd fails us). The fourth stanza begins as though it were about to conform to the same pattern, but a firm *dē* replaces *de* and a single big clause sweeps right through to the end of line 16. The vocabulary swells out to match: from line 14 onwards most of the words are of four or five syllables.

This unusual amplitude of expression suits the tenor of Sappho's thought, for she is dealing here with something lofty and rather mysterious. Religious experience is paradoxical: it seems to clarify and illuminate the understanding, and yet its nature seems to be inexplicabie in human language. Sappho's words mirror this strange combination of lucidity and obscurity; there is not the slightest doubt about the meaning of the sentence (apart from textual problems), and the syntax could hardly be more straightforward, but the uncertainty that we are bound to fell about the implications of Sappho's description – is it metaphor, symbol, or reality? – reflects the uncertainty with which we must approach any account of religious experience. These last lines manifest the luxurious enjoyment of the beauties of nature which pervaded the earlier stanzas, but in a new way. The process of elegant transition from one mood to the next is itself a source of literary pleasure, and the combination of unity and diversity is a testimony to Sappho's skill.

In the spring a young man's fancy lightly turns to thoughts of love. We all know that; and what could be more natural than to celebrate Aphrodite in the spring with a joyful outdoor festival? But some readers have wanted to go further and have found in the poem a succession of sexual symbols, identifiable perhaps by reference to *The Interpretation of Dreams*. The most extravagant of Freudian interpreters has been Robert Bagg, whose article raises questions of general principle that deserve examination. Certainly, the Greek poets were capable of using the beauties of nature for metaphorical or symbolical purposes, but when they did so, they made their intention unambiguously clear. We only have to look at such famous passages as fr. 286 of Ibycus or the address to Artemis that Euripides puts into the mouth of Hippolytus (73 ff.) to see how different they are from Sappho's poem. Indeed they provide the refutation of one part of Bagg's thesis. Gardens, he claims (p. 53), represent 'the sleepy darkness of sex (like the garden from which we have been expelled)'.[32] This is fantasy: in Greek poetry, as in the Old Testament for that matter, the symbolic significance of gardens is innocence and virginity. Bagg's only argument in favour of associating sex with gardens rests on a misunderstanding. Pausanias tells us (1.19.2) that at Athens Aphrodite was worshipped *en Kēpois*; but it turns out that *kēpoi* is the name of a district. To argue from this 'evidence' that Aphrodite was associated with gardens is no more reasonable than to deduce that St Martin must be the patron saint of agriculture because there is a church of St Martin-in-the-Fields. In-

---

[32] The parenthesis is nonsense: it should be needless to observe (*a*) that the garden of Eden does not represent sex; (*b*) that it belongs to Semitic not Hellenic mythology.

deed it is rather less reasonable, because we know from other sources that the associations of gardens were commonly different.[33]

Bagg is not much luckier with the other 'voluptuous physiological symbols' which he detects in Sappho's text (p. 53): apples, horses, cold water, flowers. The first two of these look the most promising. Apples are associated with ripening and fruitfulness, they were given in Greece as love tokens, and there was a cult of Aphrodite as the Apple Goddess (*Aphroditē mēleia*) at Magnesia. Indeed, it is likely that the Lesbians worshipped her in an apple grove because of her known association with the fruit. But this means that if Sappho wanted to describe the grove in which she and her friends communed with the goddess, she was compelled, willy-nilly, to describe an apple grove; and therefore it need not follow that the apples have any *literary* significance, either conscious or unconscious. We have no reason to doubt that Sappho is describing a real place, a spot that she knew and delighted in; and our confidence is increased by the similarity to the scene described in fr. 94, which no one has yet ventured to allegorise. In fact there are no apples in this poem, only apple trees, and this for a very simple reason: Sappho is describing the spring, and apples do not ripen until late summer. If anything, we could say that apples are chiefly notable in this poem by their absence. When Sappho wanted to turn an apple into a metaphor, she did it with unforgettable clarity and splendour (witness fr. 105a); when she wanted to express sexual passion, she could do it with vividness and power, as we know from fr. 31; but a vague blur of sub-Freudian innuendo is not at all her style.

Horses, Bagg claims, represent the 'graceful energy' of sex. It is true that they appear in amatory poetry: Anacreon, for example, in one fragment (346) describes a boy as sporting in fields where Aphrodite has tethered her horses, and in another (417) develops the comparison of a girl to a filly in elegant language that is none the less veiled thinly enough to leave no doubt of its meaning; Horace was later to adapt this poem, adding repulsive elaborations of his own (*Carm.* 2.5). But to recognise the difference between Horace and Anacreon or between Anacreon and Sappho might well serve as a test of literary sensibility; and in any case the two later poets make their meaning plain. As a matter of fact horses barely appear in Sappho's landscape and perhaps not at all. The meadow is *ippobotos*, 'horse-grazed'. She does not explicitly state that there are horses in the meadow at the actual moment, and even if there are, their presence is restricted to half a compound epithet. *ephippos* was among Aphrodite's cult titles,

---

[33] I am not denying that seeds, plants, vineyards etc. may have the sort of associations that Bagg wants them to have, only that *gardens* as such will naturally do so. The Greek evidence on this point is clear.

and Sappho makes a passing allusion to the goddess's association with youthful animalism and grace; to equate this with introducing symbols of copulation is to deny the poet all possibility of subtlety whatever.

The rest of Bagg's edifice is even flimsier. 'The cold water suggests a chilly *frisson*.' The notion that cold water is sexually arousing seems, to say the least, eccentric; indeed, it is said that cold baths were once employed at boarding schools for their supposedly antaphrodisiac properties. The *kōma* 'does not mean the sleep of fatigue at all, but of magic exhilaration'. How can sleep possibly be 'exhilarating'? It may be magical, or hypnotic, but it is none the less sleep, that is, a *relaxation* of the consciousness. Here Bagg has been led astray by the vagaries of the English language, in this case by the euphemistic use of the word 'sleep' to denote sexual intercourse; we may note that Sappho avoids a word such as *katheudein* which might risk such connotations. 'The roses fill the darkness of the lawn with the damp skin of the loving body.' This is fantasy once more, Swinburne rather than Sappho; no evidence exists for this flight of the imagination and none is even suggested.

But the fundamental reason why we should not apply Dr. Freud's do-it-yourself psychoanalysis kit to this poem is that is destroys the very qualities in which its true value consists. Above all, it is so bookish. Most of us, when we enjoy trees and flowers and sunshine, do not bother ourselves with the possible uses to which a literary symbolist can put these things; it is only when we get back into the study that we start to do so. Sappho's fr. 2 is a vivid and perceptive recreation of real experience, and it is a pity to vapour away this vividness into allegory. I am far from denying that the theme of love hovers in the background of this poem, but Sappho has the skill – and here is one of the charms of the piece – to *keep* it in the background. The grove and meadow are instinct with the spirit of Aphrodite; the mood is very still and yet tremulous with expectancy. Such an account may superficially sound similar to Bagg's; in reality it is very different indeed. The difference is between the sharp, particularising power of imagination and the abstracting tendency of symbolism.

It is enlightening to compare Sappho's poem with Ibycus' fr. 286, which does plainly use the beauty and cruelty of nature as symbols:

ἦρι μὲν αἵ τε Κυδώνιαι
μηλίδες ἀρδόμεναι ῥοᾶν
ἐκ ποταμῶν, ἵνα Παρθενῶν
κῆπος ἀκήρατος, αἵ τ᾽ οἰνανθίδες
αὐξόμεναι σκιεροῖσιν ὑφ᾽ ἔρνεσιν
οἰναρέοις θαλέθοισιν· ἐμοὶ δ᾽ ἔρος
οὐδεμίαν κατάκοιτος ὥραν.
†τε† ὑπὸ στεροπᾶς φλέγων
Θρηίκιος Βορέας

ἀίσσων παρὰ Κύπριδος ἀζαλέ-
    αις μανίαισιν ἐρεμνὸς ἀθαμβὴς
ἐγκρατέως πεδόθεν †φυλάσσει†
ἡμετέρας φρένας

[In the spring the Cydonian quinces bloom, watered from flowing rivers,
where the inviolate garden of the Maidens is, and the vine flowers bloom,
growing beneath the shady vine sprays; but for me love sleeps at no
season. Like (?) the Thracian North Wind, flaming with lightning, shoot-
ing from the Cyprian, with parching frenzy, dark, shameless, it mightily
shakes (?) my heart from its foundations.]

The first half of the fragment is presented as a double contrast, between the unchanging violence of the poet's passion and the changing
rhythm of the seasons, and between the restlessness of his love and
the calmness of the spring; but the description carries other associations apart from the overt points of comparison. The ancient garden
was an enclosed place, carefully tended and surrounded by walls or
fencing; the half-wild parkland which is every Englishman's notion of
what a garden really ought to be would not have appealed to a Greek
or Roman at all: he would have thought it a negation of a garden's
practical and aesthetic purpose, which was on the one hand to grow
produce, on the other to tame nature, reducing its irregularity to
symmetry and order. The enclosed garden of antiquity was a natural
symbol of virginity, as in a famous verse of *The Song of Songs* (4.12),
one of those later books of the Old Testament in which Greek influence
is said to have been detected: 'A garden inclosed is my sister, my
spouse; a spring shut up, a fountain sealed.' Much closer to Ibycus is
a passage in Euripides' *Hippolytus* (73–8) where the virgin hero de-
dicates a wreath to the virgin goddess Artemis: 'Mistress, for you I
bring this woven garland that I have fashioned from an unmown
meadow, where neither does the shepherd dare to feed his flocks nor
has the scythe yet come, but the meadow is unmown and the bee
passes through it in springtime, and Reverence tends it like a garden
with river waters.' Twice Hippolytus describes the meadow as *akēratos*, a word which literally means 'unharmed' and is regularly used in
the sense 'virgin' or 'undefiled'. If we turn back to Ibycus, we find that
his garden is *akēratos* too. And there are other parallels between the
two passages. The season of spring is an obvious metaphor for youth
and innocence, and sure enough, the spring appears in both Ibycus
and Euripides. Water, especially running water, is a natural symbol
of purity; we are not surprised to find running water mentioned by
both poets. To make the symbolism yet more plain Ibycus calls the
nymphs to whom his garden belongs *Parthenoi*, 'Maidens', a title which
is found nowhere else.

Ibycus' symbols are conventional, but he breathes life into these dry bones. Many Greek inscriptions survive forbidding animals to be pastured or timber to be cut on land sacred to a god; Ibycus would doubtless have known places himself where mowing was taboo. So when he tells us that the garden is *akēratos*, we feel not only that this is an image of virginity, but also that he is describing a holy place. The nymphs are there, at least in part, to enhance this impression; there is a hint of that numinous atmosphere which was evident in Sappho's poem. The garden is not merely a pretty place; Ibycus views it – and by implication views the purity of his beloved also – with respect and reverence. Similarly the running water is not just a symbol but contributes to the evocation of an atmosphere. It can hardly fail to suggest refreshing coolness, always an essential part of any idyllic landscape in the poetry of Mediterranean lands; coolness is implied again by the 'shady sprays' of the fifth line, and further emphasised, as we shall see, by contrast with the second half of the fragment.

The first extant line begins *ēri men*, which it takes seven lumbering words to translate: 'In the spring on the one hand.' We know at once that the spring is to be contrasted with something else; but with what? At the end of the sixth line we shall discover that the contrast is with the poet himself, but up to this point we are kept in suspense, and one would naturally expect the coming comparison to be with some other season of the year. So even before he has begun to describe the spring the poet has reminded us that it is not lasting; and this sense of impermanence is maintained throughout the description. He mentions two kinds of blossom, both of them belonging to plants that are cultivated for the fruits into which those blossoms will develop. In the second case this process of maturation is emphasised: the vine flowers are illogically described as *auxomenai*, or 'swelling to strength' as Bowra puts it. The repetition of the *oin-* root in *oinanthides* and *oinareois* reminds us that when the vine blossoms have ripened into grapes, they will make wine, and wine is a well-nigh universal symbol of sensuous gratification. *hernos*, a shoot or sprout, also adds to the picture of vigorous, developing growth. The word is common in Homer, but always in a simile, as a symbol for a beautiful youth; these epic associations make it especially apt in this context.

The other fruits in the garden are not less judiciously chosen. 'Cydonian apples', that is quinces, were love tokens, like ordinary apples, symbols of maturity, fecundity and so forth. Ibycus writes of the blossom, but in the context we are bound to think also of the luscious fruit, especially since the words are juxtaposed with *ardomenai rhoan ek potamōn*; we realise that these waters will make the quinces ripe and juicy. We do not know whether the poem began where our fragment begins. If it did not, then presumably Ibycus had already spoken of love. If it did, then he revealed the subject of his poem only gradually; the first two lines hinted, the succeeding lines amplified the hint, and the theme of love was not directly announced until the sixth and seventh lines – an attractive way of holding the audience's interest.

With the words *emoi d'eros oudemian katakoitos hōran* Ibycus finally reveals the contrast that we have been waiting for since the first line. But then he surprises us by producing a further six lines of elaborate metaphor, impressive in themselves and also serving to accentuate by antithesis the imagery in the earlier part of the fragment. He compares his love to a violent wind, by which his heart is shaken or crushed (depending on how we try to heal the corruption of the text). This image, which had already been used by Sappho, is direct and vivid, but Ibycus gives it an unusual slant: 'It is not a winter wind, which can at least be foreseen, but a stormy wind that may blow in or out of season, the modern *meltemi* that scourges the Aegean even in summer,' wrote Bowra (p. 262), a veteran of Swan's Hellenic Cruises. The storm is dark, the wind is strong; we might at least expect the temperature to drop, but even this small blessing is denied; the wind is 'flaming with lightning', it comes 'with parching madness'. By means of this simile we feel the violence of the poet's desire, the suddenness of its assault, the dizziness, the loss of self-control; fire and thirst, too, are strong, if conventional, images of sexual passion. Loss of control is expressed in other ways: adjectives and adverbs are piled up recklessly, and the sentence is constructed in such a way that image and reality are confused and we can hardly tell which parts of it are simile and which parts are not. Moreover, the description of the north wind keeps recalling the idyllic garden of the nymphs: the parching heat contrasts with the refreshing rivers and by analogy we feel that the other characteristics of the tempest bring out other features of the garden which may have been implied but were never made explicit. Rushing wind is contrasted with tranquillity, darkness with radiant light, shamelessness with virginal modesty, madness with the orderliness of a place where nature is under control and plants grow steadily to ripeness according to the regular rhythm of the seasons. Each half of the fragment complements the other. Ibycus' garden in springtime is not presented in the form of a simile, and indeed it is not even a metaphor, but a term of comparison. The garden must be an actual garden; otherwise no comparison would be possible. (I suspect that Ibycus invented the garden of the maidens for this particular occasion, but this does not affect the argument. Suppose that I wished to liken myself to a garden; I could compare myself to Hyde Park, which exists in London, or to the Municipal Gardens, Coketown, which I have invented. Neither place is metaphorical, even though one is part of the real world and the other is actualised only in a fictional world of my own creating.) The garden, the quinces, the vines, the streams in Ibycus' poem are not metaphorical, but they do stand for something other than themselves; it is therefore convenient to call them symbols. But this word must be used with caution. No ancient poet was a symbolist in the sense that (say) Blok or Mallarmé were symbolists. We must remember, too, that symbolism in itself is of no value; it is good only if it enriches in some way the poetry or prose in which it is used. In all too many cases one is tempted to dismiss it, in the words with which Dr Johnson dismissed pastoral poetry, as 'easy and therefore disgusting'. ('I'm seeing the professor this afternoon,' said the creative writing student, 'and we're going to put in the symbols.') Ibycus escapes censure because his symbols are expressive and illuminating. His description of the garden reveals something of the nature and the complexity of his emotions; he shows us that he prizes the freshness and purity of his beloved and yet that the very qualities which he loves must pass away for his desires to be fulfilled.

I have examined this piece of Ibycus in detail, partly for its intrinsic merit, partly to demonstrate the differences between it and Sappho's fr. 2. Let us consider some of these. 1. Ibycus makes it crystal clear that his language is intended figuratively. He explicitly compares (or contrasts) the fruit trees in spring with his own passion: *ēri men hai ... mēlides* is formally set against *emoi d'eros*. Moreover, the description of the garden is also balanced by further figurative language which, however we mend a corrupt text, must have been presented as a formal simile; so even if the first lines are 'symbolical', their symbolism is remarkably close to conventional metaphor. Sappho, on the other hand, offers no hint that her poem has a symbolical meaning, and it is entirely coherent and effective if we take it in a purely literal sense. If we are to look for symbols here, we must suppose that Sappho was writing simultaneously on two levels; that beneath the surface meaning runs a second, hidden significance. I see no evidence that Sappho, or any other archaic Greek poet, proceeded in this way. 2. Ibycus uses very basic, simple symbols: flowers, fruit, water, the spring. That there are natural affinities between youth and spring-time, water and purity, and so on, would have been recognised by Ibycus' audience and in many other cultures beside the Greek. Sappho's symbolism, if it existed, would be both idiosyncratic and obscure. 3. Symbolism enhances Ibycus' poem. Here judgment is perhaps bound to be subjective, but I do not see that Sappho's poem is in any way improved by having symbolical significances read into it; on the contrary, it is surely impoverished.

If we compare Sappho and Ibycus, we find that her achievement is at least the more unusual. Ibycus' poem, for all its skill and complexity, remains in its total effect restricted (this is not necessarily a criticism of it): the direction that our response is to take is plainly indicated and there are clear bounds beyond which it may not stray. Sappho's fragment gives us more room to expand in: the solidity or authenticity of her imagination is such that a reader who comes to it with expectations derived from the nature poetry of the Romantics, with memories perhaps of Shelley's

> Under the green and golden atmosphere
> Which noontide kindles through the woven leaves
> *(Prometheus Unbound* 2.2.75f.)

will none the less be satisfied, although Sappho's own feeling for nature was of another kind. Henry James once observed *(Partial Portraits*, ch. 4), 'There are two kinds of taste in the appreciation of imaginative literature: the taste for the emotions of surprise, and the taste for the emotions of recognition'; fr. 2 gratifies both. As an evocation of mood and scenery it speaks to our own experience, and yet at the same time it depicts a place enough like a paradise garden for the presence of Aphrodite to seem possible. Indeed, Sappho seems unconscious of any distinction between consecrated grove and divine pleasance: she inhabits a world in which a goddess might readily be expected to join her worshippers in a setting familiar to them in their natural, waking lives; or at least she so persuades us. Kilvert, too, found a religious feeling about an orchard, but with what a difference:

> At the lower house the orchard boughs were so thick and close that the sun could not penetrate them, and the sunlight only got into the orchard at a gap in the west side through which it came streaming in low in a long bright streak along the brilliant green rich velvety-looking grass like sunshine through a painted Cathedral window. (Diary for 3 June 1870)

Here, in a mere diary, is a complexity of thought and emotion greater than Sappho puts into a formal poem. The grass is *like* velvet, the quality of light is *like* the interior of a church; but for Sappho the orchard simply *is* the domain of Aphrodite. In some sense her depiction can be called suggestive, but it is not suggestive through a power of association such as comes instinctively to Kilvert. Throughout her verse her words, even when they are many-sided, seem to have a kind of lucidity unlike the aura of association usual in English poetry. The contrast between her imitators and herself if often revealing; between, for example, *ēros angelos imerophōnos aēdō* (fr. 136) ('the lovely-voiced nightingale, the messenger of the spring') and the words of Ben Jonson that it inspired *(The Sad Shepherd*, act 2, sc. 2.85f.): 'the dear, good angel of the spring, The nightingale'. *imerophōnos* is certainly an evocative word, awakening ideas of both beauty and desire, but it remains essentially descriptive, whereas 'dear, good' is evaluative, and tugs overtly at the emotions. The English adjectives are variously suggestive of virtue, preciousness, affection in the speaker, kindness in the bird; no single signification predominates. Sappho's nightingale sings out plainly; the English poet presents us with a mist of warm vague emotion in the hearer. Most obviously, Jonson's 'angel' transforms the Greek *angelos* by giving it a double meaning; the messenger has become a minister of grace as well, and a flood of associations comes surging into the verse. Sappho's idea of the bird as herald is striking – particularly so for a Greek, in its independence of the myth of Philomela – but it is as simple as it is bold.

4

Fr. 2 displays, perhaps for the first time in European literature, the 'sentiment of place' – not just a 'feeling for nature', but a feeling for what it is like to be in a *particular* place at a *particular* time. This is rare in the Greek poetry of any period; even the *Oedipus Coloneus* of Sophocles does not possess it to the same extent as Sappho's poem, and she was not to be equalled until Theocritus composed the closing lines of his seventh Idyll, in which, by a marvellous evocation of the sights and sounds and smells of a hot afternoon, he expressed the individual quality of a particular place, a homestead on the island of Cos, at a particular time of year, late summer, and indeed on a particular day of the year, the festival of Thalysia or Harvest Home. None the less, we must not suppose that Theocritus' or Sappho's 'feeling' for nature is anything like ours. The difference is well brought out by Otho Laurence, one of the imaginary speakers in W. H. Mallock's once famous satire, *The New Republic* (bk. 4, ch. 2). 'Once,' he says, 'I started to find myself quite lost in staring at a red rock, gleaming amongst shrubs and ivy, which a plant of periwinkle spangled with a constellation of purple flowers. The colour, the shape, the smell of every leaf and flower – each seemed to touch me like a note of music; and the bloom of morning mist was over everything.' This experience, he explains, gave him a strange sense of kinship with Nature (with a capital n, let us note). 'It is a mixing together of inward and outward things – our whole inward lives passing out of us into Nature; Nature melting into us, and growing part of our inward lives.' Laurence goes on to explain that if he had attempted to describe his state of mind to an inhabitant of the ancient world, that man 'would not have understood: he would have thought me raving. And my case is not peculiar. These feelings are not private things of my own. They belong to our whole age.'

This sense of oneness with nature is generally associated with the name of Wordsworth, and it is widely realised that the feeling hardly existed at all before the later eighteenth century. It is more seldom appreciated that until this period very few people looked closely and steadily at nature in an attempt to see what it was really like. Those who did were for the most part painters, and even among painters the phenomenon was surprisingly rare. The fascinated attention with which nineteenth-century writers and painters examined the quirks and quiddities of things, the knottiness and irregularity of the world, was something new in the European experience. Gerard Manley Hopkins trying in his journal to describe the *exact* curvature and motion of a wave; Ruskin analysing in detail the *exact* shape of mountains or leaves; the fictional Otho Laurence transported by the *especial* form and colour of a periwinkle – such minute and loving investigators were practically unknown before the Romantic age. Wordsworth thought that Peter Bell was a poor benighted creature in that

> A primrose by the river's brim
> A yellow primrose was to him,
> And it was nothing more.

Yet for the greater part of its history the world has been populated entirely by Peter Bells; and Sappho is no exception to this rule. It is a pleasant sensation to drowse in an orchard, to watch the leaves and the sunlight, and Sappho evokes that sensation with skill and beauty; but when Proust (for example) describes the sun through apple trees we feel that something completely different is being attempted, something that Sappho would not have valued or even understood (*Swann's Way*, vol. 1, p. 200): 'It was while going the "Méséglise way" that I first noticed the circular shadow which apple-trees cast upon the sunlit ground, and also those impalpable threads of golden silk which the setting sun weaves slantingly downwards from beneath their leaves, and which I would see my father slash through with his stick without ever making them swerve from their straight path.' Proust observes with an almost scientific precision: natural objects are treated like works of art, things to be prized for their own sake and analysed with passionate minuteness. Sappho's poem is unscientific and impressionistic; natural beauties are described, of course, but only in their relation to the poet herself; they are not valued except as a pleasant setting for sleep, wine and worship.

A modern analogy may help to bring out the distinction between Sappho and Proust. The man who puts Berlioz on the hi-fi as a background to food or conversation may possibly derive acute pleasure from the experience; but in some sense he takes the music less 'seriously' than the man who sits score in hand watching for the entry of the cor anglais; he places less value on the music *qua* music, though he may (for all we know) derive a keener pleasure from it than the more serious-minded student. This is, crudely put, the difference between the 'modern' and the 'ancient' attitudes to nature. Proust *con-*

centrates on nature, and uses it as a source for new and sophisticated sensations which without concentration he would be unable to enjoy. Sappho is more spontaneous; she lets the beauties of nature wash over her, and describes this luxurious submersion with a fine sensitivity, but she does not think to seach nature, to seek for original or unusual impressions. Perrotta's claim (for instance) (p. 40) that her 'delicate sensibility . . . made her contemplate with eyes ever new . . . the sights of nature' is wildly mistaken. The ancients never dreamed of taking nature for a guide or a mistress; she has no charms except as the servant of man. Sappho's impressionism is, however, perfectly suited to convey a sense of drowsy ease and a mildly mysterious awareness of the numinous. To venture a simple paradox, she depicts the imprecise with great precision. She looks at her surroundings through half-shut eyes; and indeed for this purpose the exalted pantheism of a Wordsworth or the microscopic attentiveness of a Proust would be out of place. It is precisely because Sappho is, within her limits, so remarkably sensitive to natural impressions that we are liable, unless we are careful, to attribute to her a modern sensibility. In an odd way she is indeed ahead of her time – only a rigid historicist would seek to deny that – but not by so much as two and a half thousand years.

A lively visual sense and a feeling for nature – two separate but connected capacities – may have been distinctive features of Lesbian poetry and the Lesbian character. Consider the case of Alcaeus. Few modern readers who compare his ancient reputation with the surviving fragments of his work will escape a feeling of disappointment. Is this the Alcaeus whom Quintilian characterised (10.1.63) as 'terse and magnificent'? Is this the man whom Dionysius of Halicarnassus praised (*Opusc.* 2, p. 205 UR) for his 'nobility and concision and sweetness . . . and above all the moral quality of his political poems'? We possess stretches of his poetry eight lines long or twelve or even more that seem to be almost entirely devoid of merit; frs. 129, 60 and 70 may stand as examples. Such verses as these are not even particularly bad; they are merely null. Bowra (p. 174f.) bravely did his best for Alcaeus, applauding his 'toughness', his 'rare quality of directness', his 'balance and clarity and unaffected vigour'; but I doubt whether this is much more than a polite way of describing straightforward grammar and an absence of subtlety.

Yet when he has a chance to talk about objects that are attractive to the eye, he suddenly comes to life. When his brother returns from distant Babylon, where he has been leading the dangerous life of a mercenary, how does Alcaeus greet him? 'You have come from the ends of the earth,' he says (fr. 350), and then continues immediately, 'with your sword-hilt of ivory and bound with gold.' Another fragment (357) describes a great house gleaming with bronze: all over the ceiling there are shining helmets with white horsehair plumes hanging down from them; the pegs along the walls are concealed by gleaming greaves, while tunics of new linen and hollow shields lie thrown upon the floor. The poet seems more interested in the appearance of this armoury than in his rather perfunctory exhortation to his comrades to remember these weapons and buckle down to their task. He is good at creating atmosphere when he has something 'picturesque' to describe that can stimulate his imagination: in fr. 338 wine and cushions in front of a roaring fire while the rain pelts down outside, or the shipwreck in fr. 148, the bilgewater rising above the masthold, great rents in the sails so that one can see right through them, feet tangled up in the sheets. It would not be hard to find other examples. More remarkable, coming from this bluff tough warrior, are one or two strangely evocative fragments of natural description. Somewhere (fr. 319) he spoke of *blēchrōn anemōn acheimantoi pnoai*, 'the stormless breaths of gentle winds'. Somewhere else (fr. 367a) he wrote of the rustle of spring: *ēros anthemoentos epaion erchomenoio*, 'I heard the flowery spring coming.'[34] And in the badly mangled fr. 115 there is what seems to have been a striking picture of birds among marshland. These are brief fragments, it is true;[35] none the less, if they had come down to us under Sappho's name, no one would have suspected that they had been misattributed, and I fancy that we should have detected in them certain of Sappho's most distinctive characteristics.[36]

Perhaps the most 'Sapphic' verses in Alcaeus' extant poetry occur in a stanza of fr. 130, a piece which is otherwise entirely typical of him. He complains that his political fortunes are at a low ebb; banished from the city, he is holed up in the backwoods, living in a precinct dedicated to the gods. Somewhat disconcertingly, he then proceeds to describe this place in terms which make it sound enchanting:

ὄππαι Λεσβίαδες κριννόμεναι φύαν
πώλεντ᾽ ἐλκεσίπεπλοι, περὶ δὲ βρέμει
ἄχω θεσπεσία γυναίκων
ἴρας ὀλολύγας ἐνιαυσίας

[Where the Lesbian girls, being judged for beauty, walk up and down in trailing robes, and around reverberates the wondrous sound of the sacred yearly cry of the women.]

With their calm vision of graceful femininity, these lines come like a cooling breeze after the resentful, rugged truculence of the previous

---

[34] Lobel, followed now by Page, emends to *archomenoio*, 'beginning'.

[35] One should add the charming fr. incert. 16LP to them, if it is by Alcaeus; but Sappho is almost certainly the author.

[36] When two and a half lines of Alcaeus fr. 347 were believed to be by Sappho, Wilamowitz and others compared them to the rest of the fragment and detected striking differences in the attitudes of the two poets to nature. Now that the whole fragment is by general consent assigned to Alcaeus, the moral, if any, is different.

stanzas. The use here of *elkesipeplos* ('with trailing robes') is a fine example of a Homeric epithet being brought to new life – a thing that has been commonly admired in Sappho. The tinge of epic colouring lends a solemnity to the processional movements of the women, but at the same time it brings the scene vividly before the mind's eye; we seem to see the long draperies of the women trailing elegantly along the ground as they walk to and fro. But what really gives the stanza its special atmosphere is the combination of the 'beauty competition' with the numinous spirit produced by the *ololugē* of the women, a cry that is 'wondrous' '*thespesia*', a cry of celebration that is yet, as the sound of the word suggests, weird and almost uncanny. Indeed the sound of the last two lines of the stanza is altogether haunting.

Here, then, is the craftsmanship that we associate with Sappho; here, too, is something very like the 'sentiment of place', the feeling for the *genius loci*. Alcaeus is not just describing any festival or any precinct, but something singular and distinctive. It is difficult not to be reminded of Sappho, and indeed the phrase *achō thespesia* is to be found in her poem about the marriage of Hector and Andromache (fr. 44.27); but for once Alcaeus comes best out of the comparison. In Sappho the expression seems to mean little more than 'an amazingly loud noise', while in Alcaeus it suggests an almost unearthly cry. It is impressive to find Alcaeus sounding so 'Sapphic', and unexpected; but perhaps we should not have felt surprised had more of his poetry survived. In antiquity he was famous not only for his political verses but also for his erotic poetry, which drew mutterings of tight-lipped disapproval from Cicero and Quintilian. All these are lost; but if they were ever to rise again from the sands of the Sahara, we should be able to compare the two poets' treatment of similar themes, and our understanding of the whole of Lesbian poetry, Sappho as well as Alcaeus, might be transformed. As it is, we have to make do with the fragments.

5

Even when she is using nature for a manifestly figurative purpose, Sappho is able to retain the keenness of her visual sense, as we may see from fr. 105a:

οἶον τὸ γλυκύμαλον ἐρεύθεται ἄκρωι ἐπ᾽ ὕσδωι,
ἄκρον ἐπ᾽ ἀκροτάτωι, λελάθοντο δὲ μαλοδρόπηες,
οὐ μὰν ἐκλελάθοντ᾽, ἀλλ᾽ οὐκ ἐδύναντ᾽ ἐπίκεσθαι.

[As the sweet-apple reddens on the top bough, at the end at the very top, and the apple-gatherers forgot it; no they did not quite forget it, but they could not reach it.]

This simile is preserved for us by the rhetorician Himerius, who explains that the comparison is with a bride who has remained untouched in spite of the zeal of her pursuers; there is little doubt that the fragment comes from one of the epithalamia or wedding songs for which Sappho was famous.

ereuthetai, 'reddens'. Sappho uses a strong visual verb to describe the process of ripening, and puts it in the present tense so that we seem to see the apple maturing almost under our eyes. And it is not just an apple, but a 'sweet-apple': *to glukumalon ereuthetai* – the two words, one appealing to our taste-buds, the other to our visual sense, are put side by side so that the delight of the eyes and the delight of the palate seem to be fused into one single delicious experience. Moreover, the movement of the verse mimics the process of growth: *akrōi* in the first line is a bud which blossoms into *akron ep'akrotatōi* in the second line, and *lelathonto* in the second line ripens into *eklelathonto* in the third. At the same time, as *akrōi* is stretched out into *akron ep' akrotatōi* we seem to see the apple-pickers stretched on tiptoe, straining after their prize. Then in the words that follow we watch the gatherers turn away, and then suddenly check themselves, turn back, and try for the apple which they had almost – but no, not altogether – forgotten. When the verb *lelathonto* is repeated, is acquires the compound *ek-* in front of it: 'they did not *quite* forget it'. This is a particularly exquisite touch, enhanced by the slight slowing of the dactylic rhythm by the long monosyllables *ou man ek-*. *akros* can refer either to the top of an object or to the end of it; I think that both senses must be present here. With the double repetition of the word our attention is focused on to the position of the apple not merely at the top of the tree but at the end – the very end – of the branch. Sappho's description is so vivid that perhaps we can even see the branch bending under the weight of the fruit at its extremity. After all, the simile is not static, it describes a process; Sappho does not say, 'Like the red apple . . .', but, 'Like as the apple *reddens* . . .' As an apple reddens, it grows bigger, it matures. And what happens to the apple when it has reached full maturity? Sure enough, its own weight pulls it from the branch and it drops to the ground below. With great subtlety Sappho uses her simile to suggest not only the desirability and inaccessibility of the apple but also, simultaneously, that it is about to fall into the hands of whoever may be waiting below when the time is ripe.

This last consideration brings us to the other aspect of the simile. So far we have seen it simply as a piece of natural description, but one of its glories is that it belongs, like Viola's 'Patience on a monument', to that rare class of similes in which the comparison and the thing to which it is compared are both equally and intensely vivid. Now the ancients seem to have expected a curiously equivocal attitude from the bride at a wedding. On the one hand, she should rejoice at the fulfilment of her desires: 'Call to her home the mistress of the house, full of desire for her new husband,' Catullus prays to Hymen, god of marriage, in the first of his two wedding hymns (61.31ff.). 'Bind her heart with love, as the clinging ivy, straying hither and thither, winds about the tree.' But later (79 ff.), 'An honourable shame delays her . . . she weeps because she must go.' And in the second and finer of Catullus' wedding hymns, the chorus of maidens utters an apparently passionate protest (62.20 ff.): 'O Evening Star, what crueller star than you is borne through the sky? For you can have the heart to tear the daughter from her mother's embrace, the clinging daughter from her mother's embrace, and give the chaste girl over to the burning groom. What crueller injury do enemies inflict when they have captured a city?' Similar sentiments are less extravagantly implied in another remnant of Sappho's wedding poetry, fr. 114. Although the reluctance of the bride must be much more commonly observed in cultures where marriages are arranged by the parents, it is a phenomenon which perhaps appeals to a primitive folk feeling; a feeble relic of this feeling survives, or survived until recently, in the tradition of the blushing bride. With this traditional sentiment in mind, we can better appreciate the skill of Sappho's simile of the apple. She has managed both to glorify the untouched purity of the girl (she escaped 'gathering' when so many other young girls were indiscriminately 'harvested'), and at the same time to suggest how right and natural the marriage is; for when the apple is fully ripe, it drops. Moreover, by bringing the apple-gatherers into the picture, she has flattered both bride and groom. Just as the apple represents the bride, the apple-pickers stand for unsuccessful suitors; Sappho implies that many men sought the girl's hand, and sought in vain, but also that when the time came, her bridegroom captured her easily and without effort.

Sappho's simile, then, is original and individual; yet in a way it is also traditional. Apples were used by the Greeks as love-tokens; a man would give apples to the girl that he loved, or a girl might flirt with a man by throwing apples after him. The reasons for this are not far to seek. Any fruit might symbolise maturity, and the seeds within it the promise of children, but the apple is perhaps particularly suitable to symbolise a girl in the early prime of her womanhood, being ripe, yet firm and crisp. The rosy cheeks of the fruit resemble a girl's rosy cheeks, and in a different way apples are also like breasts, especially the breasts of a young girl; in *Jude the Obscure* (pt. 3, ch. 9) Hardy contrasts the shapes of Sue Bridehead, young and virginal, and the older, more voluptuous Arabella: 'the small, tight, apple-like convexities of her bodice, so different from Arabella's amplitudes'. Dicaeopolis in the *Acharnians* (1199), to take a less remote comparison, describes the breasts of young girls as *sklēra kai kudōnia*, 'firm and like quinces'.[37] I am not suggesting that all the possible associations of the apple are present in this fragment – indeed I have already discussed the dangers of such an assumption; my point is rather that Sappho has taken a traditional symbol, something that would strike her listeners as profoundly natural and appropriate in the context of a wedding song, and used it to create a simile that is individual and acutely perceptive. This combination of traditional and personal elements is not the least of the beauties of the fragment.

Fr. 105c is cruelly tantalising, since not even the whole of the simile survives.

οἴαν τὰν ὑάκινθον ἐν ὤρεσι ποίμενες ἄνδρες
πόσσι καταστείβοισι, χάμαι δέ τε πόρφυρον ἄνθος

[As the shepherd men trample the hyacinth on the mountains with their feet, and on the ground the purple flower . . .]

These lines are quoted by Demetrius, who does not name the author, but they can confidently be attributed to Sappho on the basis of circumstantial evidence. Part of this evidence comes from Catullus' *Vesper adest*, in which the simile of the flower appears to be imitated. If this evidence is accepted, it is a reasonable presumption that Sappho and Catullus employed their flower similes in similar contexts.[38] In Catullus we again encounter the ambivalent attitude towards weddings that we met before: when the bride loses her virginity (62.43–7) she 'loses her flower', she is even 'polluted'. If Sappho's simile is a figurative description of the same subject – a bride's loss of her virginity on her wedding night – it suddenly springs to life. Unlike the Romans, the Greeks had no equivalent to our metaphor of 'deflowering', but the word *anthos* was frequently used to mean the bloom of life or the flower of youth, and the careless crushing of a wild flower is therefore a natural metaphor in Greek to describe the end of girlhood and the loss of virginity. Equally, the growth of a young plant is an obvious but charming metaphor for childhood. Homer used it in the eighteenth book of the *Iliad* (55–7), where Thetis recalls the childhood of her son Achilles: 'I bore a son noble and strong, the greatest of heroes, and he shot up like a sapling; and I nurtured him as a plant in a fertile garden.' Much later, Sophocles in the *Trachiniae* (144–50), and in a context not so very different from Sappho's, compared the childhood of Deianeira to the growth of a garden plant: 'The young plant is nurtured in such places on its own, and the heat of the sun does not harass it, nor rain, nor any wind, but it rejoices in an untroubled life of pleasures, until the time when a woman is called wife

---

[37] The quince is a kind of apple as far as the Greeks are concerned.
[38] Fränkel takes a different view; see Appendix 2.

instead of maiden, and receives her portion of anxieties in the night, fearful either for her husband or her children.' The flower, therefore, still more than the apple, is natural, even 'obvious', as a figurative representation of a bride, but once again Sappho has put upon an 'obvious' simile her own distinctive stamp. The shepherds are not simply *poimenes* but *poimenes andres*, shepherd *men*; this small detail leaps into significance if the simile is about the loss of maidenhead. There are other pleasing details: *possi* (men, the poet suggests, have such big clumsy feet), and *katasteiboisi*, a heavy lumbering compound verb, perhaps coined by Sappho herself. Shepherds are huge hulking things compared to a little hyacinth flower, and Sappho's language nicely brings this out. The thoughtless destructiveness of the male is likened to the groom's triumph on his wedding night, the unthinking destruction of the maidenhead that, as fr. 114 tells us, will never come back to the bride, never again.

The purpose of other details is likely to elude us in the fragmentary state of our knowledge. Why *en ōresi* ('on the mountains'), for example? It is unlikely to be purely decorative. In Homer, in Sophocles, in Catullus the young plant is tended and cultivated; it grows in a garden, orchard or vineyard. Perhaps the mountains represent the wild, free growth of the girl, before the restraints and responsibilities of matrimony overtake her. Or maybe *en ōresi* should be taken with *poimenes*: perhaps we are meant to contrast the freedom of the young men to roam over the hillsides with the defencelessness of the hyacinth, literally rooted to the spot. We can only speculate. I offer one speculation, however, which does appear to me to have some plausibility. There seems to be an undertone of brutality in this simile, a faintly sinister suggestion of blood and death. Blood would be appropriate in this context because of its shedding when the hymen is broken on the wedding night; it used to be the custom in Greece until recently, and may still be so, to display the stained sheets as proof of the bride's virtue.[39] Unlike Homer, Sophocles and Catullus, Sappho names the plant in her simile: it is not just a 'flower', a 'shoot', or a 'sapling', but specifically a hyacinth. Now according to Greek myth Hyacinth was a beautiful young man, beloved of Apollo, who accidentally slew him with a discus – another instance of the destructive thoughtlessness of the strong. The grief-stricken god caused a flower to spring from the drops of his blood, its petals blood-coloured also, and this flower was duly called by the name of the dead youth. With

---

[39] Compare Burton's *Anatomy of Melancholy* 3. 3. 2: 'In some parts of Greece at this day, like those old *Jews*, they will not believe their wives are honest, *nisi pannum menstruatum prima nocte videant*: our countryman *Sands* ... saith, it is severely observed in *Zacynthus*, or *Zante*; and *Leo Afer*, in his time at *Fez*, in *Africa*, *non credunt virginem esse nisi videant sanguineam mappam* ... Those sheets are publicly shown by their Parents, and kept as a sign of incorrupt Virginity.'

this myth in mind, we observe with interest that in the very next line Sappho draws attention to the colour of the hyacinth flower. The Greeks' use of colour epithets is notoriously difficult for us to appreciate, but it is worth noting that the adjective *porphureos* was used to describe the colour of blood. Pliny the Elder, discussing purple dye, tells us (9.135) that its highest glory 'consists in the colour of congealed blood, darkish at first glance but gleaming when held up to the light. It is for this reason that "purple" blood is spoken of by Homer' (*Il.* 17 361f.). And there is one small touch that seems to contribute to Sappho's picture of the death of the flower. The second (incomplete) clause of the fragment begins with the word *chamai*, 'on the ground'. Why? After all, the Greek hyacinth is a small flower that grows close to the ground in any case. Now *chamai* is a word which occurs commonly in Homer, often in place of *chamaze*, 'to the ground'; warriors fall to the ground, they are cast to the ground, they perish on the ground. In a context where soft hints of blood and death have already (as I suspect) been insinuated into the texture of the poetry, there is probably meant to be an unquiet stirring of our memory; not necessarily a direct reminiscence of some particular passage in Homer, but an association of ideas, a recollection that down in the dust, down on the ground, is the place where men expire. 'On the ground the purple flower . . .' – does what? If only we had the rest of the simile, or even the verb alone, how many mysteries might be made plain.

Anacreon, writing perhaps a hundred years after Sappho, employed a technique similar to the one that I have attributed to her here. Ten lines survive from the end of a poem (fr. 347) in which he reproached the boy whom he loved for cutting his hair. '. . . And of the hair that shadowed your delicate neck. But now you are cropped; your hair has fallen into rough hands and flowed down in a heap into the black dust, falling miserably at the stroke of the iron. And I am distressed and pained . . .' Here scholars have rightly perceived the shadow of heroic poetry falling across these tender little verses. The collapse of the boy's hair into the dust and the cruel edge of the barber's razor are implicitly compared to the deaths of Homeric warriors and the strokes of sword or spear that lay them low. The comparison is not overtly made but merely hinted; the essence is in understatement. It is 'witty', it is 'conceited', in the old sense of that word; but though the fragment is usually dismissed as merely humorous, it seems to me to mask the most tender feeling, the sensitivity of a man who laughs for fear he should weep. This is not the place to argue the point; but the parallel with Sappho is perhaps instructive, although it must be admitted that Anacreon is a poet whose teasing use of Homeric echoes is considerably more marked than Sappho's.

The question of Sappho's influence on Catullus is intriguing. The kind of proof that will convince a sceptic is not to be had, but there are good grounds for thinking that Sappho's poetry inspired Catullus as it so sadly failed to inspire Swinburne. Catullus is a poet who writes mostly about attitudes and emotions; outside three or four poems he is not particularly remarkable for the brilliance of his imagery or the liveliness of his sense perceptions. However, in two separate places where the influence of Sappho is arguably to be detected, he creates imagery of superb quality. The first of these comes at the end of his Poem 11. This is one of his two surviving attempts at the Sapphic metre; the other, as we have already seen, is for the most part a paraphrase of Sappho herself. This cannot be the case with the present poem, but it would hardly be surprising if Catullus had Sappho particularly in mind when attempting a metre so closely associated with her. It was, after all, a distinctly unusual metre for a Roman poet to use at this time. Horace boasted that he was the first Roman poet to sing Aeolian song in Italian strains (*Carm.* 3.30.13f.); the example of Catullus is enough to prove the claim to be inaccurate – he was perhaps thinking only of Alcaeus – but it could not possibly have been made if Aeolian metres had been at all common in Republican Latin poetry.

In the fifth stanza of his poem Catullus reviles his mistress for her infidelities in violently exaggerated language. Then in the sixth and final stanza the mood is dramatically transformed; coarse abuse gives way to tender pathos:

> *nec meum respectet, ut ante, amorem,*
> *qui illius culpa cecidit velut prati*
> *ultimi flos, praetereunte postquam*
>   *tactus aratro est.*

[Nor let her look for my love, as in the past; through her fault it has fallen like the flower at the very edge of the meadow, after it has been touched by the plough passing by.]

This is a masterly simile, and the mastery is in two words, 'ultimi' and 'tactus'. The flower was right at the *very* edge of the field, and it was just *grazed* – merely 'touched' – by the plough as it was passing by; but so delicate was it that this was sufficient to destroy it. 'Only just . . .' – the precision and the vividness with which our attention is directed to this idea bring out beautifully the contrast between the brute strength of the plough, utterly careless of whether it happens to cut down one mere flower in its passage,and the frailness and vulnerability of the flower itself. This precision and vividness, this focusing on to one exact point, recall the quality and technique of Sappho's poetry. But is this more than chance? We cannot prove that it is. The superlative 'ultimus' recalls the superlative *akrotatos*, used similarly to 'focus' concentration, in Sappho's simile of the apple; Catullus uses, like Sappho in her other simile, the image of a flower being destroyed; but there is no direct echo or imitation of any lines of Sappho that are known to us. César Franck played Wagner's music on the piano in order to stimulate his own creative powers; in Poem 11 Catullus may similarly have been stimulated by Sappho's example to produce something distinctive and beautiful of his own.

With the other passage of Catullus we are on firmer ground; this is the famous simile of the flower in Poem 62. A connection between this poem and Sappho's wedding-songs can hardly be denied. To begin with, it is an epithalamium, and Sappho was the most famous exponent of the genre. Furthermore, it is written in hexameters, which we presume to have been one of Sappho's epithalamian metres. And it also appears from independent evidence that Catullus took more interest in Sappho as a source than any Roman poet before Horace. Another morsel of Sappho must now be mentioned, fr. 104. On metrical grounds the second line must be assumed to be incurably corrupt, but even in a mutilated state it is strangely memorable.

Ἔσπερε πάντα φέρων ὅσα φαίνολις ἐσκέδασ᾽ αὔως
†φέρεις ὄιν, φέρεις αἶγα, φέρεις† μάτερι παῖδα.

[Evening Star, bringing all that the bright dawn scattered, you bring the sheep, you bring the goat, you bring the child to its mother.]

The metre is hexameter; moreover, the address to the evening star is paralleled in Catullus' poem; in fact his choirs even use the Greek vocative 'Hespere' instead of the usual Latin 'Vesper' or 'Vesperugo', the very same word that Sappho uses and in the very same place in the line. We are surely right to deduce that Sappho's fragment comes from an epithalamium, and that this epithalamium was imitated by Catullus. The resemblances 'are far from striking', Professor Fordyce comments dryly (p. 255), but influences may pass from one poet to another without close verbal imitation. I said that Sappho's fragment was strangely memorable – memorable enough, as it happens, to have been three times echoed by Tennyson,[40] and even to have had some small influence on the most famous poem of the twentieth century:

At the violet hour, the evening hour that strives
Homeward, and brings the sailor home from sea,
The typist home at teatime, clears her breakfast, lights
Her stove, and lays out food in tins.

These lines come from the third part of *The Waste Land*, and we know from Eliot himself that they were inspired by Sappho; but even with-

---

[40] *Leonine Elegiacs*, line 13; *The Hesperides*, line 96; *Locksley Hall Sixty Years After*, line 185.

out this information I think that someone who knew Sappho's lines might have guessed that they were at the back of Eliot's mind. Yet there are no verbal echoes, nothing that can be easily pinned down. In Catullus' poem, on the other hand, verbal echoes can be found (if we had the whole of Sappho's piece there might be more), as well as similarities of subject-matter and metre. These ought to suffice.

Sappho's simile of the apple so crept under the skin of George Eliot that she alludes to it in no less than three of her novels. The reference in *Middlemarch* (ch. 6) is explicit: 'He was not one of those gentlemen who languish after the unattainable Sappho's apple that laughs from the topmost bough.' (Notice, incidentally, how with the word 'laughs' George Eliot unconsciously intrudes an element of the pathetic fallacy quite alien to Sappho's clear simplicity.) The reference in *Romola* (ch. 9) is equally obvious to the reader who knows Sappho: 'Tito was used to love that came in this unsought fashion. But Romola's love would never come in that way: would it ever come at all? – and yet it was that topmost apple on which he had set his mind.' But for our purposes the passage in *Adam Bede* (ch. 19) is more intriguing: 'And there was Hetty, like a bright-cheeked apple hanging over the orchard wall, within sight of everybody, and everybody must long for her!' Since we know independently that George Eliot loved Sappho's fragment, there can be little doubt that she had it in mind when she wrote this sentence; yet the resemblances are far less close than in the other two examples. She seems, in fact, to have combined Sappho's simile with another taken from the *Vesper adest* of Catullus (62.39–47):

> *ut flos in saeptis secretus nascitur hortis,*
> *ignotus pecori, nullo convolsus aratro,*   40
> *quem mulcent aurae, firmat sol, educat imber;*
> *multi illum pueri, multae optavere puellae:*
> *idem cum tenui carptus defloruit ungui,*
> *nulli illum pueri, nullae optavere puellae:*
> *sic virgo, dum intacta manet, dum cara suis est;*   45
> *cum castum amisit polluto corpore florem,*
> *nec pueris iucunda manet, nec cara puellis.*

[As a flower is born secretly in an enclosed garden, unknown to the cattle, wrenched up by no plough, a flower which the breezes caress, the sun strengthens, the rain rears; many boys have desired it, many girls; but when it has been plucked by the thin fingernail and lost its flower, no boys have desired it, no girls. Even so a maiden, while she remains untouched, is dear to her friends; when she has lost her chaste flower and her body has been sullied, she does not remain delightful to boys or dear to girls.]

This passage displays a union of verbal beauty, perceptiveness and tenderness of feeling which is found nowhere else in Catullus, nor in any other Latin poet except Virgil, whose spirit indeed these lines so strangely anticipate. In the first place, the sound of the verse is attractive: in the first of the quoted lines, for example, there is an elegant patterning of the consonants r, s and t. Secondly, the movement of the lines reinforces their meaning, and even adds to it. Catullus begins his simile with a line which is entirely spondaic except for the fifth foot. Then gradually the verse gathers momentum. Whereas the first line is a single indivisible unit, the second is broken into two phrases and the third into three separate clauses. The effect of these lines is beautifully to convey a sense of expansion and growth. In the first we are present at the 'birth' of the flower ('nascitur'); a hushed tone, almost a tone of reverence, is given by the slow spondees, the s sounds and the word 'secretus'. The short participial phrases and the still shorter clauses that follow express the growth of the flower as it presses upward steadily but little by little. Much must depend, obviously, on the way the poem is read; it is not so very hard to make the three tiny clauses 'mulcent aurae, firmat sol, educat imber' suggest both shy hesitancy and firm, strong growth – the delicacy of the flower and at the same time its healthy, expanding vigour. In the two lines which describe the plucking of the flower ('idem cum tenui carptus defloruit ungui' and 'cum castum amisit polluto corpore florem') there are by contrast no pauses; the growth of a plant is a gradual, uncertain business, its destruction easy, the affair of a moment.

The occasion is a wedding; we are supposed to imagine that these lines are sung by a chorus of girls (who are in turn answered by a chorus of young men). Earlier in the poem the men remark that the girls have been rehearsing. Spontaneity would therefore be out of place, and there is a certain formality and regularity to the girls' lines; just as in a piece of music one phrase answers another, so here 'multi ... multae ...' is answered by 'nulli ... nullae ...', and 'dum ... dum ...' by 'nec ... nec ...' These symmetries have a charm of their own, but they also contribute to the sense; to each phrase describing the desirability of the young girl corresponds another telling of her 'downfall', so that we seem to feel a natural rhythm of rise and fall, of growth and decay. The nice balancing of one phrase by another feels 'just right', and thus the girls' chorus seem to persuade us that their analogy between the flower and the maiden is a fair one. The flower grows, the flower is plucked and ruined; the girl grows, the girl is plucked and ruined – yes, we say to ourselves, it *is* so. (But then in the next lines the men produce a quite different analogy, and we have to think again. It answers the girls' analogy point by point, clause by clause, and so it again seems inevitably right.)

Catullus also exploits the resources of language to bind the comparison to the thing compared. Within the simile he employs words which could be used as naturally if not more naturally of a person as of a plant: 'nascitur', 'mulcent', 'educat', 'defloruit'. Conversely, when he comes to speak directly of the girl, he uses words which would be equally appropriate in a description of a flower: 'intacta', 'florem'. Naturally, the traditional use of the enclosed garden to symbolise youth and virginity contributes greatly to the charm of these lines; they reverberate with echoes from the poetry of the past. But at the same time he adapts his literary models to produce something that is distinctively his own. Sophocles had written of the young plant that 'the sun does not trouble it nor rain nor any wind'; Catullus acutely perceived that his metaphor could be turned on its head, and sun, wind and rain be described as contributing to the plant's healthy growth, as indeed they must do. The beauty of this is that the bride is simultaneously given two different but equally desirable qualities: she carries about her the strength and freshness of the open air, and yet she is the delicately nurtured product of the 'enclosed garden' formed by her parents' protective care. We are made aware of both the loveliness of cultivation and the loveliness of untrammelled nature.

Sophocles knew, of course, that some amount of sun and rain is needed to make things grow; however, once he has created his metaphor of the young plant protected from the violence of these elements, he has done with it, and is not interested in exploring its further possibilities. Catullus is different; to borrow the phrase that Matthew Arnold plucked out of Wordsworth, he continues to compose 'with his eye on the object', even when he is speaking figuratively. In the first line we really seem to *see* the plant 'being born': the hushed tone and the epithet 'secretus' suggest the first appearance of something that is just visible to the eye, only just. As in Poem 11 our attention is fixed and focused on a particular point. Four lines later Catullus describes the plucking of the flower in precise and vivid detail. 'Tenui . . . ungui . . .' – 'by a thin fingernail' – we see the nail cutting sharply into the stalk; and this focusing on the precise moment of contact is picked up two lines later by the use of the concrete adjective 'intacta'. It is amusing to observe that when Quintilian came to quote this line (9.3.16) he bowdlerised it, no doubt unintentionally, writing 'innupta' in place of 'intacta'. 'Innupta' is the obvious word, but one has only to substitute it in the text to appreciate with how perfect a judgment Catullus chose his words.

For all the fineness of his visual imagination, Catullus does not forget that his flower is only a metaphor, a symbol of something other than itself. In the first line of the simile we feel something of the privacy and secrecy surrounding that great feminine mystery, the moment of childbirth. The sun and rain of the third line naturally suggest to a modern reader the smiles and tears of childhood, and Catullus shows that he too intends this implication by using with 'imber' the verb 'educare'. The plant must suffer the rain as well as enjoying the sun if it is to grow; even so, the child must be disciplined and corrected if she is to be well brought up, and tears as well as caresses will be a part of her experience. These lines of Catullus are a superb fusion of metaphor and reality; they are also, we may surmise, a fusion of two of Sappho's similes, the apple growing in the orchard and the flower growing on the mountainside. In her turn George Eliot seems to have combined Sappho and Catullus, perceiving, whether consciously or instinctively, a kinship between the two poets in these places. We have found in the last stanza of Catullus' Poem 11 and in the flower simile of Poem 62 a special quality absent from most of his surviving work; the two passages even have a number of words in common: 'flos', 'aratrum' and 'tactus' (in Poem 62 'intactus'). Even the cases in which the words appear are the same. If we take either of the two poems separately, we find good reasons for thinking that Catullus had Sappho particularly in mind when he wrote them; when we find them so like each other and so little like the rest of his verse, we may well suspect that Sappho could inspire in him poetic qualities which otherwise lay dormant.

6

Fragment 16, lines 1–20:

οἰ μὲν ἰππήων στρότον, οἰ δὲ πέσδων,
οἰ δὲ νάων φαῖσ᾽ ἐπὶ γᾶν μέλαιναν
ἔμμεναι κάλλιστον, ἔγω δὲ κῆν᾽ ὄτ-
τω τις ἔραται·

πάγχυ δ᾽ εὔμαρες σύνετον πόησαι   5
πάντι τοῦτ᾽, ἀ γὰρ πόλυ περσκέθοισα
κάλλος ἀνθρώπων Ἐλένα τὸν ἄνδρα
τὸν πανάριστον

καλλίποισ᾽ ἔβα 'ς Τροίαν πλέοισα
κωὐδὲ παῖδος οὐδὲ φίλων τοκήων   10
πάμπαν ἐμνάσθη, ἀλλὰ παράγαγ᾽ αὖταν
   . . . σαν

   . . .αμπτον γὰρ . . .
   . . .κούφως τ . . .   . . .οη . . ν
. . με νῦν Ἀνακτορίας ὀνέμναι-   15
σ᾽ οὐ παρεοίσας,

τᾶς κε βολλοίμαν ἔρατόν τε βᾶμα
κἀμάρυχμα λάμπρον ἴδην προσώπω
ἢ τὰ Λύδων ἄρματα καὶ πανόπλοις
πεσδομάχεντας.   20

[Some say an army of horsemen, some say a host of infantry or ships is the most beautiful thing upon the black earth, but I say that it is what one loves. It is very easy to make this understood by all, for she who far surpassed mankind in beauty, Helen, left her husband, the noblest of men, and went sailing to Troy, and had no thought at all for her child or her dear parents, but was led astray by ... bent ... lightly ... has now put me in mind of Anactoria, who is not here. I would rather see her lovely way of walking and the bright sparkle of her face than the Lydians' chariots and infantry in full armour.]

The first sentence is in the form that has become known by the German name *priamel* ('preamble'); that is to say, the main subject is introduced as the culmination of a series of contrasts. But to give a label to a trick of style is not to explain it, and we must still ask why poets have found it so attractive. Obviously the answer will depend to some extent on the context. Shakespeare uses it in his ninety-first sonnet to create a formal and symmetrical pattern: he begins,

Some glory in their birth, some in their skill,
Some in their wealth, some in their bodies' force ...

– and so on. Then exactly half way through the sonnet, in lines 7 and 8, he pauses:

But these particulars are not my measure;
All these I better in one general best.

Then in the second half of the sonnet he goes through the list of other men's preferences again, this time contrasting each one with his own love:

Thy love is better than high birth to me,
Richer than wealth, prouder than garments' cost ... etc.

The shape of the sonnet is elegantly symmetrical – and yet not quite, for the second list is terser than the first, and there is space at the end for a bitter couplet which gives a savage twist to what is otherwise rather a quiet poem. Expectation is aroused, only to be cheated; a mirror-like pattern is created, but the mirror proves to be slightly distorted.

The sonneteer can calculate his symmetries (or asymmetries) more nicely than most poets, since each of his pieces must be exactly fourteen lines long, neither more nor less. We must expect to find other writers using the priamel somewhat differently. Usually it is a device for creating suspense, for gripping the reader's attention and drawing him onward. This function is evident even in Shakespeare's sonnet: 'Some glory in their birth,' he begins, and the 'some' is emphatic. We know at once that a contrast is coming, but the poet is in no hurry to reveal what it is. Some do this, he tells us, some that, some the other; 'some' is repeated again and again, and not until line 7, with a firm 'but', do we get the contrast that we have been expecting. The same trick is played on a much larger scale by Horace in the first ode of his first book. After two brief lines of address to Maecenas, he launches into a priamel no less than twenty-six lines long. Some people desire victory in the Olympic Games, he informs his bemused patron, others political success; some enjoy farming, others trading, others lazing about doing nothing. And this long catalogue of other people's ambitions and pleasures is stretched out still further by the insertion of little vignettes: the hunter in the winter, the drinker dozing in the shade. What is the tone of all this? Horace is writing nominally to Maecenas, in reality for a general audience of cultivated readers. How should they imagine the poet's patron reacting to such a dedication? Surely with puzzlement, or at least with amused impatience. 'Sunt quos curriculo pulverem Olympicum/collegisse iuvat' ('there are some who delight to raise the dust of Olympia with their chariots') – what a curiously impersonal beginning after two lines of respectful but also remarkably affectionate address. As Horace proceeds to catalogue the different ways of life that men choose Maecenas no doubt realises that the poet's own preference will come at the end of the list; but when, oh when, will he get to the point? The poor man is not put out of his misery until line 29, which begins, without connective, with a stark and emphatic 'me'. In other words, the 'suspense' is of a humorous kind: Horace is teasing his patron (and his readers) by growing more and more digressive until he finally brings his priamel to an end with a jolt.

A similar technique can be found in that most Horatian of English poets, Andrew Marvell (*To His Coy Mistress*):

> *Had* we but world enough, and Time,
> This coyness Lady *were* no crime.
> We *would* sit down . . .

And so on for twenty lines. The coy mistress is being paid out in her own coin as the poet coyly delays the introduction of a verb in the indicative mood. The tone again is teasing; but the priamel also gives a shape and strength to the poem. When Marvell at last begins his twenty-first line with 'but', the little word carries enormous weight:

> But at my back I always hear
> Time's winged chariot hurrying near . . .

Similarly the 'me' in Horace's line 29 is mightily emphatic.

These examples suggest that it would be difficult, though not impossible, for a priamel of great length to be entirely solemn. Sappho's priamel is short, but here too we may find not humour exactly, but a certain lightness of tone. We have to wait until the very last word of the extended third line to discover what it is that Sappho thinks most beautiful; by delaying the word *eratai* until this moment she gives it strong emphasis, but perhaps she is also teasing us a little: as we have seen before, the structure of the Sapphic metre lends itself naturally to an effect of lingering at the end of the stanza. The 'philosophy' of this poem has been taken very solemnly: we have been told that Sappho anticipates Protagoras' assertion that 'man is the measure of all things' and that she 'is writing a sketch on the abstract notion of desire. At least as important as Anaktoria is the poet's attempt to move towards logical thought' (Du Bois, p. 91). Neither common sense nor common sensibility support such views; this is a love poem, and the blurry abstractions of the early part of the fragment have a subordinate role, preparing for and contrasting with the climactic appearance of Anactoria herself. The fifth stanza is more intently focused on a *particular* beloved and her *individual* personality than any other passage of Sappho known to us – more intently, maybe, than anything in ancient poetry before the time of Catullus.

The priamel is 'short-circuited', in Garry Wills's phrase: its natural completion – 'But I love Anactoria's walk and gleam' – is held back, and the poet turns aside to declare, in blank, colourless pronouns, that the most beautiful is 'that thing which a person loves'. *tis*, she says, a trifle coyly, but of course we know immediately that she is thinking of herself. So we are agog to learn the object of her passion; 'Who is it this time?' we ask, like Aphrodite in fr. 1. But Sappho is still dallying with us; having whetted our interest she puts us off with the prosaic statement that 'it is entirely straightforward to make this understood by everybody'. It cannot be denied that lines 5 and 6 are curiously wooden; their cumbrousness is perhaps best explained as indicating a kind of poker-faced sobriety that is not to be taken with entire seriousness. In any case, it does seem to be Sappho's practice on several occasions to concentrate the expression of intense feeling into particular areas of her poems, leaving other areas that are emotionally thinner, either because they are plainer or because they are, on the contrary, more ornamental. The generalities of lines 3 to 6 set off the individuals who matter to us: Helen, Anactoria and Sappho herself. Anactoria's name is not revealed until line 15, and then it is slipped in quietly and almost casually. One of the beauties of the piece – and it is a playful kind of beauty – is that Sappho seems to have rambled her way to Anactoria almost by accident, and yet all the while she was moving serenely towards the priamel's destined fulfilment.

Page feels that lines 6 and 7 are inelegant: Sappho is going to explain that Helen considered her lover to be the most beautiful thing in the world, and she confuses the issue by saying that Helen herself surpassed all mortals in beauty. The criticism is perhaps fair, but the blemish is not grave: *perskethoisa kallos* and later *panariston* have inverted commas around them, as it were; they represent the objective, conventional standards against which Sappho sets her own subjective view. She emphasises Helen's supreme beauty because she intends to show that this woman could have anything that she wanted; and what is more, she had got by conventional standards all that a woman could desire: an outstandingly noble husband. (Unfortunately there is a gap in the papyrus at line 8, but some form of *ariston* ('best') seems certain. With the plausible supplement *panariston* (or indeed *meg'ariston*), Menelaus' excellence is especially emphasised: he is as exceptional in his way as Helen in hers. This would be an exaggeration, if we are to go by what Homer tells us, but it would serve to bring out Sappho's point with the greatest possible clarity.) Menelaus is not mentioned by name and Paris was probably not mentioned at all – characteristically Sappho concentrates entirely on Helen and her emotions – but the implication is unmistakable: the king of Sparta was a far better man than the Trojan bounder, but Paris just happened to be the man that Helen loved.

Sappho's thought is more complex than may at first sight appear. Most obviously, she is asserting the terrible power of sexual passion. It can break every tie of family obligation, and sweep away all other natural affections. Husband, parents, child – all are abandoned, and Sappho declares that Helen did not even give them a thought. Sappho combines this idea of the strength of love with another: its utter unreasonableness and illogicality. How could she possibly prefer Paris to her husband? Simply because he was *kēn'ottō tis eratai*. 'Parce que c'était lui; parce que c'était moi'; there is no other reason. To enquire what moral attitude Sappho takes towards Helen is to ask a question so inappropriate that any answer to it is likely to be misleading. Sappho contemplates the destiny of Helen with a pure wonderment – I had almost said a tragic wonderment, but that would be to use an adjective at once too strong and too precise, for it is a part of the poem's largeness that we are simply shown Helen's act with great clarity, without having our opinions directed to a specific conclusion. Sappho seems also to have a third idea, related to the other two, which one can perhaps call a feeling for the individual and his individuality. In the first stanza the sights which 'other people' prefer involve mankind in the mass: infantry, cavalry, ships. Sappho uses plural nouns in the first two and a half lines, but when she describes her own preference she uses singulars: that one thing (*kēno*) that an individual (*tis*) loves. Helen prefers one thing to a multitude of other blessings.

The poet herself prefers two small, particular and rather unexpected-qualities in Anactoria to Lydian chariots and foot-soldiers, weapons and all.[41]

The fourth stanza is too fragmentary for anything much to be made of it, but we can still detect the dying fall of line 16. The name of Anactoria in the middle of the last line of the stanza forms a climax, and then in the lingering extension to that line Sappho adds touchingly and simply, *ou pareoisas*, 'who is not here'. From this point the verse surges forward to a climax; this much we can say with confidence, even though we do not know whether the poem ended at line 20. After so much plainness of expression the strange and unforgettable phrase in line 18 shines out with a captivating charm. The word *amaruchma* is used not merely of flashing or twinkling eyes, but also of any quick, light movement. Sappho speaks of the *amaruchma* of the girl's face; so we see not just the sparkle in her eye, but the bright mobility of her whole expression. Mobility, indeed, is the essence of Anactoria, for the other thing that especially entrances Sappho about her is the lovely way she walks. We all know how full of character a person's gait can be;[42] with exquisite economy Sappho has suggested not only the girl's physical charms but the gaiety and liveliness of her personality. She does not describe this directly (and in the reticence lies half the beauty), but we feel the fine discrimination of a love that can choose out two characteristics so plainly visible and external, and yet so expressive of the inner nature.

The last two lines extant recur to the subject-matter of the first two, providing a neat example of 'ring composition'. The purpose of the fifth stanza is, in part, to compare something slight and inconsequential with something vast and magnificent, and yet Sappho, as Page has explained (1955, p. 57) finds likeness between things apparently unlike: 'It looks as though Sappho observed that what captivates the spectator of an army of cavalry or infantry, or of a fleet under sail, is their *movement*, the grace of orderly and rhythmic procession, and their *amaruchma*, the sparkle and flash of innumerable spears or chariots or sails.' The idea, as Page says, is 'a little fanciful'; it is

---

[41] I see no good reason to doubt, either, that there is an element of conscious femininity in Sappho's outlook: her own view contrasts with the masculine enthusiasm for armies and navies.

[42] So did the Greeks. The Chorus of the *Agamemnon* sing that when Helen deserted her husband, she 'stepped lightly through the gates, daring what must not be dared', and the seers lamented, 'Alas for the marriage-bed and the husband-loving *steps*' (*Ag.* 407 and 411). For a moment we *see* Helen, and there is horror in the contrast between her girlish footstep and the dreadful significance of her present deed. We meet something a little similar in Euripides' picture of poor vain silly Glauce tripping through the palace, 'stepping delicately with whitest foot', carrying the robe which will torture her to death (*Med.* 1163f.). These parallels suggest that *kouphōs* (line 14) may possibly have stimulated visual memories in Sappho that 'put her in mind' of Anactoria.

'conceited', to use that word again in its seventeenth-century sense; but this does not mean that it vitiates the poem. The sequence of moods, like the subject-matter, takes the form of a ring; in the centre is a stark illustration, drawn from mythology, of the power and irrationality of love, but on either side of it the mood is more personal, more intimate. I have used words like 'coy', 'teasing', 'humorous', but these are coarse exaggerations, for Sappho establishes a tone which eludes precise description. She writes with a certain wit, a certain melancholy; and it would be crude to suppose that the two qualities are incompatible. Indeed it is their combination which is so tender and so touching.[43]

Nowhere else in her surviving verse is anything like 'conceited' writing to be found, a fact which serves to remind us how far we are from being able to make any general assessment of her work. How much variety was there in her love poetry? There are signs, at least, that she sometimes wrote in a manner more metaphorical and more richly wrought than we have so far seen. 'Love shook my heart,' she declared in one poem (fr. 47), 'like a wind falling on oaks on a mountain.' Homer had used the simile of a tree battered by storm to describe warriors under assault; Sappho applies it to a purely mental experience. The comparison of love to a tempest is simple but strong; perhaps, though, the simile was not only strong but subtle. Remembering fr. 31, we might surmise that Sappho was rooted to the spot by the sudden assault of love and yet shaken to the very core of her being, a state which would be finely evoked by the battered oaks of the simile. But this, of course, is guesswork. Another fragment (130) runs,

Ἔρος δηὖτέ μ' ὁ λυσιμέλης δόνει,
γλυκύπικρον ἀμάχανον ὄρπετον

[Love, looser of limbs, shakes me again, a
sweet-bitter resistless creature]

Even in isolation these are impressive lines. *Bitter Sweet* is the title of a musical by Noël Coward, a facile mixture of tears and laughter; the expression has become a cliché. But when Sappho wrote, it was still fresh; indeed, she probably invented it herself. And even now *glukupikros* does not seem a hackneyed word in its context here, because she has combined it with another epithet that has a similar ambivalence. In Homer *lusimelēs* is an epithet applied to sleep; Hesiod uses it to describe love (*Th.* 121), and here he too is thinking, as far

---

[43] It is possible, I suppose, that Sappho means to indicate that Anactoria has gone off with a Lydian, but the idea is unappealing. A *double entendre* in line 19 would seem to me merely vulgar: 'I prefer Anactoria's gait and face to the chariots of the *Lydians* (get it ?).' Of course on this interpretation the *quantity* of what is expressed is greater.

as one can see, of the loosening of the limbs in slumber. Alcman used it brilliantly (fr. 3.61f.):

λυσιμελεῖ τε πόσωι, τακερώτερα
δ᾽ὕπνω καὶ σανάτω ποτιδέρκεται

[. . . with desire that loosens the limbs, and she casts glances more melting than sleep or death.]

For the first time in European literature sexual desire is associated, though most gently, with death; and *lusimelēs* is faintly – very faintly – sinister. When Sappho takes the word over from Hesiod, she sets it in a context which enriches its meaning: followed by *glukupikros*, it suggests an experience at once terrible and delightful: a sensation of helpless collapse and loss of control, and yet a luxurious feeling of relaxation and surrender. *lusimelēs* is reinforced by the vigorous verb *donei*; Sappho is shaken, and again we are left to wonder whether the thrill or the agony is the greater. She follows Hesiod in personifying Love, but again with a difference. In the *Theogony* Eros is 'the most beautiful among the immortal gods', but Sappho deliberately refuses to think of him as a handsome young man: to her love is an *orpeton*. The word can be used of anything that goes on four feet or creeps or crawls: to Sappho love is a beast, a creature, a thing, and she declines to be any more precise. The vague and sinister effect of *orpeton* is intensified by *amachanon*. The adjective often means 'irresistible', and this sense is clearly present here, but it also means 'clumsy', or 'unmanageable', and sometimes 'extraordinary', 'enormous', 'inconceivable'. In the last sense it is often used, like *orpeton*, of monsters. In the context we see love not merely as irresistible but as a blundering, bludgeoning force. What sort of monster is love? We do not know, and the vagueness is all the more threatening.

'Love struck me again,' wrote Anacreon (fr. 413), 'like a smith with a great axe, and soused me in a wintry torrent.' In places such as fr. 47 Sappho seems to anticipate this sort of style, though even here there are differences: Anacreon is more 'clever', more fanciful, more artificial. She might also handle amatory themes, it would appear, in the sumptuous, decorative manner that we associate with Ibycus: in one poem (fr. 54) she described Eros as 'coming from heaven wrapped in a purple cloak'. This Eros must have been the handsome young man that we met in Hesiod, and a far cry from the Eros of frs. 47 and 130. But further speculation would be futile; we are given just a tantalising hint that Sappho may have written of love in a more traditional and mythological manner than we are otherwise aware of, and no more. Elsewhere (fr. 198) she said that Eros was the son of Earth and Heaven, but the context is entirely unknown. Pausanias tells us, 'Sappho of Lesbos sang about Eros many things that contradict one another' (Sappho, ibid.). That is as we should expect: Sappho thought of Eros in different ways on different occasions, sometimes as an emotion personified, sometimes as a god.

The bulk of her extant verse is either about love or about the personal concerns and emotions of herself and her friends. The two themes, of course, are closely related. But we may reasonably ask if her range was as restricted as the accidents of survival make it appear; after all, Alcaeus was remembered by Horace for his amatory lyrics, and of these barely a trace survives. Sappho wrote a fair number of hymns, if fragments such as 17, 53, 127, 128 are any indication, but to judge by the deities invoked (mainly the Graces and the Muses) these were personal appeals for help with private problems. She also wrote about Selene and Endymion, about Prometheus, about Leto and Niobe and a number of other such subjects, but we cannot say whether any of these were narrative poems or whether the mythological personages were introduced merely as examples, like Helen in fr. 16. Our longest fragment of Sappho, 44, has an ostensibly mythological theme, but it is only an apparent exception to the general run of her extant verse. The subject is the marriage of Hector and Andromache, but in the thirty-five lines or so that we possess there is no narrative to speak of; Sappho's one purpose is to paint a picture of jubilant celebration. And though her style in this poem has certain epic features, there is nothing Homeric about the scene which she describes. The myrrh, cassia and frankincense, and the *satinai* (or light barouches) for the women to go about in, do not belong to the heroic age, but they would have been familiar to Sappho herself. So under the guise of mythological narrative she is really giving her audience a vivid picture of contemporary life. In any case, it cannot be said that this fragment adds to her reputation. Quaint, lively and fluent, it is the work of an able poet; but there is no subtlety in it, and no inspiration.

Subtlety is the last thing for which we should look in some of the verses that Sappho wrote for weddings. Little need be said about such fragments as 110a and 111 except to record pleasure that this much romanticised poet could turn out such simple silly stuff. But others of these fragments stick strangely in the mind, though we may not easily be able to say why. We have seen how fr. 104a impressed Tennyson and Eliot; the two verses of fr. 114a seemed to Lesky (p. 139) 'as tender in their feeling as anything in Greek poetry':

παρθενία, παρθενία, ποῖ με λίποισ᾽ ἀποίχηι;
†οὐκέτι ἤξω πρὸς σέ, οὐκέτι ἤξω.†

[Maidenhood, maidenhood, where do you go away to, abandoning me? 'No more will I come to you, no more will I come.']

These fragments have often been compared to folk poetry; certainly, with their constant repetition of words they are unlike most of the rest of her work. Their simplicity is of a different kind from the simplicity that we meet in some of her larger fragments; and yet we shall hardly be right to call it naiveté. Let us consider, for example, fr. 102, not from a wedding poem, but a piece which has seemed to some to have a similar folk quality:

γλύκηα μᾶτερ, οὔτοι δύναμαι κρέκην τὸν ἴστον
πόθωι δάμεισα παῖδος βραδίναν δι᾽ Ἀφροδίταν.

[Sweet mother, I cannot weave the web; I am overcome by desire for a boy because of slender Aphrodite.]

This is the model for Landor's well known poem:

Mother, I cannot mind my wheel;
    My fingers ache, my lips are dry;
Oh! if you felt the pain I feel!
    But oh, who ever felt as I?

No longer could I doubt him true;
    All other men may use deceit;
He always said my eyes were blue,
    And often swore my lips were sweet.

The contrast shows how far any folk element there may be in Sappho is from 'folksiness'. Landor creates a self-conscious naiveté in the girl's belief that her passion is unique and in the gauche anticlimax of the lapse from 'always' to 'often'; there is nothing like this in Sappho. But nor on the other hand does Sappho exhibit the cultivated hyper-restraint that we sometimes get from Callimachus (Epigram 19Pf.):

δωδεκέτη τὸν παῖδα πατὴρ ἀπέθηκε Φίλιππος
    ἐνθάδε, τὴν πολλὴν ἐλπίδα, Νικοτέλην.

[Philippus, a father, buried his twelve-year-old son here, his great hope, Nicoteles.]

Such bareness is the conscious archaism of the sophisticated. Sappho is neither austere nor naive, she is just luminously direct; whereas Callimachus goes for calculated understatement, she provides statement merely. Eliot once said that she remains in one's mind as setting the standard 'for having fixed a particular emotion in the right and the minimum number of words, once and for all'.[44] If this is so, it is a high achievement, but one not readily subject to analysis.

[44] *To Criticise the Critic* (London, 1965), p. 127.

7

Fragment 94, lines 1–11:

τεθνάκην δ᾽ ἀδόλως θέλω·
ἄ με ψισδομένα κατελίμπανεν

πόλλα καὶ τόδ᾽ ἔειπέ μοι·
ὤιμ᾽ ὡς δεῖνα πεπόνθαμεν·
Ψάπφ᾽, ἦ μάν σ᾽ ἀέκοισ᾽ ἀπυλιμπάνω.   5

τὰν δ᾽ ἔγω τάδ᾽ ἀμειβόμαν·
χαίροισ᾽ ἔρχεο κἄμεθεν
μέμναισ᾽· οἶσθα γὰρ ὤς σε πεδήπομεν.

αἰ δὲ μή, ἀλλά σ᾽ ἔγω θέλω
ὄμναισαι . . .   . . . αι,   10
κα . . .   καὶ κάλ᾽ ἐπάσχομεν . . .

[. . . and honestly I wish I were dead. Weeping much she left me and said
this: 'Ah, how dreadfully we have fared; Sappho, truly it is against my
will that I leave you.' I answered her thus: 'Farewell; go, and remember
me; for you know how we attended upon you. But if you do not, I wish to
remind you . . . and we had beautiful times . . .']

This poem is written in a three-line stanza consisting of two glyconics
and a third glyconic with dactylic expansion. Glyconic lines are used
by Anacreon in poems, such as frs. 348, 357, 359 and 360, that have
a certain seriousness underlying the levity, or at least the simplicity,
of their surfaces. Sappho does not have Anacreon's sophisticated and
sometimes ironic tone, but her poem too is marked by a blend of
seriousness and simplicity. It is spare and direct. The construction of
the sentences is plain and paratactic. The parting words of Sappho
and her friend are introduced baldly by the phrases *kai tod'eeipe moi*
and *tan d'egō tad'ameiboman*. There is a stark asyndeton between the
first and second lines. The language of the two women is direct but
restrained.

Despite this plainness (or because of it), the poem is affecting. Essentially this is because Sappho shows us the strong feeling underlying
the apparent ordinariness of what is being said. *ōs deina pepontha-*
men, says the departing friend, in words which could perfectly well be
colloquial. *deinos* is one of the commonest of Greek adjectives, as
ubiquitous and as various in its application as 'nice' or 'awful' in
English. It is one of the staple epithets of everyday speech ('dreadful',
'strange', 'odd', 'clever'), and yet it can also be used in very solemn
contexts, often when a sense of wonderment is being expressed. *deinon*
to tiktein estin, says Clytemnestra in the *Electra* of Sophocles (770): to

give birth to a child is a strange (mighty, wonderful) thing. The guilty queen would like to be able to hate and reject her daughter, but she cannot. Many things are *deinos*, sing the chorus of the *Antigone* (332f.), and none is more *deinos* than man. *deinos* is the womb, Antigone declares in the *Seven against Thebes* (1031), from which she and her brother were born; she means that the bond of sisterhood is powerful, and also mysterious. Sappho's friend uses a word which is ordinary but very suggestive. It is also especially apt in this place: parting is 'such sweet sorrow'; it is 'all we know of heaven, And all we need of hell'; when friends or lovers say goodbye, they seem to find their own emotions hard to understand, for the experience is painful, and yet in a way beautiful; they are brought up against those great mysteries, the passing of time, the force of circumstance. Something of this is in the commonplace adjective *deinos*.

peponthamen is another restrained but powerful word. In origin the verb *paschein* is emotionally neutral: 'to have something happen to one.' But as early as Homer it comes to have, without any qualifying adverb, a more specific meaning: 'to have something unpleasant happen to one', to 'suffer' in the usual sense of that word in modern English. Sappho's friend has spoken a sentence which could be as colourless as 'What a strange thing has happened to us'; but the words that she uses imply that she means much more.

A similar austerity can be found later in Sappho's reply. *chairois' ercheo*, she says. The regular way of saying goodbye in Greek is to use an imperative form of the verb *chairein*, and similarly the participle can also be used as a formula of farewell. *chairōn aphikoio*, Helen says to Telemachus in the *Odyssey* (15.128), as he prepares to quit Sparta for home. When the imperative mood is used as a greeting or goodbye, the literal meaning of *chairein*, 'to rejoice', is probably quite forgotten, but where the participle is found, the speaker usually proves to be putting emphasis on the word; it is as though he were saying not just 'farewell' but 'fare*well*'. Telemachus is going back to face his mother's suitors, and so there is particular point in Helen wishing him luck; in fact she says specifically, 'May you *arrive* with gladness', not (as would be more usual), 'Go with gladness.' In Euripides' *Alcestis* (813) the servant says to Heracles, *chairōn ith'; hēmin despotōn melei kaka*. There is a deliberate contrast: 'Do *you* go *gladly*: the *trouble* concerns *our* master.' In the *Trachiniae* (819f.) Hyllus speaks of Deianeira with bitter sarcasm:

ἀλλ' ἑρπέτω χαίρουσα· τὴν δὲ τέρψιν ἣν
τὠμῶι δίδωσι πατρί, τήνδ' αὐτὴ λάβοι.

[Let her go *gladly*, and may she receive the same *pleasure* that she gives to my father.]

The most touching example of the usage comes in the *Hippolytus* (1440f.) when the hero dying bids adieu to the goddess Artemis:

χαίρουσα καὶ σὺ στεῖχε, παρθέν᾽ ὀλβία·
μακρὰν δὲ λείπεις ῥᾳδίως ὁμιλίαν.

[Do you go with gladness, blessed maiden; easily you leave our long companionship.]

chairousa here is very pathetic. For Hippolytus the parting is a tragedy, but to the goddess it is easy; the death of her devotee will not disturb her divine serenity. She is indeed *olbia*; she will indeed go her way with gladness.

And so with Sappho: *chairois'ercheo* means 'goodbye', but it also means 'go gladly'. Through the conventional words of parting an overtone of pathos can be heard: Sappho wishes her friend happiness even though the separation is a sadness to herself. There is even an implication that the friend may cheerfully forget her former companion, as we see from the next two lines. Sappho has only one very small request to make: 'Remember me.' This is not much to ask, 'for you know how we attended upon you'; none the less, the poet fears that the friend does not appreciate how she has been valued. This fear is expressed in just three tiny words: *ai de mē* ('but if not'). There are no reproaches, no angry complaints, no self-pity; just the plain assertion, put in the simplest words possible, that she at least (*egō* is emphatic) wants to remember the happy times that they had together. One of the beauties of the poem is the restraint with which Sappho expresses the sorrow of parting through words that are all of comfort and remembered happiness.

It has been maintained that the papyri discovered in the last hundred years have lessened Sappho's stature. Frs. 1 and 31 are exceptional, so the argument goes; no doubt they were picked out by Dionysius and Longinus because their quality was unusually high. We now have considerable if incomplete pieces of Sappho's other verse, and they are markedly inferior to the two great poems; we may deduce, therefore, that her poetry was, on average, not very distinguished.

A consideration of fr. 94 shows the dangers in such a view. I argued that fr. 16 is a work of skill and subtlety; the whole poem does not survive, and we cannot be sure where it began or ended, but at least the fragment that we have is sufficiently self-contained for us to be able to judge it more or less fairly. With fr. 94, however, we are not so fortunate. It begins in the middle of a stanza. The second word is *de*; very likely there was a contrast with the clause that went before, but what was in that clause we have no means of guessing. And what is the tone of those first four words? Is this a stark statement of appalling grief, or is it a typically colloquial exaggeration? *adolos* is a word found in solemn treaties and in drinking songs; how is it being used on this occasion?

This first line presents a vexing problem: is this Sappho addressing us in her own person, or are these words the end of a speech by the friend?[45] If it is Sappho who speaks, the poem contains three layers of time: the desolate present, the parting, and memories of a still more distant time of happiness. On this account one of the beauties of the poem is that Sappho, bitterly grieved herself, speaks words of comfort, although it is the girl, for all her sobbing, who will sooner find consolation; in the plain but understated contrast between the two women much of the pathos of the piece resides.

If line 1 belongs to the girl, Sappho's sorrow at parting still remains, by delicate implication, in lines 7ff., but we can no longer speak so strongly of desolation or bitter misery. Anne Burnett wishes to go further, contrasting an effusively tearful friend with a Sappho who insists that 'there is refreshment, even joy, in memory' and means it. This is not so much wrong as misleading because it ignores the extent to which we are not told what to think. The friend may have all the words of overt grief, but they are still plainly expressed; the grief may be exaggerated, but we are not compelled to believe so; the poet may not know the answer herself. Sappho simply presents the scene; as in real life, so in the poem, we are left to make our own judgment. She does not say that memory will console; she does not say that it will fail to console; she makes no comment at all. However we take the first line, the poem's clarity and lack of authorial intrusion are remarkable on so personal a theme, and a source of pathos and (in a literary sense) veracity. The contrast with the subjectivity of fr. 31 is great.

From the tenth line onwards the fragment is badly damaged, but so far as we can judge, this part of the poem seems to have been largely static. Sappho has said that she wants to remember the past, and she slips into a daydream in which the senses of touch and sight and smell are all indulged; the verses drift idly among garlands, beds, perfumes and soft flesh without apparently going anywhere; the comfortable flow of the lines contrasts with the stiff, terse language that preceded them. The tensions of personal encounter have perhaps proved too much; at any rate, the unhurried memories seem to avoid the personal and work indirectly, dwelling upon fair objects, physical comforts and shared ceremonies. But it is impossible to be confident about the effect of this without knowing the overall structure of the poem. Suppose, for the sake of argument, that it was yet another example of ring composition. It might have begun by describing how the friend came

---

[45] Most scholars have taken the former view; the case against them is forcefully argued by Burnett.

to take her leave of the poet, with perhaps some account of the reason for the separation. The exchange between the two women would have followed, and Sappho's extensive reminiscences of past pleasures. Her transitions are sometimes abrupt; she might have returned suddenly to her original starting point: the friend's departure. The effect would have been of a rough awakening, the poet jolted out of a happy dream into harsh reality.

All this, of course, is speculation; but it would explain why Sappho's remembrances of things past are so long and leisurely. On this account the static, dreamy quality of these lines would be an essential part of the whole scheme of the poem: had they been fewer, the rude awakening would have been less rude. But taken purely in isolation, they may seem, at least to an unsympathetic judge, a little slack or dull. Obviously no weight can be put upon an unevidenced guess about verses not extant; but we can see how rash it may be to judge an incomplete fragment simply on the basis of the surviving lines.

Fr. 96 is also constructed on a glyconic base, though in this case each one of the three lines of the stanza is different in metre, and within the stanza a word may freely run across from one line into the next. At a casual glance the piece appears flexible, loose, simple at any rate; but it has caused much puzzlement. After three lines in which we can make out the phrase 'often directing her mind hither' and probably the name of Sardis, the fragment continues:

σε θέαι σ᾽ ἰκέλαν ἀρι-
γνώται, σᾶι δὲ μάλιστ᾽ ἔχαιρε μόλπαι·   5

νῦν δὲ Λύδαισιν ἐμπρέπεται γυναί-
κεσσιν ὡς ποτ᾽ ἀελίω
δύντος ἀ βροδοδάκτυλος σελάννα

πάντα περρέχοισ᾽ ἄστρα· φάος δ᾽ ἐπί-
σχει θάλασσαν ἐπ᾽ ἀλμύραν   10
ἴσως καὶ πολυανθέμοις ἀρούραις·

ἀ δ᾽ ἐέρσα κάλα κέχυται, τεθά-
λαισι δὲ βρόδα κἄπαλ᾽ ἄν-
θρυσκα καὶ μελίλωτος ἀνθεμώδης.

πόλλα δὲ ζαφοίταισ᾽ ἀγάνας ἐπι-   15
μνάσθεισ᾽ Ἄτθιδος ἰμέρωι
λέπταν ποι φρένα κ.ρ . . . βόρηται . . .

[She . . . you like a goddess manifest, and delighted most of all in your song. But now she stands out among the women of Lydia, like the rosy-fingered moon after the sun has set, surpassing all the stars. Its light spreads alike over the salt sea and the fields full of flowers; the dew is shed in beauty and roses bloom and tender chervil and blossomy melilot.

Wandering to and fro, she remembers gentle Atthis with yearning and
. . . devours (?) her tender heart . . .]

At line 8 Schubart, followed by most editors, mended the unmetrical
a brododaktulos mēna of the papyrus by replacing *mēna* with the
commoner word for moon, *selanna*; but A. J. Beattie once tentatively
suggested that it might be the adjective which was corrupt: something
like *brododaktulēa* ('rosy-ringed') should be read.[46] Homer's *rhodo-
daktulos*, a fine epithet for the dawn, does not make obvious sense
applied to the moon; however, a rosy halo can sometimes be seen
around the moon: Aratus mentions it as a sign of a coming storm
(*Phaen.* 796f.). If Beattie's idea were right, Sappho would have taken
a formulaic adjective out of Homer and transformed it by the alteration
of a letter or two into something fresh and perceptive – an elegant
sleight of hand.

But attractive as the idea seems, it is likely to be an instance of
modern sentiment misguiding the critic. Schubart was probably right,
and we should compare 'rosy-fingered Moon' here to 'rosy-armed Dawn'
in fr. 58 and 'golden-sandalled Dawn' in frs. 103 and 123; that is to
say, the moon is half way to being a mythological figure, and realism
is not Sappho's intention. Certainly the picture of nature here functions very differently from that in fr. 2, to which it has too often been
likened. Here is no unusual perceptiveness in the interpretation of
things seen, but a plain account that expands calmly and regularly,
developing almost into a catalogue when the names of the flowers are
reached. Three kinds of flowers are listed, of two, three and four
syllables respectively; the stanza in which they appear contains three
descriptive epithets, one in each line, and again of two, three and four
syllables in length. Indeed, if we look back over the three stanzas of
the simile, we find one descriptive epithet in the first of them, two in
the second, and three in the third. Sappho's procedure in this part of
her poem is cool and slow, not imaginative in investigating landscape,
but wholly apt for the cool, empty scene that she puts before us.

It is widely agreed that the description of the moon passes beyond
simile and turns into a picture of a real night; so much was allowed
by a critic as sober and sceptical as Page. But I doubt whether this is
the whole truth; even in the lines about the dew the element of simile,
though secondary, seems to have been not altogether forgotten. Sappho
calls the chervil *apalos* ('tender'); this is a favourite advective of hers,
but on the other extant occasions when she uses it, she applies it
either to people or to parts of their bodies (hands or necks).[47] Here, for
once, it is used of objects, but we may well suspect that Sappho has

[46] JHS 77 (1957), 320.
[47] I exclude from consideration fr. 94. 22, where the noun with *apalos* is unknown.

people in mind. Flowers, so frequently and so naturally mentioned by her in association with young womanhood, surely in this place correspond to the girls who surround the absent friend in Lydia. We have already been told that the friend excels them as the moon excels the stars; now we learn, through the medium of imagery, that her radiant beauty enlivens those about her (there was a belief that the moon nourished the dew). This interpretation – essentially Bowra's, purged of some extragavance – has been censured as fanciful and even tasteless, but it seems to me to emerge easily from the shape of the poem.

To our own sensibilities moonlight seems beautiful, but also a little mournful. Perhaps we recall Milton's description of the melancholy life in *Il Penseroso* (65–70):

> I walk unseen
> On the dry smooth-shaven green,
> To behold the wandering moon,
> Riding near her highest noon,
> Like one that had been led astray
> Through the heav'n's wide pathless way . . .

Or Sidney's sonnet to his Stella (*Astrophil and Stella*, 31.1f.):

> With how sad steps, O Moon, thou climb'st the skies!
> How silently, and with how wan a face!

When we read in Sappho of the moonlight flooding down upon fields and waters, we think that there is something melancholy in the beauty of the scene. *We* think so; but did she? For myself, I believe that she did and that on this basis we can make sense of the simile's structure. Page complains that the transition at the end of the simile is abrupt, and logically no doubt it is; but this is surely not the impression with which most readers are left. As the night and the moonlit sea and fields are set before us, we are prepared for the sad, restless wanderings of the absent friend – in a night, we cannot help feeling, just like the one described – so that they seem not greatly to alter the mood of the poem when we hear about them. We have become aware that the splendid isolation of the moon in the heavens is lonely as well as glorious; the poem modulates, as it were, into a minor key. After all, we know that Sappho wrote about the Moon's love for Endymion (fr. 199); it was not unnatural for her to associate the bright disc in the night sky with yearning desire.

And yet, on another level, the simile is emotionless. We have seen the calm, lingering style of its construction. It is empty of all human beings or other living creatures,[48] and although Sappho loves depicting

---

[48] C. Carey aptly contrasts *Il.* 8. 555ff., where the simile of a moonlit night ends, 'And the shepherd is glad in his heart.' (p. 367n.)

people and things in motion, it is entirely static: the perfect tenses of *kechutai* and *tethalaisi* show us that the dew has already been shed and the flowers have already grown. We have found or suspected areas in other poems of Sappho which were 'irrelevant' in literal terms but important to the total emotional structure. Here, similarly, there is an area in the centre of the poem which by its stillness and emptiness contrasts with and enhances the human drama on either side of it.

This account of the poem may appear to be self-contradictory in making the simile emotional and emotionless at the same time; but the contradiction is apparent only, and of a kind that may be quite common. Here, by way of analogy, is another famous moon, from Milton's *Samson Agonistes* (86ff.):

> The sun to me is dark
> And silent as the moon,
> When she deserts the night
> Hid in her vacant interlunar cave.

These lines are obviously the expression of fierce pain, but they work upon our feelings through the creation of a scene wonderfully cold, pure and austere. In a comparable way, Sappho uses a picture that is itself pale, vacant and drained of emotion to excite an emotional response. If this interpretation is right, her restraint is remarkable: the simile speaks only of light and beauty; nothing is overtly said of the girl's sorrow. Schadewaldt went further: no word is spoken, and yet the poem is full of Sappho's own love and longing. It may be so; but in the present state of our knowledge the idea is no more than a guess. If we could only make more out of lines 18–20, we should be much better placed to understand the piece; but here the scene is dark, with no kindly moon to light our way.

The simile in fr. 96 is recalled by fr. 34:

> ἄστερες μὲν ἀμφὶ κάλαν σελάνναν
> ἂψ ἀπυκρύπτοισι φάεννον εἶδος
> ὄπποτα πλήθοισα μάλιστα λάμπηι
> γᾶν

[The stars around the beautiful moon hide away their bright faces when she is full and shines the most over the earth]

The similarity between the two passages suggests that here again Sappho is speaking of a girl who excels all her companions in beauty. Further evidence of this is provided by *men* in the first line, implying that the moon and stars are about to be compared or contrasted with something else, and by the words *apukruptoisi* and *eidos*, which strikingly personify the stars and suggest that Sappho had something more than the beauties of the night sky in mind.[49] Once again, we are liable to have our feelings about the fragment influenced by later literature; English-speaking readers will probably recall Wotton's poem *On His Mistress, the Queen of Bohemia*:

> You meaner beauties of the night,
>   That poorly satisfy our eyes,
> More by your number, than your light;
>   You common people of the skies,
>   What are you when the moon shall rise?

Even without this association we should, I think, have found the fragment memorable. Memorability is an elusive quality; it has been called the test of very good poetry and of very bad poetry. For better or worse Sappho's poetry is insistently memorable; there are so many thoughts and expressions that refuse to be forgotten.

We are told by the emperor Julian that somewhere in the same poem Sappho described the moon as *arguria* ('silver'). We are freely accustomed to use the English adjective in a transferred sense to mean 'like silver in appearance'. *argureos* preserves its literal signification – 'made of silver' – much more strongly, and is only rarely used as a metaphor. 'Silver' is an excellent adjective to describe the colour and sheen of the moon; so much seems obvious to us, but Sappho had noticed it for the first time and was prepared to use language quite boldly to make her point. And she may also have had another aim in view. The one metaphorical use of *argureos* elsewhere occurs in Alcman's first Partheneion (fr. 1.55), where Hagesichora's face is so described. Maybe this is to give the effect of the pale light of early dawn on her features, but it may rather refer to the use of white lead as a cosmetic. Pindar speaks at line 8 of his second Isthmian about *argurōtheisai prosōpa ... aoidai*, 'songs whose faces have been silvered'; he is referring to poets who accept fees, but the phrase is wittier and more pointed if faces were silvered literally as well as metaphorically. If this is correct, it is probable that when Sappho used the adjective, she was thinking not only of the moon but also of the girl to whom the moon is compared. As in the fragment about the apple-gatherers, her language would have given vividness both to what was within the simile and to what was outside it.

Another reason for not judging Sappho as a whole by frs. 1 and 31 is that in important respects they would appear to have been unlike a great part of her poetry. These two poems concentrate on Sappho

---

[49] Bacchylides too uses the moon putting the stars to shame as a simile (8. 27–9), and it is plausible to suppose that his imagery was inspired by Sappho's. As Perrotta observed (p. 71), our appreciation of her art is enhanced by comparison with the later passage.

and her emotions to the virtual exclusion of all else. None of her friends or rivals is named; that would be entirely inappropriate. But Sappho's poetry was full of names: Atthis, Gongyla, Anactoria, Dica, Gorgo, Andromeda, Gyrinno, Archeanassa – all these in just a handful of fragments. Moreover, if the bulk of our biographical information about Sappho derives ultimately from her own poetry, as seems likely, she must have revealed a good deal about her life and circumstances in her works. This again would be at variance with the method of frs. 1 and 31, in which she ignores external circumstances in order to focus attention on to a particular mood or moment.

Greek love poetry, it has often been said, fixes its attention on the lover: it was left to the Romans to give the personality of the beloved a place in their verse. This just generalisation is exemplified by frs. 1 and 31, but fr. 16 is perhaps a partial exception, for here the reader is suddenly made aware of Anactoria's physical presence, and in such a way that her personality also is suggested. And in a few other fragments there are tantalising hints that Sappho might have been feeling her way towards a sense of the subjectivity of a lover's choice. It may be the implication of frs. 41 and 50 that physical beauty alone is not enough; character and the sheer irrationality of personal preference are fundamentally important. Fr. 49 may indicate that it was the very fact of Atthis being small and gauche that made Sappho fall for her.

Certainly she talked about the doings of herself and her friends. In various fragments (133, 82a, 144) she tells us that Andromeda has been nicely paid back, that Dica (or Mnasidica) has a better figure than Gyrinno, that some people have 'had quite enough' of Gorgo. More than once she draws attention to the importance of dress sense, and wonders where she can get a suitable headband for her daughter (frs. 24, 57, 98a, 98b); she complains that Atthis has deserted her for Andromeda and laments that those that she befriends do her the worst harm; she declares that somebody or other has never come across anyone more tedious than Irana, she observes with a sneer that Archeanassa will be called wife of Gorgo, she exults over a rival who will be forgotten after her death because she lacks poetic ability, and protests that she is not a spiteful person (frs. 131, 26, 213, 55, 120). How trivial is all this? It is difficult to judge without having more of the poems from which these fragments come. Three lines about her daughter (fr. 132) have softened even the stern heart of Page: 'I have a beautiful daughter, my beloved Cleis, who looks like the golden flowers, whom I would not [exchange] for all Lydia or lovely . . .' This is charming but slight. Yet the very slightness may serve a purpose. Let us suppose that the complete works of Sappho had survived. We should have had, if we may judge from the existing fragments, a remarkable picture of the daily life and concerns of a circle of friends (and enemies). Sappho might have looked less like Sarah Bernhardt and more like Jane Austen. And the backbiting and tittle-tattle, apparently so trivial, could for all we know have been as significant and as subtly used as by that novelist.

Throughout antiquity people were fascinated by Sappho's life and personality; few Greek writers attracted so much biographical specu- lation. This was partly, perhaps, because she was a woman, and pas- sionate; but there were other female singers, and other poets of love. Sappho was unique, however, in offering a series of glimpses into the life of a real society; her poetry was such that of its very nature it was liable to excite the inquisitiveness of later generations. She was not writing her memoirs, of course, and evidently there was not sufficient information in the poems to enable biographers to reconstruct the story of Atthis or Anactoria or to relate the tale of Sappho's amours; but there was enough, surely, to make people long for more, and in some cases to supply it from their own imaginations.

Here once again it may be helpful to compare Sappho with Catullus. Today he enjoys a high reputation which extends beyond the circle of professional scholars, and rightly or wrongly his fame in the wider world rests almost entirely on his shorter poems. He wrote little verses about the guest who pinched the napkins and the man who overdid his aspirates; he giggled at goings-on in the back streets, and assaulted his friends with gross and jovial obscenity. No one supposes that any of these poems is profound, but they are extraordinarily direct, and cumulatively they give us, as no other Latin poet does, a partial but authentic picture of a certain society. A typical modern assessment of Catullus' shorter poems is this from E. A. Havelock (p. 75): 'The total of a hundred and nine poems and fragments deserves to be regarded as a single body of work displaying certain common characteristics of style and substance.' In other words, his poetry exhibits that 'signifi- cant unity' which Eliot named as one of the marks of a major poet; and we can certainly say of him that the knowledge of a very large part of his work 'makes one enjoy more, because it makes one under- stand better, any one of his poems.'

We are not lucky enough to have a 'very large part' of Sappho's work, but clearly enough it possessed the sort of unity that is found in Catullus. One cannot be entirely confident of any negative proposi- tion about Sappho when we have lost so much of her, but it is surely remarkable how much she does *not* put into her poems. In sharp contrast to Alcaeus, she says next to nothing about the turbulent politics of Lesbos; it is ironically appropriate that the principal allusion to a political event that we have from her comes in a poem about ladies' headgear (fr. 98b. 7–9). That fear and hatred of old age which haunted Mimnermus and Anacreon and which seems so natural an emotion in any poet of love does not appear to trouble her; she thinks only of the immediate moment. The mutability of fortune was a topic that enthralled the Greeks; it dominates the history of Herodotus, it underlies a great part of Greek tragedy, and among lyric poets we find it as a recurrent theme in Simonides; but Sappho does not dwell upon it at all. The fear of death, so important in so much Greek poetry from Homer onwards, seems to have passed her by. Aristotle tells us that she thought death an evil, but for an oddly uncompelling reason: 'The gods have judged it so; else they would have died long ago' (fr. 261). This does not seem to be the language of one much possessed by death; the context may have been almost frivolous. In one poem (fr. 95) she welcomed the prospect of dying and seeing the 'dewy lotus flowers on the banks of the Acheron' – a surprisingly optimistic vision of the underworld. Contrast Homer: the ghost of Achilles tells Odysseus that he would rather live as the serf of a poor landless peasant than be ruler over all the dead (*Od.* 11.489–91). Contrast Mimnermus' description of the childless man who 'lacks children and goes down beneath the earth to Hades longing for them above all else' (fr. 2.13f.). Contrast the supposedly light-hearted Anacreon (fr. 395.7–12):

διὰ ταῦτ᾽ ἀνασταλύζω
θαμὰ Τάρταρον δεδοικώς·
Ἀίδεω γάρ ἐστι δεινὸς
μυχός, ἀργαλῆ δ᾽ ἐς αὐτὸν
κάτοδος· καὶ γὰρ ἑτοῖμον
καταβάντι μὴ ἀναβῆναι.

[Therefore I often sob, fearing Tartarus; for the little room of Hades is terrible, and the way down to it hard; and it is certain that one who has gone down cannot come up again.]

Even in the brief words of Mimnermus there is a strong feeling for the reality of the underworld as a place literally below the ground, literally beneath our feet; we seem to see the dying man still calling out for children as he is dragged away, downwards to Hades. This sense of the physical actuality of the underworld is far more intense in Anacreon's poem. In the previous lines he has been lamenting the constricting effects of old age: the grace of youth has gone from him, his teeth are rotting and 'there is no longer much time of sweet life left'. A modern poet would probably proceed from such a sentiment to speak, whether with dread or resignation, of his impending extinction; not so Anacreon. To him death means not annihilation but further constriction and hardship;[50] it could almost be described as the process of ageing intensified. The way to the underworld is *argaleos*, 'difficult'

---

[50] For this sense of constriction compare the black words of Aeschylus (*Eum.* 339f.): *thanōn d'ouk agan eleutheros* ('Once a man is dead, he is not too greatly free').

or 'painful'. Anacreon clearly means this literally; it is not a symbolic statement like Virgil's 'facilis descensus Averno' (*Aen.* 6.126). And the way is *downward*; the physical location of Tartarus is emphasised. The last two lines begin with the words *katodos* and *katabanti*, and in the second of them *katabanti* is balanced by the contrasting *anabēnai*. And above all the place of Hades is a *muchos*, a word that was used of the little dark room that formed the innermost part of a house; Anacreon feels vividly that to be dead is to be imprisoned in a small, cramped cell, without light or space. (There may also be a bitter joke: the *muchos* was where the stores were kept, and the underworld is a 'storehouse' of dead souls.) No wonder that he sobs aloud – *anastaluzō*, a striking word.

Anacreon's means are economical; he uses few words, and employs a light metre more often used for drinking songs. Indeed much of the strength of the poem derives from the painful contrast between the apparent flippancy of the manner and the grimness of the content. Catullus attempted something similar more than five centuries later. Writing in hendecasyllables, a metre normally used for skits and lampoons, he urges his mistress to live and love with him and cock a snook at censorious greybeards. Then suddenly his tone grows serious (5.4–6):

> *soles occidere et redire possunt;*
> *nobis cum semel occidit brevis lux,*
> *nox est perpetua una dormienda.*

[Suns can sink and return, but we, when our brief light has once sunk, must sleep throughout one eternal night.]

Once again there is an effective conflict between the gay metre and the grave matter; and yet the emotional atmosphere is very different from Anacreon's. Whereas the Greek poet shudders at the prospect of the life (of a kind) that awaits him after death, the Roman looks forward to nothing better or worse than oblivion. Yeats once remarked (*Explorations*, p. 438) that no one 'has ever trembled or been awestruck by nymph-haunted or Fury-haunted wood described in Roman poetry.' Similarly one might say that no one has ever shuddered with dread at the prospect of a Roman Tartarus. Lucretius, writing at the same time as Catullus, alleged that his contemporaries were tormented by fear of the mythological terrors of the underworld, but he had a particular axe to grind, and it is difficult to believe him; we more readily credit Cicero's opinion that even among women and children these fears had by his time been dissipated (*Tusc.* 1.37). Greek mythology was a living part of Greek religion, both Hades and Olympus, both chthonic deities and Homeric gods; the Romans, though they took over a mythological system from the Greeks, could only accept it indirectly, as allegory or as literary fiction. Herein lies one of the great differences between the experience of the two races.

Sappho, however, seems to have lacked the typically Greek feeling about death. Certainly she had a lively devotion to the Olympian gods and especially Aphrodite. When we read fr. 5, in which she asks Aphrodite and the Nereids that her brother repent of his misdeeds and do honour to his sister, we feel that we are overhearing a private prayer. Indeed this is perhaps the reason why the poem, as a poem, appears to be so dull: Sappho wants to obtain a favour from the gods, and she has no specifically 'literary' purpose whatever. The nearest she comes to the language of Homer or Anacreon about the underworld is in fr. 55, an assault on an unknown woman:

κατθάνοισα δὲ κείσηι οὐδέ ποτα μναμοσύνα σέθεν
ἔσσετ᾽ οὐδέ †ποκ᾽† ὕστερον· οὐ γὰρ πεδέχηις βρόδων
τὼν ἐκ Πιερίας· ἀλλ᾽ ἀφάνης κἀν Ἀίδα δόμωι
φοιτάσηις πεδ᾽ ἀμαύρων νεκύων ἐκπεποταμένα.

[When you have died, you shall lie there, nor shall there ever be any memory of you thereafter, for you have no share in the roses from Pieria; but unseen in the house of Hades also you shall walk among the dim dead, having flown away from here.]

This is splendidly vivid invective. Sappho's visual imagination is keen, as usual, and she uses it to create a lively picture of fluttering ineffectuality. The woman's departure from the land of the living is shown to us in literal, physical terms; we see her first flying away (the aorist participle is nicely calculated) and then wandering about among the dead. *phoitan* means to 'roam about' or 'go to and fro'; Homer uses the word of the ghost of Achilles (*Od.* 11.539), and other writers use it of dreams. It is an apt word for the spirits of the dead and equally apt to express futile or flustered activity. *aphanēs* ('unseen') is a two-edged word; it is used especially of the dead, but it is also applied to living people in the sense of 'mean' or 'insignificant'. There is a telling detail in *kan'Aida domōi*, 'in the house of Hades *also*'; the woman is obscure among the living and she will be obscure among the dead. *amauros* is another cutting epithet; like the English 'dim', it is applied both to ghosts and to undistinguished people. Sappho's victim is a thoroughly dim creature and the dim underworld is where she belongs.

As an insult this is admirable, if insults can ever be that; and as well as being magnificently offensive, she has set before us a scene of the underworld which we seem to see with our own eyes. Her imagination is vivid here, but it is a literary imagination: her real reason for crowing over her enemy is not that her ghostly existence will be miserable but that she is a woman of no importance, with no skill as a poet; the visual details are essentially a gloating development of this idea. Not for one moment does it cross Sappho's mind that the same fate may await herself after death; and it would surely be mistaken to suppose that she is expecting, by contrast, to go to the isles of the blest. She just does not think about the matter at all. The spirit behind her words, therefore, is very different from Homer's, even though the terms used may be similar.

8

A brief fragment (976 in PMG) commonly attributed to Sappho but denied to her by Lobel and Page provides a fascinating if subjective test of whether we can sense a 'Sapphic' quality in her surviving verses:

δέδυκε μὲν ἀ σελάνα
καὶ Πληϊάδες, μέσαι δὲ
νύκτες, παρὰ δ᾽ ἔρχετ᾽ ὤρα,
ἐγὼ δὲ μόνα καθεύδω.

[The moon has set and the Pleiads, it is midnight, the watch passes, but I sleep alone.]

The facts bearing on authorship are, very briefly, these. The poem is quoted by Hephaestion;[51] he does not name the author. Elsewhere, however, he quotes Sappho without giving the author's name. The dialect is not Aeolic, and in three places the metre forbids the restoration of normal Aeolic forms. This metre ('enoplion' or acephalous hipponacteum) is not found in the extant fragments of Sappho or Alcaeus.

On this basis it might appear that there is nothing positively to indicate Sappho's authorship, and some evidence against it. Unfortunately, the matter is a little more complicated. Hephaestion quotes the lines at the end of a passage in which he discusses the practice of 'the Aeolians', that is, Sappho and Alcaeus; and since the speaker is a woman, one strongly suspects that he or his source attributed the poem to Sappho. On the other hand, this very suspicion may tell in the opposite sense: poems with female speakers would naturally tend to be attributed to the most famous of female poets, and as we shall see, the character of this speaker provides arguments against Sappho's authorship.

Parallels for the non-Aeolic forms can be found in the fragments of the Lesbian poets, but the appearance of three of them in so short a

---

[51] Also, in the fifteenth century, by Apostolius. His son Arsenius attributes the lines to Sappho; it is hard to know what weight to give to this testimony.

space remains deeply suspicious; if these lines had been found in isolation on a papyrus, we should not give them to Sappho. And for three further reasons I find it hard to think that they are hers. The first of these derives from the last words, 'I sleep alone.' The girl is obviously waiting for her lover. The night wears on and he has still not arrived: when will he come? Now this is the sort of theme which belongs to the world of Hellenistic epigram and love poetry, and which would, indeed, be equally at home in the verses of Horace, Ovid or Propertius: we are given a vignette, a glimpse of a dramatic situation, and seduced into supplying for ourselves a whole little *histoire d'amour*. I have been sceptical about historical generalisations, but I do venture one now: this method is surely alien to archaic lyric; we certainly know of nothing else in Sappho like it. Indeed, in no fragment of hers is the narrative persona anyone other than Sappho herself. But whoever the imagined speaker is in these lines, she is clearly not Sappho. It is beyond reasonable doubt that she is waiting for a *man*, since whereas she must stay at home her lover is free to roam through the streets by night; we are in a world of heterosexual intrigue far removed from Sappho's ethos. The fact that the speaker is a woman is a red herring; she is a dramatic persona, and her sex is in itself no justification for attributing the lines to Sappho rather than any other poet, male or female.

Another reason for doubting Sappho's authorship is to be found in the third line. The manuscripts read *para d'ercheth' hōra*, literally 'the hour passes by'. This has commonly been taken to mean 'time passes by', but *hōra* does not mean time in this sense. The words could perhaps mean 'the opportune moment is passing by' – the girl can only be with her man during the hours of night – but even this seems a little odd. Lavagnini's suggestion (p. 189) that *hōra* means 'the time of youth' is poetically unattractive; the admirable particularity with which the girl marks the slow passage of time, measuring it by moon, Pleiads and midnight, is destroyed by this hopelessly vague and sentimental reflection. The situation in the poem is similar to that in an epigram of Asclepiades (*Anth. Pal.* 5.150): 'Nico swore that she would come to me tonight, but she has not come, and the night watch has gone past . . .' The similarity of the phrase about the night watch, *phulakē de paroichetai*, to the third line of the present poem had already been noticed by Lavagnini when Maas pointed out that according to the *Etymologicum Magnum* the *phulakē* was called *ōra* in some parts of Greece.[52] Taken together these two pieces of evidence are surely decisive, and we should read *para d'erchet'ōra*. Simplicity and exactitude are restored. The words now add to the

---

[52] Lavagnini, p. 188, supposing Asclepiades to be imitating our poem but to have misunderstood the meaning of *hōra*; Maas, p. 131f., alluding to *Et. Mag.* 117.120.

dramatic vividness: the woman lies awake, waiting; she hears the watchmen go past; and *still* he has not come. But the night watch was a part of the highly organised civic society of Hellenistic cities; we do not readily associate it with the early sixth century B.C.

Some scholars – recently Gomme and Clay – have suggested that the poem is complete in its present form. If this appealing theory is accepted, it provides a last reason for doubting Sappho's authorship. For to risk another generalisation, it is not likely that Sappho wrote little gems only four lines long. That again is a manner, so far as lyric poetry is concerned, which belongs to another age. But because Sappho's remains are so fragmentary, critics are easily tempted into thinking that a miraculous brevity was a characteristic of her poems.

It is a tribute of a kind to Sappho that scholars have defended her claim to these lines with such warmth of emotion. Gomme (p. 265) wrote of 'that short poem, which can charm most men's ears, but of which both Lobel and Page have such a hate that they have banished it not only from Sappho, but from Lesbian, and leave it lying about, not telling us what, if it is not Lesbian, it is.' Clay declares sorrowfully (p. 120), 'To the friends of the midnight poem perhaps the strangest thing that philologists have had to say about it is that it cannot belong to Sappho. It is a disappointment that the friends of Sappho have not been friends of the poem ...' Agreeable though it is to find such passion invading the chaste pages of the learned journals, the issue is not a matter of friendship or hatred but of fact; we cannot give the piece to Sappho just because we like it. There is a certain irony in the scholars supplying the emotionalism which the fragment so finely lacks. Its beauty lies especially in the economy with which we are invited to imagine so much: the man's promise, the lonely night (that melancholy moon again), the stages of long sleepless waiting (now the moon sets, now the Pleiads, now the watch *passes*, step by step). The poem's plainness is a world away from Housman's self-pitying para-phrase, with its insistent use of the pathetic fallacy, irrelevant pic-turesqueness and whining repetitions:

The *weeping Pleiads* wester,
   And the moon is under seas;
From bourn to bourn of midnight
   Far *sighs* the rainy breeze:

It *sighs* from a *lost* country
   To a land I have not known;
The *weeping Pleiads* wester,
   And I lie down alone.

The contrast brings out the simplicity and immediacy of the Greek.

These are qualities that we might well wish to call Sapphic; yet the creation of concise dramatic anecdote is not, I believe, what we should expect from her. At all events, a consideration of this fragment concentrates our attention upon what we may suppose the range and limits of her art to be.

9

It may be doubted whether we can hope to discover a unity in the work of every great writer, however much we may enjoy such unity when we find it.[53] But if the work of a writer or of any artist is unified, the unity may be achieved in either of two ways: there is unity by exclusion, when the artist restricts the range of his style, tone or subject-matter and concentrates upon some particular type of form or expression; and there is unity by inclusion, harder to pin down, when the artist combines within his work a variety of diverse or disparate elements in such a way that we sense the impress of a single, individual mind upon the whole. Jane Austen may serve as an example of the first kind of unity; Beethoven perhaps of the second.

Sappho limited herself to a handful of related topics, and her poetry is indeed unified by exclusion; yet in a way she also exhibits a unity of the other kind. Here once more a comparison with Catullus may help. Most of his poems, like hers, are notably restricted in range, but he treats his few themes in very varied ways. Some of his love poems are addressed in pet language to Lesbia herself, with little or no thought, apparently, for any other audience; some appeal against Lesbia to the world. Some are passionately sincere and, as far as we can tell, essentially autobiographical; others, notably the verses addressed to Iuventius, are elegantly 'literary', to use that question-begging word. Some are tersely epigrammatic, some are tirades, some are highly wrought, some careless, some introspective, some recklessly self-indulgent. We know far less about Sappho than Catullus, but all that we do know suggests that her work displayed a diversity in unity which, if not the same as that so much admired in Catullus, was at least comparable. Love and friendship were her topics, but even in the few fragments that have come down to us we can see a striking variety of mood and manner. She may be trivial, she may be profound; she enjoyed bright surfaces, but she knew something of the interior darkness. She dealt with the most slight of human experiences, and the most solemn; we encounter in her few surviving verses jokes and jealousy, religion and picnics, gossip and goddesses, children, passion, tenderness, haberdashery, orchards, lovers, enemies. She writes sometimes plainly, sometimes with amplitude; she can be subjective or

[53] On this question see below, p. 88f.

objective, humorous or melancholy, quietly wistful or violently emotional. These are not simple antitheses: it is a combination of different qualities, varying in their relative proportions from poem to poem but seldom altogether absent, that unifies her work. In almost every fragment of hers that we have examined we have discovered some distinction of mood or tone that sets it apart, sometimes slightly, sometimes markedly, from the other extant pieces; yet her readers have always found in all but the most paltry of her fragments a common quality – a quality that, helplessly, one can only call Sapphic. We know very little about her personality, and yet reading her poetry we are always aware of a voice with a distinctive timbre. Indeed, though she could be so nice in her choice of vocabulary, there seem to have been one or two words of which she was particularly fond: *kalos*, *abros, apalos*. Catullus, too, has his favourite epithets: 'venustus', 'ineptus', 'iucundus', 'bellus', 'lepidus', etc. In his case we can say with fair confidence that some of these words are ordinary colloquialisms, some vogue expressions of the society in which he moved, while some may possibly be individual mannerisms. In Sappho's case we are more uncertain of the nuances.

We have found poets and literary men exuding a somewhat indeterminate enthusiasm for Sappho's irresistible charm. What is fascinating is to discover this kind of enthusiasm reappearing in the work of professional scholars; criticism of Sappho is not, as it has been with many another ancient poet, a matter of *belles lettres* on one side ranged against *Altertumswissenschaft* on the other. Schadewaldt (p. 49), Treu (p. 158) and Lesky (p. 143) all speak of her 'magic', a magic, Lesky adds, that is 'hard to capture in words'. Treu writes of words gleaming out, clear as crystal (p. 137); Schadewaldt declares (p. 176), 'In her hand the most prosaic thing, a box, a scent, a woman's tunic, turns into a little poetic miracle', a remark which recalls Schumann's claim that when Beethoven wrote a scale of C major it was a world away from the scale of C major written by any other composer. Charm is the most elusive of literary flavours – if it were not elusive, it would surely not be charm? – but we cannot leave it out of account in considering Sappho. And where such a variety of readers has testified to finding a peculiar, unanalysable excellence, it is hard to deny that there is genuinely some quality to which they have responded.

None the less, it is easy to get carried away by Sappho and to read portentous significances into puny fragments. In the second chapter of *Vainglory* Ronald Firbank describes the party thrown by Mrs. Henedge to celebrate the discovery of a new Sapphic fragment. Professor Inglepin reads it out to his expectant audience. Then someone awkwardly asks what is means in English.

'In plain English,' the Professor said, with some reluctance, 'it means: "Could not" [he wagged a finger] "Could not, for the fury of her feet!" '

'Do you mean she ran away?'
'Apparently!'

The spell of course is broken. None the less, the professor is rhapsodic:

> 'We have, at most, a broken piece, a rarity of phrase . . . as the poet's
> *With Golden Ankles*, for instance, or *Vines trailed on lofty poles*, or *With
> water dripped the napkin*, or *Scythian Wood* . . . or the (I fear me, spurious)
> *Carrying long rods, capped with the Pods of Poppies.*'

Firbank's satirical fantasy is not as remote from reality as one might
suppose. Consider this sentence: 'All study of her work is, must be, a
frantic raking over scrapheaps whence some verbal splinter may shine
out golden before the darkness closes in once more – "the herald of
the spring, the sweet-voiced nightingale" – with that genius for economy and the *mot juste* ("whiter than eggs"), those adjectives expressing
tenderness, slenderness, brightness which form her private stock-in-
trade, the glimpses she offers us of a small, suffering, beautiful, sunlit,
intense, hedonistic world . . .'[54] If this passage and the professor's
speech in *Vainglory* were set before one without any indication of
their origin, one might well guess that the latter was a parody, and
by no means an extravagant one, of the former (unless, indeed, one
concluded that the parody was the other way round); but in fact
Firbank anticipates the critic whom he seems to be burlesquing by
some fifty years.

Among Ezra Pound's shorter poems there is one entitled *Papyrus*.
Here it is in its entirety:

Spring . . . .
Too long . . . . . .
Gongula . . . .

These words are derived, at least in theory, from Sappho's fr. 95.
Pound wanted to show how eloquent and enticing a few torn remnants
of a poem can be; in some cases they may be more suggestive than the
poem complete. (If nothing of Lucan had survived except a few battered
fragments, would we not rank him among the greatest poets of Rome?)
It is all too easy to fall in love with the very fragmentariness of
fragments; when a critic writes about verbal splinters shining out
golden before the darkness closes in – a messy metaphor – one suspects
that he may be in danger. There is a romantic charm about many a
ruined abbey and headless torso, and a fragment of lyric poetry may
exercise the same attraction; there is no harm in indulging this emotion as long as one is aware that it is a different activity from appreci-
ating the poetry; we should be enjoying not Sappho but the eloquence

---

[54] Peter Green, *The Shadow of the Parthenon* (London, 1972), p. 191.

of time and chance. The trap is not as obvious as it may seem. It is evident that some of those who have written on Sappho have seen her as a sort of archaic Emily Dickinson, composing brief verses of jewel-like perfection. Consciously they may agree that this is not so, but subconsciously they have been unable to break the spell.

Sappho has continued to fascinate poets and writers in this century as in the last. Firbank himself, although he mocks the Sappho-worshippers, was entranced by her. He translated the *Ode to Aphrodite* (not very well, it must be admitted) into English Sapphics, and inappositely inserted the whole of it into *Vainglory*. And her simile of the hyacinth crushed by the shepherds gave him a superb title for another of his novels: *The Flower Beneath the Foot*. J. D. Salinger owes her a similar debt: *Raise High the Roof Beam, Carpenters*, the title of his story about a wedding in New York, is a quotation from one of her epithalamia. 'Like Ares comes the bridegroom,' the poet continues; in the story the words prove to be ironical, because the bridegroom in question funks the ceremony. In Salinger's *Franny and Zooey*, the poet appears again: 'I think I'm beginning to look down on all poets except Sappho,' the heroine writes. 'I've been reading her like mad, and no vulgar remarks, please . . . "Delicate Adonis is dying, Cytherea, what shall we do? Beat your breasts, maidens, and rend your tunics." Isn't that *marvellous*? She keeps *doing* that, too.' This is the enthusiasm of Symonds – 'Every word has . . . a seal of . . . inimitable grace' – translated into modern terms. Lawrence Durrell has written a verse drama about her (in which we are offered the frisson of incest), and Peter Green a novel, historically curious as a late representative of the Louÿs tradition; to these writers her life and personality have been as strong an enticement as the poetry.

The question of Sappho's character, and especially the nature of her feelings towards other women, has dominated much of the discussion about her, but the truth is that we know little about it.[55] In her surviving fragments she gives us extraordinarily vivid and convincing accounts of moments of experience; through her poetry we can empathise with certain of her emotions, but we cannot analyse with any precision the personality which gave rise to them. If we had all her poetry, we should doubtless be wiser, but perhaps not greatly so: the psychologists have taught us that we do not understand the true nature of our own feelings; how then are we to understand Sappho's, with nothing but her writings to go by? Every writer must be selective, and in any case there perhaps never was a poet, no matter how direct

[55] M. L. West discusses the topic judiciously (pp. 320–4). He argues that the fragments in themselves provide no evidence for the physical gratification of homosexual desires, but he points out that the pederastic poetry of male writers (e.g. Theognis) is comparably reticent.

and sincere, who did not fictionalise his experience to some extent; moreover, to analyse the nature of sexual feelings, love and deep friendship, and the relation between them, is a very difficult and delicate business at the best of times. To use the old analogy once more, we hear a good deal from Catullus about his joys, griefs and passions, but in the end we have hardly any idea of what he was really like; still less are we in a position to discuss his complexes and repressions or to analyse his ego and his id. Besides, we cannot see ourselves as others see us, and any writer who encourages us to enter into his feelings and share them is liable in the process to rob us of the capacity to assess them objectively. And anyway lyric poetry is simply not a medium for self-revelation in the sense in which a reader of Proust or Pepys or even Cicero would understand the term. Even on the basis of the extant verse it would be foolish to deny that there was a sexual element in Sappho's attachments to her female friends; we can hardly go further, and perhaps even with ten thousand of her verses before us we could not say much more.

Romanticism, sentimentality and not seldom lubricity have helped to draw people to Sappho, but it would be unfair to her admirers to suggest that the merits which they claim to see in her are not really there at all. I have argued that Sappho fulfils the conditions laid down by twentieth-century critics for qualifying as a 'major' poet, or at least that she would have fulfilled them if a substantial proportion of her work had survived. But in the end it may not be very important whether a poet is major or not; what counts is the quality of each individual poem, or in this instance each individual fragment. The case for saying that Sappho's claim to greatness must rest entirely on frs. 1 and 31 is not a derisory one, but I believe it to be misguided; I have tried to show that in many other remnants of her verses we can discern poetic merits of a high order. Sometimes one must speculate, sometimes one has to give her the benefit of the doubt, but in the circumstances these are not unreasonable methods of proceeding. I have tried to indicate where the uncertainties lie, but even when all these are admitted, Sappho stands out as a poet of exceptional subtlety and power. We are sometimes tempted to regard the methods of literary criticism practised in antiquity as crude or mechanical, but the fact remains that the ancients judged their poets and writers, so far as we can tell, with accuracy and assurance. Concerning Sappho's poetry the judgment of antiquity was unanimous; and it was surely not mistaken.

Part Two

Catullus and the Idea of a Masterpiece

Catullus' longest and most elaborate poem, 64, has not been universally admired. In the last century, for example, Robinson Ellis (p. 282) judged it too long and too repetitious; and Auguste Couat (p. 177) could find in it no dominant idea, inspiration or unity. In 1920 Pasquali (p. 18) declared that the true Catullus was not to be seen in it, since here the poet had merely wished to show off his technical virtuosity. Nineteen years later E. A. Havelock (p. 77f.) compared it unfavourably to Catullus' 'two indubitable successes' in sustained composition, Poems 61 and 63: 'The poem is read for the emotional passages that it contains . . . These are strung together with a minimum of hasty narrative into an ill-assorted series.' Kroll (p. 142) was unenthusiastic: since the poem lacks any personal element and Catullus appears here only as an imitator, one would gladly date it to the period before love taught him to find his own voice. Of recent commentators in English, Fordyce gave little away, but his approval seems to have been at best lukewarm, and Quinn (1972, p. 259), while allowing that the poem is 'in many respects a minor masterpiece', has qualified this already cautious praise with the remark that 'it doesn't in my opinion maintain the same high level of technical perfection and assurance' as the *Attis* (Poem 63). However, since Friedrich Klingner published his long, acute and sympathetic study of the poem in 1956, it has not lacked for attention or praise. Numerous articles about it, and even two slim books, have since appeared, most of them, either explicitly or by implication, placing a high value upon it. No one who writes on it today can pretend to be tilling virgin soil, nor can anyone who champions it claim the merit of originality; my excuse for returning to it is simply a belief that there is still more to be said, and that whatever recent studies may have added, the tone and intention of the poem as a whole are still largely misunderstood, perhaps less understood, indeed, than when Klingner wrote.

Peleus and Thetis (an unsatisfactory title for the poem, but there is none better) is the kind of work that is liable to suffer particularly

from the reductivism that has characterised much recent criticism of
Latin poetry. By this term I mean the tendency to look for a single
formula or critical method to apply to as many different works and
authors as possible. An extreme reductivist is Francis Cairns, who
holds (p. 32f.) that 'in a very real sense antiquity' – and he means a
period of eleven hundred years – 'was in comparison with the nineteenth and twentieth centuries a time-free zone'; all the poetry composed over this immense stretch of time, he maintains, is to be
analysed in terms of the genres into which it can be categorised, and
without such analysis an understanding of the poem (or play) is not
possible.[1] In its extreme form this theory is unlikely, I think, to convince many people; and indeed I cannot see that its assertion is anything other than an act of faith. It is perhaps the consequence of
looking at ancient poetry in isolation; I believe that most fair-minded
readers of the classics who make even a cursory study of sixteenth-
and seventeenth-century poetry will allow that much of it responds
better to a generic analysis than much classical literature. A compar-
ative study would help greatly to establish the virtues and limitations
of Cairns's method; it is clear from his own book that the theory works
better for Tibullus and Statius than for Aeschylus, and one could
probably demonstrate that it works as well for (say) Ronsard or Spen-
ser as for any of them. The natural conclusion is that it describes more
or less justly particular types of poetry which have been written both
in antiquity and in more recent times, but that it does not cope (and
how strange if it did) with all the verse written by all poets over a
period of more than a millennium.

Cairns's presuppositions, like them or not, are at least openly and
boldly stated. Commoner, and more misleading, is a reductivism that
remains below the level of consciousness. Many recent critics of Latin
poetry seem to come to their job clutching tools fabricated primarily
for dealing with Horace and the Augustan elegists, or perhaps with
Virgil. It is then assumed that the same categories of judgment should
be applied to Horace as to Virgil, or to Virgil as to Catullus. These
views can perhaps be defended – Horace and Virgil, after all, were
friends and contemporaries, and Virgil was much influenced by Catullus – but what I would stress is that they are often held simply *as*
assumptions; their validity is not questioned. And indeed they seem
to me to be false assumptions; what we now need in the criticism of
Latin poetry is not catch-all formulae, but an ever more delicate
discrimination. Rome in the second half of the first century B.C. was
anything but a 'time-free zone' (what *does* that phrase mean?); on the
contrary, it was a period of rapid and profound change, political, moral

---

[1] There is some whistling to keep the spirits up here. A *real* sense? A *very* real sense?
Compare the journalistic trope: 'Miss Evert *literally* wiped the floor with her opponent.'

and social, and it is incredible that none of these changes should have been reflected in Roman literature. So much may seem obvious; but discrimination should go further. We must distinguish the methods and intentions not only of writers belonging to successive generations, but to different writers within the same generation. In considering a period of which we have an instinctive understanding, we do this automatically; to take one example, Oscar Wilde's *Picture of Dorian Gray* and Henry James's *Portrait of a Lady* were written within a few years of each other by men who moved widely in the more cultivated circles of London society, and yet no one supposes that it is appropriate to assess them by the same criteria. Most people, no doubt, will conclude that one of these books is superior to the other, but this is not the point at issue here; the point is rather that whether they fail or succeed within their own terms, those terms are substantially different, although both works belong to the same genre, the novel. James may be tackled with the same tools that are applied to Jane Austen and George Eliot; Wilde may not. Have we reason to think that the literature of late Republican Rome should be treated any differently? We have enough information about the period to know that it was a time of intense and fundamental disagreement about the nature of poetry and the proper course for modern writers to follow, with Cicero hoping for works that would be masculine in style and elevating in content, while the neoterics held to a Callimachean viewpoint which has been compared, not inappropriately, to the nineteenth-century belief in art for art's sake; I could well imagine Cinna the Poet reading Professor Cairns's book with a lively enthusiasm, and Lucretius, if ataraxia did not restrain him, throwing it across the room in displeasure.

We should be prepared, too, to discriminate within the work of a single poet. Virgil himself has perhaps suffered from reductive critics, for I suspect that recent attempts to find moral vigour in the *Eclogues* spring from a desire to identify a single, unifying method common to all his works. This is to underestimate him; we do better to admire the astonishing transformation that made an Augustan master out of the neoteric creator of faint, fugitive beauty. Certainly, every reader feels, if it is not too banal to say so, that in all his poetry, from first to last, he is always intensely 'Virgilian'; certainly there remain neoteric elements in the *Aeneid* just as there are the seeds of Augustanism in the *Eclogues*; but the unity of his works is a nebulous and perhaps indefinable thing, whereas their variety is plain, definable, and an important part of his conscious intention. When he began the *Georgics*, taking the severe Hesiod as his nominal model in place of the Hellenistic Theocritus, he surely meant to attempt something new, to assume the earnest tone so carefully excluded from his pastoral verse. It is to his credit that he succeeded; to make him into a moralist throughout his creative life is to make him not a better but a more limited poet.

Virgil's art changed as he grew older, but there is no *a priori* reason why a poet should not use two different styles or methods simultaneously; to take Catullus himself, what merit is there is trying to show that the poet of *Vivamus mea Lesbia* is the 'same' as the poet of *Peliaco quondam*? In 1961 Michael Putnam published an article, 'The Art of Catullus 64', maintaining that the poem is really concerned with Catullus' feelings about Lesbia and his dead brother. Clearly Putnam proposed this theory because he believed that it was right, but evaluative judgments and judgments about matters of fact are not wholly independent, and no one would be likely to put forward such a hypothesis unless he thought that it enhanced the value of the poem.[2] Putnam himself is frank about his motives: he wants to have a 'unified picture' of the poet's mind and personality, and he means to supply it by showing that all the poems of Catullus are autobiographical.[3] In other words, we are to look not just for the deep and obscure kind of unity that I have already mentioned, but for unity in its simplest and most superficial form; we are to try and show that all the poems of Catullus are on the same subject. Is this not, when we consider it, an unattractive project? Let us imagine ourselves in the shoes of an able and ambitious poet in the middle of the first century B.C. Will this man not want to try his hand at a diversity of styles and subjects? Will he thank the critic who assures him that he had only one theme? To look for that single theme is to think not like a poet but like a don. Putnam's kind of unity, in fact, is too superficial to be worth having.

A unified picture of the poet's personality is a deeper matter, but in the case of Catullus we know far too little to be able to attain it. I am not even certain that it would be desirable. Shakespeare probably wrote *Hamlet* and *The Phoenix and the Turtle* at about the same time. If we fail (as surely we shall) to discern the unity of mind behind these two works, we should not be too greatly scandalised; instead we should stand astonished before the protean character of Shakespeare's art. This is a difficult and subtle matter, on which it is unwise to be absolute. It is amazing that the same man should have written *King*

---

[2] I cannot myself see evidence to support Putnam's theory. As for evaluation, I agree with T. E. Kinsey's judgment on Putnam's identification of Catullus with Ariadne and Lesbia with Theseus: 'There is nothing in the poem to suggest such an identification, and if appreciation of the poem depends on making it, then this is a defect' (p. 912).

[3] 'Nor are we justified,' he writes, 'in assuming that the epyllion could never be a vehicle for personal statement (an argument which seems to imply that Catullus could only be himself when writing in shorter verse forms)' (p. 199). It is clear from the context that he identifies 'being himself' with 'making a personal statement' and 'making a personal statement' with 'making an autobiographical statement'. This mistake is at the heart of his argument.

Lear, A Midsummer Night's Dream and the *Sonnets*; it is also true, I think, that most readers have the subjective feeling of sensing a single mind behind these hugely diverse works; and I believe too that the recognition of this kind of subjectively felt 'unity' is a legitimate source of aesthetic pleasure.[4] The theory that Shakespeare's works were written by a committee under the direction of the Earl of Oxford and the theory that they were written by Bacon are both impoverishing because both destroy our sense of acquaintance with genius, the former by parcelling out his mind among half a dozen people, the latter by creating a picture of a mind so various and contradictory that we cannot know it or believe in it. The consciousness of unity may be agreeable, if we can attain it, but it is not something to which we should feel ourselves entitled – I have already suggested that it cannot be found in *all* Shakespeare's works –; still less should we seek it at the expense of underestimating the diversity of a great man's achievement.

Of course, I do not suppose that Catullus has anything like Shakespeare's range, nor do I doubt that there are many points of resemblance linking Catullus' shorter pieces with his longer works; all I want to do is to question the assumption that it is *necessarily* a work of virtue to minimise the differences between them. The temptation is particularly strong because in one of his poems, 68, he combined the complex and elaborate manner of his long works with the autobiographical elements of his shorter elegies;[5] but it is at just such a place as this that discrimination is most necessary. Unless we see the oddity of Catullus' procedure here, we miss his intention. The juxtaposition of varied themes in this elegy – the poet's friendship with Allius, his love for Lesbia, his brother's death, Protesilaus and Laodamia – resembles the rich diversity of *Peleus and Thetis*; what Klingner has called its *poikilia*. The long, fluid and complex sentence that opens the poem recalls the similar openings of Poems 65 and 66. Into this urbane and highly wrought texture the death of the poet's brother forces itself with a painful abruptness:

> *sed totum hoc studium luctu fraterna míhi mórs*
>   *abstulit. o misero frater adempte mihi, . . .*   20

[But my brother's death has removed from me through grief all this interest [in writing poetry]. O brother taken from me, unhappy that I am, . . .]

The awkward rhythm at the end of the first line and the jolting stop

---

[4] But a pleasure which it is dangerous to indulge too far. Consider how it has bedevilled the 'Homeric question'.

[5] Poems 65 and 66 are comparable: a shorter, personal elegy introducing a long and non-personal exercise in Alexandrianism.

near the beginning of the second are deliberately angular; the poet recovers himself, and the verse rises into an extended and plangent threnody; then the flowing epistolary manner is resumed. Less abrupt but hardly less surprising in the midst of Catullus' elegant and instructed verse are lines 70ff:

> *quo mea se molli candida diva pede*   70
> *intulit et trito fulgentem in limine plantam*
>   *innixa arguta constituit solea . . .*

[Thither my bright goddess stepped softly, and placed her shining foot on the worn threshold, pressing with brisk sole . . .]

Suddenly Catullus focuses on a single point of time and space, brief, simple and private. With a sharp tap Lesbia's gleaming foot hits the worn threshold; the neat sound and the contrast of textures arouse our auditory and visual imaginations, and mark the individuality of the place and moment. Then in the next line we are back with Protesilaus and Laodamia in the literary world of Greek mythology. To appreciate the force and originality of what Catullus is doing, we need to realise that the brother's death and Lesbia in the doorway have intruded into a kind of poetry in which they do not naturally belong; and to understand this, we must appreciate that the longer poems and the shorter are kettles of different fish. This, then, is one practical example of how a poet's meaning eludes the reductive critic.

In reading recent discussions of *Peleus and Thetis*, or at least those written in English, I have been struck by how frequent are the attempts to make Catullus into a moralist. Thus David Konstan (pp. 101, 84) calls the poem a 'penetrating critique of Roman values'; 'The causes of the decline lie, for Catullus, in the development of civilisation itself, symbolised by the voyage of the Argo and the marriage of Peleus and Thetis.' The superb description of Peleus' palace at lines 43ff. is a favourite hunting-ground for this type of critic. 'The turn to decadence has begun, as the luxurious setting . . . implies' (Harmon, p. 314n.); 'The opulence and splendour of Peleus' palace may . . . be symbols of corruption rather than greatness' (Konstan, p. 33); 'Throughout, Catullus emphasises wealth and artifice . . . I think the normal Roman reaction to an exotic scene of this kind would have been one of disapproval' (Bramble, p. 39). Behind these judgments I suspect that there lies a form of historical reductivism. It is common enough in the works of established historians to find statements such as 'The Elizabethans hated the mob' or 'The Victorians were prudish'. Such statements do little harm so long as it is recognised that they are no more than a form of shorthand for 'Many Victorians were prudish' or 'Most upper-class Elizabethans hated the mob'; but they can easily lead to a blunting of the historical imagination. We have often been told that the Romans were grave and moralistic, or that Roman writers disapproved of luxury; and we tend to forget what such generalisations really mean, or ought to mean. Bramble expresses himself with a proper caution, but I doubt whether even he has been immune from this tendency. Simply as a historical judgment, his view of 'the normal Roman reaction' is strangely misguided;[6] it is true that a good many Roman writers – not all – inveigh against luxury, but why do we suppose that they did so if not because a great many of their contemporaries wallowed in the indulgences that they deplored? But in any case Bramble's argument is fundamentally mistaken in method. The Romans were not a body like the Conservative Party or the Mormon Church to which we may legitimately ascribe a collective opinion, but a vast number of unique individuals; and in the last years of the republic they differed violently on every subject under the sun. The one thing of which we can be absolutely certain is that not all the readers of the poem reacted to it in the same way. Even if it could be shown that a substantial majority of literate Romans held identical views about the decor of legendary palaces, still the only proper question would be: what views did Catullus hold? He is the one individual with whom we have to deal. For my own part, I confess that I cannot understand how anyone who reads lines 43–9 aloud to himself, and reads them in context with the forty-two lines that precede them, can fail to see that Catullus is revelling in the sensuous luxury of what he describes.

To turn away from the text itself to generalisations about society is almost always a mistake, a kind of failure of nerve or concentration. This is not to say that the literary critic should seal the poem off into a kind of vacuum, safe from contamination by the messy complexities of history; quite the reverse. The essence of the true historical imagination is to perceive the relation between the particular and the general; to seize the larger pattern without losing sight of the quiddity of individual men and events. To read the poems of Catullus is inevitably to have an experience of history; it is to receive some kind of impression, however dim and incomplete, of a particular society, and a particular milieu within that society, and a particular man within that milieu. Poetry, in short, is a part of history; and at the same time a wider historical study may illuminate particular poems. The critic may, and indeed should, examine the background against which Catullus wrote, and consider what kind of poet we might *expect* him to be, knowing what we do about the literary and social attitudes of the time. These investigations will not interpret the poetry for us, but they will give us a yardstick to measure it against. The individual

[6] See Griffin.

poet may fit the yardstick very accurately or he may not; only his own words can tell us that.

The moralising interpreters of *Peleus and Thetis* receive apparent support from its concluding lines, in which Catullus sternly denounces the vices of mankind. But most critics of the poem, in calling this ending a 'tailpiece' or 'epilogue' have recognised that there is something odd about it. Whatever its function may be (and we shall consider this question later), it is manifestly at variance with most of the piece. It is the last of the many surprises which Catullus has carefully distributed throughout his poem. When it opens with a rich evocation of the voyage of the Argo, we do not suspect that this will be a poem about the wedding of Peleus and Thetis; when we reach the wedding, we do not anticipate that it will be interrupted by a description of a tapestry occupying more than half the entire piece; after reading the elaborate account of Ariadne's grief and lamentation, we are taken unawares when Catullus reveals that what the coverlet really depicts is Bacchus about to bestow upon her a supreme privilege; after the jubilation of the marriage ceremony we do not expect the wedding song to be given to the aged and sinister Parcae; and the gloomy conclusion is perhaps the greatest surprise of all. Anyone who has failed to perceive that throughout this poem Catullus is deliberately various, disproportionate and unpredictable has certainly not understood it; once Catullus' tactics of ingenious deception are appreciated, the heavy moralising of his conclusion actually confirms, by force of contrast, that the poem is not moralistic as a whole. This may seem paradoxical. Just so; we are dealing with a poem of paradox.

If we turn to the rest of Catullus' work, we do not get the impression of a man much occupied by questions of social morality. Many of his contemporaries, to be sure, wagged their heads gravely over the decadence of their age, but Catullus has told us what he thought of them at the beginning of Poem 5:

Vivamus, mea Lesbia, atque amemus,
rumoresque senum severiorum
omnes unius aestimemus assis!

[Let us live and love, my Lesbia, and reckon all the mutterings of strict old men at a single farthing!]

I see no reason to doubt that these lines reflect the attitude of the historical Catullus; and if we cast our gaze more widely still, over the circle in which he moved, we find our impressions confirmed. It is beyond reasonable doubt that the Lesbia of Catullus' poems was one of the sisters of the dissolute P. Clodius Pulcher; she has been traditionally identified with the notorious Clodia Metelli, and many scholars have also supposed the Rufus of Poems 69 and 77 to be Clodia Metelli's lover, M. Caelius Rufus, the amusing and rakish young man whose personality still lives for us thanks to his somewhat unexpected association with Cicero. If these identifications are correct, we have independent evidence that Catullus was part of a raffish, licentious society; and if they are not, the evidence of the poems themselves is good enough.[7] Catullus' friends were just the sort of people that Sallust, Livy and Horace had in mind when they lamented the decay of ancient virtue. Moreover, he associated with other poets who, as we have reason to believe, were more than usually unlikely to regard moral suasion as part of their function. This brings us to the place at which historical and literary reductivism come together; that is, where judgments about the nature of Roman society overlap with judgments about poetry's proper character.

In France, since the time of Baudelaire and Gautier, the literature of dandyism has been an important part of the native tradition, and critics have recognised that it must be examined on its own terms. England has also produced distinguished writing of this type, but the English have never felt much at ease with it, and have tended to regard it as peripheral or eccentric; rightly or wrongly, the 'great tradition' is seen as descending through writers of high moral seriousness. In America the literature of dandyism has hardly existed at all; the most conspicuous exception is the young T. S. Eliot, but he is one of those exceptions that confirm the rule, for the influences on his early poetry were largely French, and from his twenties onwards he took laborious pains to transform himself into a European. It is significant that French scholars have felt no embarrassment about praising Catullus' poem for its wayward aestheticism, while their English-speaking counterparts, the Americans especially, have desired to make him as earnest, disciplined and intellectual as they can. Boucher, for instance, is pleased by 'the astonishing diversity of the work' and the 'deliberate disequilibrium between its various elements'; he urges us not to forget that 'the accent is placed on detail and not on the whole', and concludes that the description of Ariadne 'can only proceed from an extraordinarily vivid artistic sensibility: it requires us not to minimise the role of aesthetics to the advantage of the moral elements.'[8] Putnam, by contrast, does not so much as consider the

---

[7] Wiseman has cast some shrewd doubts upon the traditional identifications; they still seem to me more likely than not. And in any case the connection with Clodius remains.

[8] Boucher, pp. 191, 194, 199. Klingner's approach is similar. I attribute this to his good judgment rather than to some form of cultural determinism; but it may be worth observing that Germany, like other continental countries, has tended to regard France, sometimes willingly, sometimes with intense reluctance, as the cultural centre of Europe. The English, being both more insular and possessing a tradition of continuous literary excellence stronger than that of any other country, have usually been innocent of such feelings. English-speaking readers of Catullus should recognise that they may be uniquely prejudiced against the kind of poetry that he is attempting in *Peleus and Thetis*.

possibility that artificiality may fascinate or that tenuousness may have a charm and beauty of its own (p. 165f.): 'If *64* is . . . a series of narrative sections strung *loosely* together by means of the most *tenuous and superficial* bonds, then we should *certainly without further ado* dismiss the poem as a piece of made-to-order Alexandrian work . . . There is no *meaningless artificiality* here.' Bramble (p. 24) deplores the possibility that we might regard the poem as a series of *unintegrated* panels', 'a mere *tour de force*, an eccentric *experiment in form*'; '[Catullus] concludes his poem with a moralistic epilogue which would be quite out of harmony with the rest of the piece, if the careful innovations and changes of tone there contained were designed to do *nothing more than charm and entertain* . . . the reader would be forced to dismiss all that had preceded as simplistic and *meaningless frivolity.*' There is an eagerness to discover that the poem is *about* something: Leo C. Curran writes (p. 173n.), 'I have in mind something more *disciplined and intellectual* than what Klingner sees as a striving for *poikilia*'; M. L. Daniels discusses (p. 95) 'the *central theme* of Catullus 64, namely the concept of the *domus*'; Konstan concludes (p. 101), 'I find it impossible to suppose that the epyllion . . . was an *occasional* composition . . . Our poem . . . is *about* Catullus' Rome.'[9]

It must be allowed that the technique of selective italicisation can easily be unfair; none the less, the picture that emerges from this accumulation of evidence is clear. It is also plain, I think, that in many cases the attitudes thus revealed have not been reached by a considered rejection of other possibilities, but have simply been assumed. Moral puritanism in literary criticism is out of fashion – the critic who shrinks from Catullus' anatomical grossnesses is regarded as pitifully unsophisticated; it is ironical that a kind of aesthetic puritanism should have succeeded it. Now it is at least conceivable that a reductive view about the content and construction proper to poetry could be defended; I believe such a view to be mistaken (for it is one of the glories of literature that it can do so many different things), and I shall try to show in due course that poetry in which purely aesthetic values are paramount can indeed be fine and moving, but for the purposes of my immediate argument it is sufficient that *as a matter of historical fact* writers have at certain periods taken the purely aesthetic line. This fact is incontrovertible, and it follows that while the reductive view of how poets *ought* to write may still be tenable, the reductive view of how they *do* write is not.

I have used the term dandyism, but without defining it. The word is normally applied to certain forms of expensive or idiosyncratic tailoring, but it may also be used in an extended sense to cover dilettantism and aestheticism as well as affectations of dress. These

---

[9] The italics are mostly mine.

phenomena are connected, but there is no English word to cover them all, and we must adopt the word dandyism for want of a better. In this wider sense the soberly dressed Pater, with his dogskin gloves and false-military moustache, is as much a dandy as the beringed D'Orsay or the velvet-clad Wilde.[10] Lord Blake has analysed dandyism thus:[11]

> It seems to be a characteristic of an era of social flux, when aristocracy is tottering or uncertain, but when radicalism has not yet replaced it with a new set of values. It flourishes in a period when manners are no longer rigidly fixed, but have not yet degenerated into mere anarchy, so that there is still a convention to rebel against, still a world to be shocked and amused by extravagance and eccentricity. The dandy must have a framework in which to operate.

These acute observations are equally true of dandyism in its wider sense. If we examine the literature of the 1890s or the 1920s, we find in it attitudes of rebellion against the establishment that are none the less strongly upper-class in character. The consequence of these attitudes is an emphasis on style, if necessary at the expense of substance, and an avoidance of seriousness, at least in its conventional forms. George Orwell was delighted by a cartoon in *Punch* which he considered to give a just impression of the literary climate of the twenties: 'An intolerable youth is pictured informing his aunt that he intends to "write". "And what are you going to write about, dear?" asks the aunt. "My dear aunt," says the youth crushingly, "one doesn't write *about* anything, one just *writes*." '[12]

Turning back to first-century Rome, another case of a social and moral order cracking up, we find some suggestive parallels. Obviously the differences are enormous; and yet there is the same combination of quasi-adolescent rebellion with essentially aristocratic attitudes. Catullus enjoys shocking grave old gentlemen, but he also likes to show up the ineptitude of Arrius, who misplaces his aitches and thinks he is being very *comme il faut*, while Marrucinus, who has left a

[10] For the idea that dandyism is as much an internal as external matter, compare Barbey d'Aurevilly: 'Minds which see things only in their most trivial aspect have imagined that Dandyism was above all the art of dress ... Dandyism is a complete mode of being, and only contingently is it materially visible' (*Du Dandysme et de Georges Brummell*, sect. 5). And for the difficulties of terminology, compare Martin Green: 'We need to associate the dandy with two other types, seemingly unrelated, the *rogue* and the *naïf*, and to see that temperamentally the three types are all first cousins. All three go in defiance of the "mature" modes of seriousness that our culture sponsors; all are "young men's styles of being" ... The aesthete and the dandy are very closely related, and frequently the same person is both. Very often the two phases are alternative ways of embodying the same idea, the same temperamental drive.' (*Children of the Sun* (London, 1977), pp. 26f., 33)

[11] Robert Blake, *Disraeli* (London, 1966), p. 78.

[12] 'Inside the Whale' (*The Collected Essays, Journalism and Letters of George Orwell* (London, 1968), vol. 1, p. 58).

dinner party with one of his host's napkins, is censured not for dishonesty but for vulgarity and lack of style. Catullus' insistence on urbanity, charm and elegance, 'lepos' and 'venustas', is an aesthetic attitude that covers literature and society alike; Marrucinus fails as a dinner guest and Volusius fails as a poet, and for reasons not wholly dissimilar. In Poem 95 Catullus contrasts the dreary *Annales* of Volusius and the endless prolixity of Hortensius with his friend Cinna's *Zmyrna*, a work which he alleges to have been nine years in the writing (presumably a humorous exaggeration). We are severely hampered by the loss of this poem and such comparable works as the *Io* of Calvus and the *Glaucus* of Cornificius, but everything that we know or can infer about neoteric poetry suggests that it was indeed the literature of dandyism in full flower. The style was mannered (Cicero noted the trick of using *spondeiazontes*, lines with a spondee in the fifth foot) and highly wrought. The point of comparing Cinna with more prolific poets was to highlight his polish and refinement. Learning and scholarship in verse were admired and the big manner shunned; Callimachus was a patron saint. Another sign of Hellenistic influence is the apparent preference for subjects with an erotic theme, often dealing with perverse forms of love; Cinna, whose poem handled the obscure myth of Zmyrna's incestuous passion for her father, had managed to find a theme both learned and decadent. It strains credibility to suggest that poems like this had a moral message or were rich in reflections upon the political and social conditions of the time. In his survey of the twenties Orwell remarked, 'What is noticeable about all these writers is that what "purpose" they have is very much up in the air. There is no attention to the problems of the moment, above all no politics in the narrower sense. Our eyes are directed to Rome, to Byzantium, to Montparnasse, to Mexico, to the Etruscans . . . – to everywhere except the places where things are actually happening.' *Mutatis mutandis* much the same could be said of the neoteric 'epyllia': art is created for the sake of art, and we are transported away from the present world into a mythological Grecian past. Even the Roman past is avoided: Volusius with his *Annales* in the Ennian tradition is the enemy.

The ending of *Peleus and Thetis* may seem to make it a partial exception to these tendencies; but does it really? Lines 397–406 have sometimes been taken as an attack on contemporary Rome, but this is surely too simple. When Catullus tells us that the gods have ceased to take part openly in the affairs of men since the earth was stained with crime and greed drove justice from men's minds, he clearly does not mean to imply that the gods were frequent participants in Roman battles and guests at Roman parties in the third or fourth centuries B.C. We are still back in the mythical past; his account of the decline of man is in a tradition that goes back as far as Hesiod, and his sweeping condemnation covers a period of a thousand years and more. Even if these lines were a reference to the Rome of his time, we could safely say that no one with a genuine interest in the moral troubles of the age would have chosen quite this list of crimes; there is nothing about ambition, corruption, ostentatious consumption, the neglect of traditional religious observances – those matters over which the true Roman moralists lamented. Catullus' list of sensational family and sex crimes is simply a throwing up of the hands in indiscriminate horror. By its exaggerated blackness it sets off the radiance of his legendary world, and it may be that this is its primary function.

One last kind of reductivism needs to be considered, the subtlest, the most tempting and, it may be felt, the most justified. Bramble's stimulating article is entitled 'Structure and ambiguity in Catullus LXIV'. Now the word ambiguity has itself become increasingly ambiguous in the last fifty years. 'Is all good poetry supposed to be ambiguous?' Empson asked himself in the preface to the second edition of his famous book; and answered, 'I think that it is.' But as he also reminded his readers, 'I claimed at the start that I would use the term "ambiguity" to mean anything I liked', and indeed he had allowed that his first type of ambiguity, arising when a word or grammatical structure is effective in more than one way at once, 'covers almost everything of literary importance'.[13] It is perhaps unwise for the rest of us to usurp the privileges of genius; such excessively vague use of language can conceal the fact that what Bramble is describing, in common with many other critics of ancient poetry, is not the kind of ambiguity possessed by all good poetry, but an effect of a much more specific type.[14] He is concerned with what, borrowing a metaphor from music, we might call an equivocation between major and minor moods, and indeed with a particular form of that equivocation: with language that seems on the surface happy or serene but holds undercurrents of pessimism or melancholy.[15] Great poetry, without a doubt, has been founded on this particular form of ambivalence: it is fundamental to the *Aeneid*, a work which we are constrained to regard at one moment

[13] Examine the entry under 'ambiguity' in the supplement to the *Oxford English Dictionary* and see the bewilderment of the learned lexicographers at the vagueness of the word's new meaning.

[14] *Seven Types of Ambiguity* is not the only book in which Empson has transformed an English word in a potentially misleading way: *Some Versions of Pastoral* deals not with pastoral but with works that may illuminatingly be *compared* to pastoral. Critics who have failed to appreciate this have got themselves into a tangle.

[15] The musical analogy is perhaps illuminating, since in music the rules governing form and language are more demanding and more absolute; in consequence aesthetic principles emerge more clearly. An equivocation between major and minor modes is easily created; but to compose a piece, not wholly dull, in which minor chords are absent for long stretches is formidably difficult. This is one reason why the exposition of the first movement of Beethoven's A flat Sonata, op. 110, has such a special atmosphere.

as the central achievement of Roman poetry, at another as one of its most eccentric productions. All I am concerned to do is to question the assumption that confronted with what appears to be a happy poem, we shall *automatically* enhance its value if we can find some darker tones concealed within it. I believe this assumption to be very wide-spread; such expressions as 'complexity', 'emotional richness', 'tension' and of course 'ambiguity' are constantly used in contexts which make plain that the users presume these qualities to be *always* virtuous. However, the kind of equivocation that we are considering is one that is comparatively easy for a poet to suggest; to sustain a mood of pure jubilation or serenity without becoming insipid is a most rare achievement. If we are tempted to find hidden dubieties in a superficially joyful poem, we should at least consider the possibility that we are making it not richer but more commonplace. It is seldom that a poet has succeeded in that most difficult task of creating for a space a world of

> ordre et beauté,
> Luxe, calme et volupté

but when we are offered admittance to such a world, should we not accept the privilege?

2

Peliaco quondam prognatae vertice pinus
dicuntur liquidas Neptuni nasse per undas
Phasidos ad fluctus et fines Aeeteos,
cum lecti iuvenes, Argivae robora pubis,
auratam optantes Colchis avertere pellem   5
ausi sunt vada salsa cita decurrere puppi,
caerula verrentes abiegnis aequora palmis.
diva quibus retinens in summis urbibus arces
ipsa levi fecit volitantem flamine currum
pinea coniungens inflexae texta carinae.   10

[Once upon a time pine-trees born on the summit of Pelion are said to have swum through the clear waves of Neptune to the waters of Phasis and the lands of Aeetes, when chosen youths, the flower of Argive man-power, desirous to carry off the golden fleece from the Colchians, dared to speed over the salt seas in a swift ship, sweeping the blue waters with hands made of fir-wood. The goddess who holds the fortresses at the tops of cities herself made for them the chariot that flew with the light breeze, fitting the pine fabric to the curved keel.]

Catullus uses the opening lines to set the tone, or rather the variety of tones. 'Peliaco quondam . . .' – the first word places us firmly in the

Greek world, the second right back in the past. 'Peliaco' has a stylistic function also; Catullus has used an adjective for a noun ('the Peliac peak' instead of 'the peak of Pelion'). The same mannerism occurs twice more in this poem (at lines 77 and 368), and twice also in Catullus' translation of Callimachus' *Lock of Berenice* (66.8 and 60): it is a feature of epic diction, but not only of epic, as the examples from Catullus' most overtly Callimachean poem show. In itself the word could be grandly Ennian or sumptuously artificial; a note of grandiosity is struck at the start, but we have yet to see to what extent the grandiosity is, so to speak, in inverted commas.

The stateliness of 'Peliaco' is continued in 'prognatae', a solemn, archaic word found in Ennius and in funeral inscriptions; 'vada salsa' in line 6 is an epic phrase. Reminiscent of old epic again is the simple and conspicuous alliteration of the opening lines: 'Peliaco . . . prognatae . . . pinus . . . Neptuni nasse . . . fluctus et fines' – three words beginning with p in the first line, two with n in the second, two with f in the third. And yet the total effect is quite unlike Ennius or Lucretius. With a studied calm Catullus distances from us the scene that he is depicting; 'quondam' in line 1 is picked up by 'dicuntur', emphatic and a touch unexpected at the start of line 2; the voyage of the Argonauts is vastly remote from us, and it may not even have happened. At other points in the poem he reminds us of the distant and perhaps fictional character of his story: 'fertur' (19), 'perhibent' (76 and 124), 'olim' (76), 'ferunt' (212). Commentators compare the tradition of 'scholarship' in Alexandrian poetry; Callimachus, for instance, wrote (fr. 612 Pf.; *Hymn* 5.56), 'I sing nothing that is unevidenced' and 'The story is not mine but others'.' The comparison is probably fair, but here as elsewhere Catullus has the power to breathe life into Hellenistic conventions; indeed a great part of the intended effect of the poem is the way in which dry mannerisms are marvellously converted into the stuff of a gorgeous voluptuousness. 'In the distance,' Novalis says, 'all becomes poetry'; Catullus' attitude is romantic, and we are invited to view the Argonauts from afar, in a sort of radiant haze, with a strange mixture of self-indulgence and detachment. This method is far different from the method of the epic poet, who for all his buskins and grand manner, seeks to confront his audience with his characters directly. Virgil, it is true, is willing at certain moments to assume the romantic tone, as in the superlative sentence introducing his catalogue of the Italian forces, where he reflects upon how faint is our knowledge of that bygone time (*Aen.* 7. 641–6);   but this is one of Virgil's un-epic procedures. A thin breeze ('tenuis aura'), he says, brings us all that we know of the past; this subtle metaphor, with its mixing of wistfulness with pleasure in the very dimness of antiquity (how inviting that soft breeze upon our faces), is indeed close to the mood of Catullus in parts of this poem.

There are yet more heroic resonances in his opening lines to be mentioned. Both in subject and phrasing they echo the beginning of Ennius' *Medea*, itself closely based on the start of Euripides' play. Scholars often exaggerate the amount of literature that Roman readers could be expected to carry around in their heads, but there is little doubt that Catullus expected his audience to remember the start of perhaps the best known of all Greek tragedies. What are we to make of these reminiscences? Different scholars have differing answers. Bramble detects a sinister note (p. 35f.): 'The echoes of Ennius' *Medea*, itself more moralistic than its Euripidean model, together with certain other linguistic details, indicate that Catullus was not merely indulging a taste for whimsical ornamentation. He does not moralise in the forthright Ennian manner ... But there are correspondences ... which request the audience to think back to a play which began in anything but a light-hearted or amoral vein.' Harmon draws the opposite conclusion (p. 312): 'In his imitation of Ennius' passage, Catullus omits the exclamation *utinam ne*: there will apparently be no cause in 64 to regret the Argo's voyage ... The opening lines of 64, which exclude the tone of regret in the Ennian passage, imply that 64, in contrast to the tale of Medea, tells of aspirations fulfilled.' These two lines of argument seem equally good, or equally bad; together they suggest that it is rash to draw too exact a moral from literary echoes. This is another difficult matter; there are indeed times when a poet alludes to a predecessor because he wants to make some quite specific point. But interpretation of this kind can easily make reading poetry an exercise rather like doing a crossword puzzle, with the reader having to pick up clues and guess their significance correctly. Not much poetry works in this way.

What both Harmon and Bramble have failed to recognise is the distinction between what we may call colour and intention; an illustration from comparatively recent literature (chosen not quite at random) may help to clarify it. In Oscar Wilde's dialogue, *The Critic as Artist*, one of his characters describes the enduring power of Homer over the imagination of the modern reader:

'Hector that sweet knight is dead,' ... Yet every day the swan-like daughter of Leda comes out on the battlements, and looks down at the tide of war ... In his chamber of stained ivory lies her leman. He is polishing his dainty armour, and combing the scarlet plume. With squire and page, her husband passes from tent to tent ... Behind the embroidered curtains sits Achilles, in perfumed raiment, while in harness of gilt and silver the friend of his soul arrays himself to go forth to the fight. From a curiously carven chest ... the Lord of the Myrmidons takes out that mystic chalice that the lip of man had never touched ...

This does not sound at all like Homer; Wilde has taken pains to give his account a medieval tone. Clearly no one would take this for genuinely medieval language; but it would no less clearly be a mistake to suppose that he intended to produce a medieval effect and clumsily failed in his aim; the reader is meant to see through the pretence, to recognise behind the obviously cardboard mask the voice of a sophisticated modernity. The colour is medievalising, the intention is not. I have taken this instance because, being close to our own time, we understand it instinctively; if it seems too remote from Catullus, other examples may be found in Latin poetry. Near the beginning of the *Metamorphoses*, in his account of the creation, Ovid assumes a manifestly Lucretian colour. No one will imagine that he has a Lucretian intention, that is, a sustained moral energy and an urgent desire to enforce philosophical convictions upon his readers; nor does he seek to deceive us into thinking that he has. Throughout the poem he borrows differing styles, tragic, high-epic, melodramatic, neoteric, and so on; and in most cases we are meant to react in a similar way. We are to realise that the virtuoso is trying out a new style; that he is adopting the manner without the substance.

The distinction between colour and intention is an important principle, but it is not absolute; Catullus (and indeed Ovid) in alluding to tragedy or epic may wish to convey some elements of tragic or epic effect. But epic and tragedy are both complex kinds of literature; which of their elements he means to carry over – grandeur? pathos? remoteness? rhetoric? artifice? – must be revealed by the poem itself as it proceeds.[16] At the same time the principle may suggest how wrong it is to speak, as one critic does (Quinn, 1971, p. 262), of 'a kind of pastiche of archaic style which is in fact the effect of a highly mannered, self-conscious art, remote from the illusion of primitive simplicity it seeks to create'. Catullus intends no such illusion; from the very first words the piece proclaims itself to be 'civilised poetry'. It is designed not to *be* primitive or simple, but to *recall* these qualities, and that from a great distance. A cultivated nostalgia is implicit in

---

[16] Harmon can justly say that the tone of regret is absent, without needing recourse to Ennius (but I cannot accept his implication, if such it is, that the reader notes the absence of Ennius' 'utinam' ('would that . . .'), and adjusts his reaction accordingly; no one, unless he be an academic, responds to poetry in such a way). Bramble, for his part, forced to admit to the 'distant setting' and the 'eccentric charm' present in these lines, must hold that Catullus has a concealed message running contrary to his ostensible meaning. But since the Argonauts, like other mythological heroes, could be handled in a great variety of ways, many of them mutually incompatible, and since Catullus emphatically declares that the time of their voyage was one of enviable happiness, how is the reader to get out of the text a moral so clear and yet so opposed to what is overtly said? The weight that Bramble places upon 'ausi sunt' ('they dared') is excessive, though I allow that there may be a hint of (pleasurable) shock in these words. He finds the delightful quaintness of lines 2 and 7 'perturbing', but his arguments for this puritanical claim are exceedingly far-fetched.

the poem from the start, although it lies beneath the surface before breaking out superbly at line 22.

For the opening lines have features which modify the epic elements. Line 3 is a *spondeiazōn* (suitably, it is an exotic proper name that makes it so). There are 30 such lines out of 408 in this poem, as compared to 32 out of more than 12,000 in Virgil; as we have seen, the *spondeiazōn* was a neoteric mannerism, and this feature alone virtually proves that *Peleus and Thetis* is a neoteric poem – that is, the kind of poem that Cicero thought inimical to the Ennian tradition. Indeed, those alliterations turn out to be no more than a bow in Ennius' direction: the technique which in him, as in Catullus' contemporary Lucretius, was used to produce a rugged solidity, here comes out smooth and harmonious. The sound is subtler than at first it appears: the n's in the middle of words in line 1 lead on to the initial n's in the second, which in turn are echoed by the *-un-* syllables in 'dicuntur', 'Neptuni', 'undas'. All the significant words in line 3 end in an s, and these combine with the intial f's to evoke the sound of the sea. There are other qualities which are less readily analysable; but any reader will grant that these lines have a delicate sonority and a buoyant variety of dactyls and spondees.

The verse construction is distinctive. To an unusual degree the lines are self-contained units; in the first sentence alone, lines 3, 5 or 7 could be removed from the text without damaging the sense. Fordyce reports that 27 lines are enclosed by a noun and its adjective (as in line 5) and 58 lines contain two nouns and their adjectives arranged in a parallel or chiastic order (including the 'golden line', where two adjectives occupy the first half of the line and their two nouns occur in the second half; line 59 is an instance). One would expect this method of construction to be stiff or monotonous; it is a testimony to Catullus' technical mastery that it is not. In part this is due to his idiosyncratic use of the present participle (e.g. lines 5 and 7), which enables him to tag on new phrases to build long sentences that are fluid and relaxed; Fordyce counts 32 such participles in the first 131 lines. These dry statistics are significant because Catullus' manner is part of his meaning; it is vital to realise that this is an almost narcissistic style. Instead of the pressure of emotion forcing the sense across the natural pauses of the verse, line after line presents itself individually and seems to ask, 'Am I not admirable?' Above all, Catullus' style makes itself conspicuous; this is a poem of display.

An appreciation of style will guide us to Catullus' tone of voice. It is a tone of a certain complexity. To the already curious blend of Ennian archaism and elegant modernism Catullus will later add a free use of diminutives, colloquial and sentimental. The periphrastic description of Minerva (who reappears at lines 228 and 395 but is not once directly named) hints at another element, the allusiveness and erudition of Alexandria, although in reality the touches of obscure learning in the poem are rather occasional.[17] He shows that he can play the game with perfect assurance, but he does not overdo it; in fact he makes his bow to Callimachus, just as he bows to Ennius, and goes his own way.

The mingling of such diverse elements of style is liable in itself to be bizarre, and it is complemented by some bizarreries of subject-matter. There is a certain gaiety in those epic pine-trees 'swimming through the clear waves of Neptune', enhanced by the especial light-ness of sound in line 2. There is grotesqueness too in line 6 with the Argive heroes 'sweeping the blue sea with fir palms', particularly if we pick up the hint of punning oxymoron in 'abiegnis . . . palmis' ('palma' can be a tree or a part of the body, like 'palm' in English).

With an extraordinary capacity to fuse style and content into one, Catullus makes these oddities serve a further purpose. His method is subjective, or 'empathetic'. The descriptions are bizarre because the first ship was indeed a bizarre sight to its beholders. They would not have the vocabulary to speak of 'ships sailing'. How else are they to describe the new marvel if not as 'trees swimming'? What are oars if not 'wooden hands'? For the same reason the ship in line 9 is called a 'currus', or chariot, for the only time in extant Latin; but on another level this is a stylistic mannerism, imitating a Greek poetic usage. The atmosphere of marvel and miracle is continued in lines 8–10: Catullus does away with the usual story that the Argo was constructed by the shipwright Argus; his Argo is to be a ship of wonder, and Minerva herself fashions it on the heroes' behalf. He thus rules out the possibility that the first voyage might be an impious challenge to the divine order; indeed one his themes in this part of the poem is unity and co-operation between gods and men. By the curiously vivid use of words with the roots *flex-* and *tex-*, and particularly by the oxymoronic phrase 'pinea texta', as though the tree trunks were as pliant as thread, he implies that to the goddess the labour of carpentry is as easy as weaving (and of course there is a neat allusion here, for weaving was indeed under Minerva's patronage). The ship speeds over the ocean, even a light wind is sufficient to make it fly; the perilous adventures that confronted the Argonauts are forgotten, and all is liveliness and ease.

The first ten lines, for all their richness of tone, set the scene fairly briskly; but in keeping with the poem's subjective tendency and also with its character as a self-conscious display, the greater part of it will consist of a series of lingering tableaux or set-pieces. The first of these now follows.

[17] 'Incola Itoni', line 228, is the most blatant example; see below, p. 125n.

illa rudem cursu prima imbuit Amphitriten;
quae simul ac rostro ventosum proscidit aequor
tortaque remigio spumis incanuit unda,
emersere freti candenti e gurgite vultus
aequoreae monstrum Nereides admirantes.   15
illa, atque <haud> alia, viderunt luce marinas
mortales oculis nudato corpore Nymphas
nutricum tenus exstantes e gurgite cano.
tum Thetidis Peleus incensus fertur amore,
tum Thetis humanos non despexit hymenaeos,   20
tum Thetidi pater ipse iugandum Pelea sensit.

[That ship by her voyage first handselled Amphitrite, untried before. As she ploughed with her prow the windy sea, and the waves, twisted by the rowing, grew hoary with foam, the marine Nereids, marvelling at the prodigy, put forth their faces from the gleaming swirl of the waters. On that day, and on none other, mortals saw with their eyes the sea Nymphs with their bodies naked, standing forth from the hoary swirl as far as the paps. Then is Peleus said to have kindled with love for Thetis; then did Thetis not scorn to be wed to a mortal; then did the father himself judge that Peleus should be joined to Thetis.]

In line 11 the Argo is launched into the sea, which with a sumptuous Grecian preciosity, heightened by the *spondeiazōn* rhythm, is called Amphitrite. And Amphitrite is 'rudis'; it is almost as though the ship's prow is breaking the goddess's virginity – another luscious, even decadent touch.[18] The keel hits the water vigorously; but by the end of the sentence the pace has slowed dramatically, and we are lingering over a scene of sensuous beauty. The lushness of the passage is controlled by a superb visual precision. Catullus focuses on the way the water twists away from the oar and is turned into foam as it twists; there is a contrast between the matt texture of the hoary foam in line 13 and the gleams of sunlight on the water in line 14, and another contrast of texture between the gleaming sea and the faces of the Nereids popping up above it.[19] The marvel of the scene is matched by the mannered virtuosity of line 15: a four-word hexameter, a proper

[18] The text is corrupt. Quinn, accepting the Oxford ms's 'proram' and a renaissance correction of the mss's 'Amphitritem', has recently revived the reading 'illa rudem cursu proram imbuit Amphitrite' ('She [Minerva] dipped the prow, inexperienced in sailing, in the sea'). This reading gets over a puzzling difficulty: if the Argo is the first ship, how does Theseus come to be shown seafaring on the tapestry at line 52ff.? But it makes line 11 a weak afterthought to line 9f.; and the Argo must be the first ship to account for the amazement of the Nereids in the succeeding lines.

[19] The character of Catullus' visual imagination would alone strongly favour the Aldine edition's 'incanuit' for the 'incanduit' of the mss. Three other arguments support the correction. 1. The d evidently slipped in because of 'candenti' in the line below. 2. 'incandeo' and 'candeo' in different senses in successive lines would be bad writing. 3. Although there are bizarreries in the poem, 'the sea grew hot with foam' seems intolerably silly. Konstan (p. 13), defending the mss, compares Ovid, *Am.* 3.6.25f., but there the conceit of the cold river water growing hot (with passion) is explicitly spelled out.

noun with a Greek nominative plural ('Nereidĕs'), and another spondaic fifth foot. But once again, technique assists meaning. The spondaic ending – 'admirantes' – slows the rhythm at the end of the sentence, to match the suspension of the narrative, and even enhances the visual picture: we imagine the Nereids stretching their eyes in amazement. And they are themselves a source of wonder, for Catullus goes on to tell us that on this occasion mortals were granted the unique privilege of seeing the sea-nymphs with their own eyes.[20] 'Viderunt . . . oculis' – the phrase is emphatic, and indeed our visual sense is still further tickled in this sentence. The nymphs are exquisitely naked;[21] the luxurious precision of 'nutricum tenus' fastens our eyes upon those lovely bodies; we know just how much we can see, and how much remains unseen. The use of 'nutrices' (literally 'nurses') as a synonym for 'papillae' is extraordinary. It seems to be inspired by the similarity of the Greek words *titthos* (breast) and *titthē* (nurse).[22] A weird preciosity, then; and yet strangely voluptuous. The crowning touch is 'e gurgite cano', emphatic because it echoes the phrases in lines 13 and 14. The sea is hoary, aged, in contrast with those lovely youthful bodies over which our eyes have been invited to linger. A visual contrast of textures, to which our mind's eye can immediately respond, is combined with another idea, the oldness of the sea, which is imaginative and fantastic. This fusion of outward precision and inner fantasy is a mark of the truly poetic mind. Catullus does not even need to tell us specifically that those naked bodies are youthful; the pressure of the poetry does it all.

In looking for a single epithet to sum up the character of this poetry, I find myself reaching for the word 'rococo'.[23] I accept it with some hesitation, because some of its associations may be misleading. What I have in mind is a combination of gaiety, mannerism, high polish, controlled ostentation, and perhaps a certain detachment. In describing the poem I may seem to have been overdoing the praise words 'marvel', 'wonder', 'superb' and so on. But my purpose is precisely to suggest that Catullus invites us to respond in this way; he is writing

[20] Unfortunately the text is slightly defective at this point. I share the general opinion that Bergk's restoration of it, 'illa atque <haud> alia . . .', is almost certainly right. With this text, Catullus is saying that the meeting of Peleus and Thetis was the moment when men had a unique revelation of the sea-nymphs, a pinnacle of human happiness and success. Bramble is too honest to reject Bergk's text ('If Bergk's correction in 16 is accepted, . . .'), but it is ruinous to his view that the voyage of the Argo is an impious act which marks the beginning of the gods' dissociation from men, and his shifts to get round the difficulty are wholly unconvincing (p. 37n.).

[21] Not 'nudo' but 'nudato corpore'; there is perhaps a suggestion that they have stripped themselves, as it were for our pleasure.

[22] 'Nutricum' is genitive plural, in which case and number the two Greek words are identical.

[23] Paul Friedländer summed the poem up as 'baroque' (p. 17).

about legendary marvels, and, style and content being intertwined, he does this through the medium of verse that is self-consciously marvellous. Indeed the sheer wonder of art and technical brilliance is, as we shall discover, one of his largest themes.

Like so much of Greek mythology, the story of Peleus and Thetis could be treated in very different ways; the citation of known literary precedents will not in itself give us Catullus' meaning. We must look to the actual poem, and as we do so, it surely becomes evident that Catullus is following the tradition that represented Peleus as the happiest of mortals, and rejecting those sources which made Thetis a reluctant bride (line 20 is emphatic on this point: 'Then Thetis did not despise marriage with a mortal'). The notion that Peleus and Thetis both fell in love at first sight, found in no other author, is probably Catullus' own invention. As ever, style *is* meaning; both the narrative method and the verse construction serve an expressive purpose. Up to line 19 we have had not a clue that Peleus and Thetis are to figure in the poem; by line 21 they are already betrothed, and with the blessing of Jupiter himself. Everything has gone with a supernatural smoothness, expressed also by the extreme symmetry of the sentence: three lines beginning with 'tum' and an elegant polyptoton, the figure by which the same noun is repeated in different cases. The air of opulent elaboration is enhanced by the Greek nouns (the proper names and the word 'hymenaeus'), the Greek accusative 'Pelea' in line 21, and the Greek rhythm of line 20, with the last syllable of 'despexit' lengthened in arsis and a four-syllable word to end the line.

From one point of view lines 19–21 are neatly self-contained; from another they lead on, with the buoyant vitality typical of the poem, to the gorgeous climax of lines 22ff.:

o nimis optato saeclorum tempore nati
heroes, salvete, deum genus! o bona matrum
progenies, salvete iterum . . .
vos ego saepe, meo vos carmine compellabo.

[O heroes born in a time of history too much desired, hail, children of gods! O gracious offspring of your mothers, hail again . . . You, you will I often address in my song.]

Catullus at last breaks out into apostrophe, and matching style to content, at last he lets a sentence flow over the division between the lines; the sense of liberation after the excessive balance of the previous lines is marvellously realised. But there is none of the roughness of personal urgency: the vocatives with 'o', emotional but strongly poetic in diction, the lavish use of anaphora and the artificial, perhaps too carefully wrought chiasmus of line 24 ensure that the operatic, rococo manner is maintained. New tonal elements are infused into the verse to enrich the blend and enhance the sense of climax. With calculated elegance the heroes are addressed three times in three different forms, 'heroes', 'deum genus', 'bona matrum progenies', each phrase being longer than its predecessor; but these varied forms of address also imitate the enumeration of cult titles in cletic prayer. Similarly, the promise in line 24 is a common feature of hymns. It is a promise that Catullus gaily disregards – an indication of the detached worldliness that is an important element in this poem; he wants the religious colour, without the religious intention. Alien to true religious feeling also is the mood of rich nostalgia introduced by the word 'nimis' in conjunction with 'o': 'a time too much desired'.[24] Here is no sharp pang of grief; the sumptuousness of the context reduces yearning to an almost luxurious sensation. The mood is not precisely definable; I should describe it as joy tempered by a regret so akin to pleasure that it seems virtually to be a part of the joy itself. Virgil, a poet who dealt much in indefinable atmospheres, remembered this passage when he celebrated the life of the Italian farmer in a passion of melancholy delight (*Geo.* 2. 458f.):

o fortunatos nimium sua si bona norint
agricolas.

[Oh farmers, too happy, did they but know their own blessings.]

Even the position of the noun and the pause in the middle of the second foot are from Catullus.

The sense of loss in line 22, subordinated though it is to the rococo mood, affords the first hint that this may not be wholly a joyful poem. We miss Catullus' mastery of poetic structure unless we see that the numinous and wistful tones make their entry at this moment; they are a means of defining the form. Like the composer thickening his orchestral texture as he approaches a high point, Catullus marks his climax by a new enrichment of the emotional colouring. He sustains the sense of climax until line 30 by moving on from the heroes in general to Peleus in particular and celebrating his wondrous good fortune with a battery of epanalepsis, anaphora and Greek nouns and formations, all reinforcing a flourish of grandly rhetorical questions. Then his sure sense of form leads him to make a heavy pause, and to resume in a matter-of-fact tone at line 31 with the prosaic connective 'quae' and the businesslike ablative absolute 'finito tempore'.

After this he works gradually and subtly towards another climax.

dona ferunt prae se, declarant gaudia vultu. 34

[They bear gifts before them, they display their joy in their faces.]

---

[24] Fordyce is wrong to translate 'nimis' merely as 'very'. The idea of excess is basic to the word.

This is a splendid line, solemn, processional, yet gay. The rest of the paragraph is formed of three clearly defined sections, the first of three lines, the second of five, the third of seven; the structure broadens out symmetrically.[25]

> *deseritur Cieros, linquunt Phthiotica Tempe* 35
> *Crannonisque domos ac moenia Larisaea,*
> *Pharsalum coeunt, Pharsalia tecta frequentant.*
> *rura colit nemo, mollescunt colla iuvencis,*
> *non humilis curvis purgatur vinea rastris,*
> *non glebam prono convellit vomere taurus,* 40
> *non falx attenuat frondatorum arboris umbram,*
> *squalida desertis rubigo infertur aratris.*
> *ipsius at sedes, quacumque opulenta recessit*
> *regia, fulgenti splendent auro atque argento.*
> *candet ebur soliis, collucent pocula mensae,* 45
> *tota domus gaudet regali splendida gaza.*
> *pulvinar vero divae geniale locatur*
> *sedibus in mediis, Indo quod dente politum*
> *tincta legit rosea conchyli purpura fuco.*

[Cieros is deserted, they leave Phthian Tempe, the house of Crannon and the walls of Larissa, they meet at Pharsalus, they throng the Pharsalian dwellings. No one tends the land, the oxen's necks grow soft, the low vine-shoot is not kept clear with curved hoes, the bull does not tear the clods with ploughshare pressed downwards. The pruners' billhook does not thin the shade of the tree, scaly rust spreads over the abandoned ploughs. But the abode of Peleus himself, as far as the opulent palace stretched back, was resplendent with shining gold and silver. The thrones glow white with ivory, the table carries gleaming cups, the whole house rejoices, resplendent with royal treasure. But the goddess's bridal bed is being set in the middle of the palace; it is smoothly fashioned from the Indian tusk and covered with a purple cloth steeped in the rosy dye of the shellfish.]

The first section is highly literary, stuffed with proper names, each line having one break in the sense at the caesura and another at the end; the style thickens, but the emotional character does not. In the next section the poetic interest quickens; the keenly observed details give Catullus' picture of the deserted countryside a sharp individuality. Finally, all the stops are pulled out for an orgy of luxurious splendour.

'Optatae . . . laetanti . . . gaudia . . .' Joy, joy is still the theme, and those scholars who suppose that Catullus means something different from what he so enthusiastically declares he means turn the poem into a game for cryptographers. Peleus is the pillar of Thessaly ('Thessaliae columen', line 26), and it should be self-evident that the hap-

---

[25] Quinn misses this point by starting a new paragraph at line 43.

piness of his people is a demonstration of loyalty which is held up for our delight. It ought to be obvious too that Catullus is revelling in the qualities of the perceptible world. The poem is rich in lavish personifications of the inanimate. Line 30 is modelled on a line attributed to Euphorion (fr. 122 Powell): 'Ocean, by which all land is encircled and bound in.' In Catullus' adaptation Ocean *embraces* the whole world ('amplectitur'); a small modification, but this massive paternal hug enormously adds to the exuberance. In line 46 the very house rejoices, and in this context of hilarity the phrase 'pulvinar geniale' ('bridal bed') in the next line cannot help but acquire the suggestion of a second meaning; it is the 'cheerful bed' as well. We shall find a similar mood at other moments in the poem. At line 280ff. Chiron fills the palace with flowers, 'quo permulsa domus iucundo risit odore' (284) ('the house smiled [or 'laughed'], caressed by their pleasant scent'). 'Permulsa' suggests the sense of touch, 'risit' of sight, 'odore' of smell; the synaesthesia is very sumptuous. Laughter as a metaphor for bright colour or sparkling light is conventional enough, but to make the house laugh at a scent, so that the visual picture is merged with an element of sheer fantasy, and to make the scent so gorgeous that it is like a caressing touch – this is indeed dazzling. And yet mingled with the rich synaesthesia is the refreshment of another tone: the bright, clear charm of an innocent primitivism. Chiron is portrayed as a simple sylvan, bringing flowers 'in unsorted garlands' ('indistinctis corollis', line 283); 'Chiron's present is an unsophisticated one,' as Fordyce says. In Theocritus' eleventh Idyll the rustic Polyphemus offers flowers to Galatea with a lovable gaucherie; there is something of the same spirit here. The centaur's flowers come from woods, plains, mountains and riversides; Catullus has packed a great variety of landscapes into a few lines. Here the outdoors and the indoors, the abundance of wild nature and the artifice of man-made beauty come delectably together; and when the house laughs, we may suspect that in its courtly fashion it is amused and charmed by the artless offering, much as at another wedding Shakespeare's Duke is pleased by the rude mechanicals. The wind and water of line 281 refresh us with the openness of the countryside; and yet even here Catullus thickens the atmosphere with another distinctive personification: the breath of the west wind upon the flowers is an act of parturition, fecund and warm.

The maternal fug is thicker at line 86ff.; it is significant, as we shall see later, that Catullus' eager immersion in the sensuous spreads over into the story of Ariadne.

hunc simul ac cupido conspexit lumine virgo
regia, quam suavis exspirans castus odores
lectulus in molli complexu matris alebat . . .

[As soon as the royal maiden caught sight of him with desiring eye, she whom her chaste bed, breathing out sweet odours, nurtured in the soft embrace of a (or 'her') mother . . .]

The languid spondaic movement of line 87, enhanced by the s's and long a's, suggests the heaviness of the perfume. The bed is luxuriously personified: it breathes out, nurtures, even seems to embrace like a mother, for the strange language of line 88 almost fuses bed and mother into one. The assonance of l in this line creates a more delicate sound; and here the diminutive 'lectulus', intimate amid the splendour, is a brilliant stroke. Catullus has created a sense of enclosure, of muskiness and close embrace; but as at line 280ff. this tight, interior world is blended (or contrasted) with an outdoor freshness:

quales Eurotae praecingunt flumina myrtus
aurave distinctos educit verna colores . . .   90

[Like the myrtles that gird the streams of Eurotas, or the varied colours that the spring breeze draws forth . . .]

Wind, water and springtime all have their part to play. On the one hand, Ariadne's setting must seem seductive to Theseus, and to the reader ('bed' and 'embrace', childlike in their superficial meaning, must carry sexual overtones in their context); on the other, she herself – so the language and imagery suggest – is a sweet young thing, girlish and innocent. The verbs in the simile, 'praecingunt' and 'educit', are strong and imaginative, and at the same time they bind the comparison closely to the thing compared; the river is girded by myrtles just as Ariadne in her scented bed is embraced, and the breeze 'brings up' the flowers just as Ariadne's mother brings up her child.[26]

To return to the early part of the poem: the scenes of the deserted countryside at line 38ff. are obviously exaggerated[27] – another touch of baroque fantasy, to which Catullus' eye for realistic detail acts as a counterpoise; he is much enjoying the visible world. 'This description owes its beauty,' R.G.M. Nisbet writes, 'to a wonderfully precise series of verbs'[28] – that, and the quantity and economy of observa-

[26] 'Praecingunt' is Baehrens's conjecture to replace 'pergignunt', the reading of the archetype. A renaissance corrector wrote 'progignunt'.

[27] The baroque exaggerations surely rule out the possibility that Catullus is speaking *au grand sérieux*. Critics who make him into a moralist here make him into a very foolish moralist indeed.

[28] Nisbet, p. 102. He rightly finds 'infertur' at line 42 disappointingly vague, and suspects corruption: 'Perhaps *increscit* would suggest the required scaliness.' Line 42 may possibly have been an afterthought. Without it we have three lines introduced by the same word leading into a lyric climax marked by enjambment – a beautifully shaped period almost exactly parallel in structure to line 19ff. The contrast between the shade at the end of line 41 and the gleaming opulence of line 43f. would also seem to be in Catullus' manner (line 308f. is somewhat comparable).

tion.[29] In a single line (41) Catullus has room for the billhook, the tree, the shade, the pruners, and by implication the heat and sweat of their labour. In line 39 we see the curved sickle bending low to get under the vineshoots, in line 40 the plough's cutting edge pressing downward into the soil, with the spondaic rhythm conveying the bullocks' effort.[30]

When we move from the countryside to the palace, the liveliness of observation remains. The description of the interior begins, 'quacumque opulenta recessit/regia.' It is as though the reader, like the Thessalians themselves, has just arrived at the doors and is catching his first glimpse of varied and distant splendours; at the same time Catullus' phrase economically implies the palatial size of the building. The sentence structure expands (first come two clauses of half a line each, then one clause of one line, then two more each occupying a line and a half); meanwhile we are drawn deep into the house, passing through a banqueting hall (45) until we come to the bridal bed in the heart of the building ('sedibus in mediis'); the sense of movement and progression adds to the verve of the poetry. Brilliant light is everywhere; the sonorous rhythm of the *spondeiazōn* line 44 evokes a thickly encrusted splendour. The upward surge of the sentence at line 45f. is admirable: two vigorous verbs, both expressive of bedazzlement, take the weight of the first two clauses; the rhythm slows; and then at the climax of the sentence Catullus flings out his exuberant fantasy: 'tota domus gaudet' ('the whole house rejoices'). The diction grows rich: the exotic touch in 'gaza', a word of Persian origin, prepares the way for the sumptuously Grecian 'conchyli' and the resplendent formality of the 'Indian tooth'. Some critics have seen an oblique criticism of Peleus' luxury in the phrase 'roseo fuco' ('with rosy dye') on the grounds that dyeing suggests deceit; but this is to lose the sophisticated piquancy of Catullus' tone. 'Fucus' is basically a descriptive word. When Virgil contrasts the blessings of country life with the

---

[29] The picture of the plough rusting in line 42 may conceivably be meant to darken the tone momentarily, but I doubt it. Bramble writes, 'Catullus here suggests wholesale dereliction. The reader has been deceived again: what he at first took for innocent *otium* turns out to be reprehensible *desidia*. The occasion itself has faded into the background, while Catullus has been intimating that at the time of the wedding man was being seduced by luxury and opulence away from his hardy agricultural existence' (p. 39). This is reductivism again. Bramble mentions Tibullus and he probably has the *Georgics* in mind too; but it is most unlikely that Catullus shared the Augustan attitude to rural labour or the Augustan interest in agricultural depression as a poetic theme. I cannot help feeling that Bramble's argument boils down to this: the possible *implication* of a single line conveys Catullus' real meaning (that Peleus' wealth was a corrupting influence), while all the lines of eager jubilation around it are so much mystification.

[30] There is a marked clash of ictus against accent in the first half of the line, and a marked coincidence of ictus and accent in the second half, reinforced by the alliteration of 'vellit vomere'. Perhaps we are to imagine the rough strain of getting the plough into motion, and then the steady pressure forward.

tedious luxuries of the city, he uses the verb 'fucare' to describe the staining of wool with Assyrian dye (*Geo.* 2. 465); with characteristic indirection he insinuates a charge of moral corruption by using words which though morally neutral in themselves, imply condemnation in their context. If 'fucare' were not fundamentally neutral, Virgil's phrase would lose its sinister suggestiveness. In Catullus' case I do not think that the word is wholly without overtones; I believe that the effect is close to that in the passage of Wilde quoted above: 'In his chamber of *stained* ivory lies her leman.' There is something luxuriously *nuancé* in the use of a word innocuous in itself but which in another context could easily have a decadent connotation. We might compare the subtle and self-indulgent paradox with which Pater describes the *purity* of Winckelmann's 'romantic, fervent friendships with young men': 'These friendships, bringing him in contact with the pride of human form, and *staining* his thoughts with its bloom, perfected his reconciliation with the spirit of Greek sculpture' (*Studies in the History of the Renaissance*, 'Winckelmann').

The radiant light that dominates this passage spreads through the poem; Catullus' self-conscious masterpiece gleams as though it were a visible artefact. 'Quanto saepe magis fulgore expalluit auri' (100) ('How much paler than the gleam of gold she often grew'). Even when pale with anxiety, Ariadne is brightly golden, like a figure moulded in precious metal by a smith, or as an operatic heroine remains gloriously melodious even in grief; we shall return to this analogy. Details, small in themselves, enhance the luminosity of the whole. At lines 16, 31 and 325 Catullus uses the word 'lux' for 'day', although he is merely indicating a measurement of time;[31] eyes are 'lumina' at lines 86, 122, and 220.[32] The poem ends sombrely, but the very last words of all are 'lumine claro'; it is as though a shaft of light from a lost and brighter world has pierced through the darkness. Ambivalence is no advantage here; this last stroke of genius would not be as moving as it is, had not the early parts of the poem been bathed in the radiance so much longed for.

---

[31] Also at line 237, if it is permissible to substitute 'lux' for 'aetas'. Baehrens made the suggestion only to reject it, but it has recently received support from Nisbet (p. 111).

[32] Like Homer, Catullus places Ariadne on Dia, which by Hellenistic times was identified with Naxos (as by Callimachus in fr. 611 Pf.). I suspect that besides suggesting Alexandrian erudition and a remote mythological atmosphere, the name Dia, 'heavenly', from the same Indo-European root as 'dies', etc., contributes to the theme of light. A passage such as line 121f., with the foam of Dia in one line and 'lumina' for eyes in the next conveys a brilliance that goes beyond the surface meaning of the words.

3

'Haec vestis . . .' After the bravura line 50 seems to have the plain, resumptive tone of line 31. Then Catullus springs a surprise: fairly soon, but at no clearly identifiable moment, the reader comes to realise that this is one of those poems, like the first and eleventh Idylls of Theocritus, the story of Aristaeus at the end of Virgil's *Georgics*, or Catullus' own *Vesper adest*, which has an inner section contained within two outer sections. Often, as here, there is a 'story within a story', but not always; in the eleventh Idyll, for example, the outer sections consist of Theocritus writing in a conversational manner to his friend the doctor Nicias, while the inner section is the song of the Cyclops Polyphemus to the nymph Galatea. What Theocritus achieves here is a contrast (not a strong but, with Hellenistic delicacy, a slight contrast) between the natural, personal tone of his consoling words to Nicias with the half pastoral, half mythological world of his inner section; Polyphemus was traditionally a monster, and also a minor Sicilian deity, but in Theocritus' treatment he is just big and awkward. Theocritus' manner is *faux naïf*; such elegantly condescending treatment of mythology is consciously artificial, and is meant to be appreciated as such.

In the first Idyll we find again, with far greater subtlety and power, similar light distinctions of tone between different parts of the poem. The outer sections, a dialogue between Thyrsis and an unnamed goatherd, are set in what has been called a timeless present; no one would call this idyllic world exactly 'realistic', but it is perceptibly closer to actuality than the inner sections, which are deliberately kept at a distance from the world that we immediately experience. The principal inner section is the famous song of Thyrsis, but earlier the goatherd describes the scenes carved on a wooden cup, a woman between two wooers, an old fisherman gathering his net for a cast, and a boy plaiting a cage for a cricket out of rushes, oblivious to a pair of foxes trying to steal his food and the grapes which he is supposed to be guarding. Plainly these scenes are not 'real' for the simple reason that the people and places do not exist, even within the universe of the poem, but are merely images. The goatherd evokes the world not of reality but of art, and the artistry of the imaginary carver is matched by the poetic virtuosity of Theocritus, who has succeeded in creating such vivid little vignettes with such brevity and economy. Indeed, these scenes, which are unreal even within the terms of the poem, are perhaps more vividly realised than anything else in the Idyll, but that is a paradox in which Theocritus takes an aware pleasure; we shall find comparable paradoxes in Catullus' treatment of Ariadne. The song of Thyrsis itself, like the cup, is designed to be a masterpiece of art, but this time the arts are those of poetry and music. In the very

first sentence of the Idyll the goatherd praises Thyrsis' piping, and
later tries to entice him to sing; the song of Thyrsis is not a spontaneous outpouring, but a performance, a party piece as it were, and
indeed the goatherd offers him a prize for it. At the same time Thyrsis'
song, which tells of the death of the shepherd Daphnis, introduces us
to a world different from that in which he and the goatherd live,
mythological, mysterious, caught only in glimpses. This is a world,
like that of Peleus and Thetis in Catullus, where divinities may talk
with men, speaking brief, suggestive and puzzling words. Why is
Daphnis dying? Why is a nymph searching for him? Who is she? And
the manner of his death – 'he came to the stream' – what does that
mean?[33] The troubling, elusive tone sets this section of the poem apart
from the rest.

The end of the *Georgics* can be seen in the same light. Both the
outer story of how Aristaeus, after losing his bees, discovered how to
get a new swarm and the inner story of Orpheus and Eurydice are
written with the highest degree of polish; this is neoteric art at its
most accomplished. And yet there are small differences: for example,
the echoes of Homeric epic, so conspicuous in the story of Aristaeus,
virtually disappear from the inner part. The exquisitely plangent tale
of Orpheus and Eurydice is put into the mouth of Proteus, a grotesque
old man, who gnashes his teeth with rage as he tells it. There is a
blatant disharmony between the speaker and the style of his speech,
and the very incongruity highlights the artifice, indeed the artificiality, of the passage. The story of Orpheus, as Proteus tells is, is partial
and allusive. It begins *in medias res*, with Aristaeus pursuing Eurydice along the banks of an unnamed river. Like Catullus' story of
Ariadne, it ends abruptly, as Proteus leaps precipitately into the sea,
leaving Aristaeus to infer as best he may the lesson he has come to
seek.

The inner section of Catullus' *Vesper adest* is, like the song of
Thyrsis, a performance, in this case a concert piece sung antiphonally
at a wedding by two competing choruses, one of men, one of women.
The consistent symmetry between the women's singing and the men's
replies indicates the thought and effort which have gone into the
composition of the recital; in the first outer section the men note the
work that the women have put into their rehearsal, adding that they
therefore deserve to win the contest (62.16): 'amat victoria curam'
('victory loves care'). Care – the very opposite of that spontaneity (or
illusion of spontaneity) which Catullus exhibits in some of his shorter
poems – will prove to be a dominant aesthetic principle again in *Peleus
and Thetis*. The outer sections of *Vesper adest* are not much less highly

---

[33] Theocritus' first readers may have been better able to answer some of these questions than we are; but the fact remains that his *manner* is mystificatory and allusive.

finished than the inner part: the richly melodious use of anaphora in the opening lines is sufficient to establish that the whole poem is to be a formal, polished display, and the outer parts, like the inner, are divided between the men and women, each section ending with the refrain used in the performance which makes up the inner part; and yet by small touches Catullus indicates that the tone in the inner and outer sections is slightly different. In the first nineteen lines there are small traces of a colloquial, or at least conversational manner: 'nimirum', 'sic certest', 'viden'. The very first word of the poem names the Evening Star in the Latinised form 'Vesper'; both choirs begin their recital by addressing the star, but this time in the Greek form 'Hespere'. Even the faint pretence of spontaneity (a pretence that we are not meant to take seriously) is to be abandoned now; for this is a concert, this is high art. The similarities of tone between inner and outer sections are so great that the closing lines are almost ambiguous: on the one hand the young men are breaking out of the antiphonal pattern of the concert and speaking directly to the bride, and yet on the other these last lines can virtually be taken as the climax and summation of their performance. The combination of a sensuous melodiousness spread over the whole poem with delicate distinctions of tone that articulate it into separate sections is the mark of an art both sophisticated and self-aware.

The scheme of *Peleus and Thetis* is somewhat similar. We have seen that the first fifty lines of the poem are lavishly decorative, but the account of Ariadne is especially so, for she is literally a decoration; she exists to adorn the bed of Peleus and his bride. The outer story of Peleus was distanced, but the inner story of Ariadne is doubly distanced, for even to the wedding guests of a long vanished age she is no more than a picture. Ariadne and Iacchus are merely 'shapes', and shapes of people who lived a very long time ago ('priscis . . . figuris', line 50); the tapestry is a work of wondrous art ('mira arte', line 51), and Catullus brings out the sheer artistry of the representation by the way in which he describes it. His account of Ariadne covers more than 200 lines, with glances backward to earlier parts of the story and forward to future events, so that we may forget (or suspect Catullus of having forgotten) that he was supposed to be writing an *ekphrasis* (that is, a description) of a picture. But at line 251 he reminds us that he has not really been so inattentive: 'at *parte ex alia* florens volitabat Iacchus' ('But youthful Iacchus was flaunting in from another part [of the picture]'). What he goes on to describe is a scene of baroque and violent action:

quae tum alacres passim lymphata mente furebant
euhoe bacchantes, euhoe capita inflectentes.   255
harum pars tecta quatiebant cuspide thyrsos,

pars e divolso iactabant membra iuvenco,
pars sese tortis serpentibus incingebant,
pars obscura cavis celebrabant orgia cistis,
orgia quae frustra cupiunt audire profani. 260

[They [the Maenads] were excitedly raging here and there with maddened
mind, revelling and shaking their heads with cries of 'euhoe, euhoe'. Some
of them were shaking thyrsi with wreathed points, some were tossing the
limbs of a bullock that they had torn apart, some were girding themselves
with twisted snakes, some were honouring dark mysteries enclosed in
caskets, mysteries which the uninitiated in vain desire to hear.]

And how does Catullus depict this alarming scene? Is his language
animated? Or the syntax agitated? Do the sentences spill across from
one line into the next? Not a bit of it. Catullus stays cool. With extreme
regularity he begins three successive lines with the word 'pars'. Each
clause is of exactly equal length, except that the word 'orgia' in the
third of these lines is picked up in a fourth line by an elegant epanalepsis, so that the last clause, in the best rhetorical fashion, is more
expansive than its predecessors. The calmness, the neatness, the control all run counter to what the words are saying. And yet here style
and content are marvellously one, for Catullus is revelling in the
paradox of visual art. Thanks to the artist's skill the most energetic
action can be brought to life, but in reality the picture is wholly static.
The Bacchic scene is exciting, and yet it is a masterpiece of carefully
planned composition. 'Pars ... pars ... pars ...' – how beautifully
the artist has arranged it all.[34]
    The same nicely balanced syntax can be found in the description of
the deserted Ariadne:

... non flavo retinens subtilem vertice mitram,
non contecta levi velatum pectus amictu,
non tereti strophio lactentis vincta papillas, 65
omnia quae toto delapsa e corpore passim
ipsius ante pedes fluctus salis alludebant.

[She no longer kept her finely woven bonnet upon her blond head; her
bosom was no longer covered, veiled by a light garment; her milky breasts
were no longer bound by a smooth stomacher; all these things had slipped
right off from her body hither and thither, and the waves of the sea were
playing with them before her very feet.]

Surely these lines are too decorative to be deeply tragic or passionate.
It is illuminating to compare a later treatment of the same scene. In
Ovid's *Heroides* 10 Ariadne batters her breast and tears her hair (line

---

[34] Moralising critics, failing to see that Catullus immensely enjoys the Dionysiac
incursion, in effect attribute to him the error that made Pentheus' last moments so
uncomfortable.

15f.); we will find nothing so indecorous in Catullus' account. At line 137f. Ovid's Ariadne declares,

> *adspice demissos lugentis more capillos*
> *et tunicas lacrimis sicut ab imbre gravis.*

[See my hair, dropping down like the hair of one who mourns, and my tunic, sodden with tears as though with rain.]

This dishevelment is notably different from the elegant déshabille of Catullus' princess, and the contrast is particularly eloquent in that we customarily (and rightly) think of Catullus as a far more direct and passionate poet than Ovid. But in the present poem Catullus is consciously attempting something very unlike his better known manner. He takes pleasure in the pictorial beauty of his damsel in distress, bringing out with loving observation the textures of her clothing against her body: the *yellow* hair escaping from under her *finely woven* bonnet, her bosom emerging from its light covering,[35] her milky breasts and the *smooth* stomacher pressing against them. Catullus' eyes travel slowly downwards with sensuous delight; it must be an insensitive reader who does not see that the poet is enjoying Ariadne's body as her clothes slip off her into the sea. Their fall has none of the clumsiness of reality; they slide from her with the fluidity of water ('delapsa', line 66) and float in the sea ('fluitantis', line 68), for waves and raiment are blent together on the marvellous embroidery. The seductive beauty of the scene is matched by the sound of the verse. In line 64 *lĕv-* is answered by *vēl-*, and there is a mixture of repetition and variation in the syllables *-ect-*, *-ect-* and *-ict-*. There are more t's and ct's in line 65. In lines 65-7 the increasing delicacy of the description is matched by a greater subtlety in the sound patterns, with the exquisite variation of the sounds *pap-*, *-aps-*, *pass-*, *ips-*. Line 67 is wonderfully sparkling; those s's, l's, u's and dental consonants ensure that we really see and hear the waves lapping. (A picture cannot be heard, of course; but we shall find that Catullus is concerned with illusion.) An irregular dancing effect is created by a hexameter that is mostly dactylic, yet with a spondee and a clash of ictus against accent in unexpected places: 'ipsĭŭs antĕ pĕdēs flūctūs sális ā-llūdebant.' The gaiety of the metre is enhanced by that last word: the waves *play* with Ariadne's garments. Throughout these lines style, sound and content remain a perfect unity.

When Ariadne runs into the sea, decorative elegance is again to the fore; we are invited to enjoy the *soft* clothing of the princess, lifted just

---

[35] The finest women's clothing was admired for its semi-transparency, and I imagine that this is the implication of the adjective 'levis'. There are thus two pictorial effects: the breasts half seen through gauzy drapery, and the breasts emerging as the drapery slips down from the body.

enough for a *bare* calf to be revealed, with the waves dancing about
her (128f.):

> *. . . tum tremuli salis adversas procurrere in undas*
> *mollia nudatae tollentem tegmina surae . . .*

[[They say that] she would then run forward to meet the rippling waves
of the sea, and lift the soft clothing covering her now bared calf.]

We may see how distinctive and unusual Catullus' method is here by
comparing him once more with Ovid; the second of the *Heroides* (Phyllis to Demophoon) is partly modelled on this poem, but when Phyllis
runs into the waves (127 ff.), there are not the visual details that
Catullus picks out, and instead of delivering a graceful speech, she
collapses in a faint. And yet Ovid had a keen eye for detail, and a
notorious weakness for speeches.[36] Catullus makes the tone in which
he has described Ariadne's distress spread over into her lament. Even
in grief her thoughts are decorative. She wishes that she might have
been permitted to follow Theseus as a slave, and to wash his feet; and
this menial office is described with almost an excess of conscious
loveliness (162): 'candida permulcens liquidis vestigia lymphis' ('caressing your white feet with limpid water'). The neatness of the chiastic word order, the graceful alternation of dactyls and spondees, the
delicacy of the few vowel sounds, the alliteration of the letter l, and
the sumptuousness of the diction – 'vestigia' for feet, the poetic 'lympha' for water, the softly luxurious 'permulcens' ('fully soothing') for
'pouring' – unite with the obtrusive prettiness of the idea: clear waters
caressing shining feet.[37] And in the next line Ariadne imagines herself
strewing Theseus' couch with a *purple* covering. At the climax of her
speech she calls upon the Furies to take vengeance upon Theseus for
his treachery in lines which Landor considered to be 'the most majestic
in the Roman language';[38] but she is not so passionate that she forgets
to mention what they look like (193–4):

> *Eumenides, quibus anguino redimita capillo*
> *frons exspirantis praeportat pectoris iras.*

[The Furies, whose brows wreathed in snaky hair display the wrath
breathing from their hearts.]

---

[36] It is true, of course, that the whole poem is a kind of 'speech' by Phyllis.

[37] Catullus presumably had in mind some lines of Pacuvius (fr. 244 R) in which
Euryclea offers to wash Ulysses' feet. Here are 'lympha' and 'permulceo' again, but the
lines are without Catullus' magic. Comparison of the two passages shows how poetic
diction is not simply a matter of words but of the manner and context in which they are
deployed. Catullus uses 'permulceo' again at line 284, and with even more luxurious
effect.

[38] *Pericles and Aspasia*, 227.

This time the alliteration is markedly conspicuous: the many t's, p's, r's and s's in a single line put the snakes, hissing and spitting, vividly before us. This sensational picture, by distracting us to some degree from Ariadne's sufferings, prevents us from becoming too greatly involved in them.

No less important than what she says is the way that she says it. Catullus tells us that he will quote her last complaints ('extremae querellae', line 130); we are perhaps surprised to be then given a speech of eighty lines. She is to speak amid sobs (131): 'frigidulos udo singultus ore cientem' ('uttering chilly sobs, her face damp'). The u's in this line mimic the gulping, as she chokes back her tears; but her speech proves to be one of exceptional fluency and ease. As with Virgil's Proteus, there is a dissonance between the manner of the speaker and the style of the speech; the purpose of this dissonance we shall consider later. Now any poet composing a long speech for a heroine in hexameters will seek to use all the artifice at his disposal; but that artifice can be directed to different ends. Ruggedness, passion and directness are qualities that can be created by contrivance; but they are not qualities that Catullus is after here. He uses the first lines of her speech, like the first lines of the poem, to establish its tone:

> *sicine me patriis avectam, perfide, ab aris,*
> *perfide, deserto liquisti in litore, Theseu?*
> *sicine discedens neglecto numine divum,*
> *immemor a! devota domum periuria portas?*　　　　　　　　135

[Faithless, faithless Theseus, have you then left me on a lonely sea-shore, after carrying me away from my ancestral altars? Are you then departing (ah, forgetful!), indifferent to the will of the gods, and bearing your perjury homeward under curse?]

Inside the repeated 'sicine ... sicine ...' is another repetition, 'perfide ... perfide ...', which in turn finds an echo in the repeated initial syllables of '*li*quisti in *li*tore.' Such complex but graceful use of anaphora is comparable to the style of Theocritus at its most melodious. The first 'sicine' introduces a heavy alliteration of p, with subsidiary alliteration of l; the second 'sicine' introduces a heavy alliteration of a, with subsidiary but strong alliteration of n and p. Ariadne makes her skill obvious; like the alliterating Holofernes she 'will something affect the letter, for it argues facility'. The 'a' of line 135, notorious as a neoteric mannerism, is melodiously pathetic rather than tragic or passionate.[39] In her first sentence Ariadne addresses Theseus with

---

[39] Cf. 'a misera' at line 70. Calvus (fr. 9 M) wrote in his *Io*, 'a virgo infelix: herbis pasceris amaris' ('Unhappy maiden: you will feed on bitter grass'); the line was echoed by Virgil at *Ecl.* 6. 47 as part of the song of Silenus, which is a sort of miniature anthology of neoteric themes. 'A' comes three times in as many lines at *Ecl.* 10. 47–9, quoted and discussed below, p. 122.

three separate vocatives judiciously distributed over the two lines. This stylistic trick resembles the mannered virtuosity of the fragments supposedly quoted from the poet Menalcas in Virgil's ninth Eclogue (lines 23–5, cf. lines 46–50):

Tityre, dum redeo (brevis est via), pasce capellas,
et potum pastas age, Tityre, et inter agendum
occursare capro (cornu ferit ille) caveto.   25

[Tityrus, till I return (the way is short), feed my goats, and drive them when fed to water, Tityrus, and as you drive them, beware of getting in the he-goat's way (he butts with his horn).]

From almost every line of Ariadne's lament the same moral may be drawn; a few examples must suffice:

quis dum aliquid cupiens animus praegestit apisci,   145
nil metuunt iurare, nihil promittere parcunt:
sed simul ac cupidae mentis satiata libido est,
dicta nihil meminere, nihil periuria curant.

[As for men, when their heart desires something and longs to get it, there is no oath they shrink from, nothing that they forbear to promise; but when once the appetite of their lustful mind is satisfied, they have no remembrance of their words, they care nothing for perjuries.]

Here the calmly formal patterning resembles the balance and symmetry of the 'performance' in *Vesper adest* (62.42–4):

. . . multi illum pueri, multae optavere puellae;
idem cum tenui carptus defloruit ungui,
nulli illum pueri, nullae optavere puellae.

[Many boys have desired [the flower], many girls; but when once it has been plucked by the thin fingernail and lost its flower, no boys have desired it, no girls.]

The condemnation in line 154ff. is too elegant to be entirely savage:

quaenam te genuit sola sub rupe leaena,
quod mare conceptum spumantibus exspuit undis,   155
quae Syrtis, quae Scylla rapax, quae vasta Carybdis,
talia qui reddis pro dulci praemia vita?

[What lioness bore you beneath a lonely rock, what sea conceived you and spewed you forth with foaming waves, what Syrtis, what ravening Scylla, what desolate Charybdis bore you, who offer me such recompense for the sweet gift of life?]

Although Virgil's Dido denounces the heartlessness of Aeneas in superficially very similar terms, we could hardly imagine her including the distractingly romantic and evocative detail of 'sola sub rupe'.[40] The hissing of the waves in line 155 is another picturesque distraction: 'quod mare *concept*um *spuman*tibus *e*x*spui*t undis.' In line 156 Ariadne manages a flawless *tricolon auctum*, as again in the fine lines 186–7:[41]

> *nulla fugae ratio, nulla spes: omnia muta,*
> *omnia sunt deserta, ostentant omnia letum.*

[There is no means of escape, no hope: all is dumb, all desolate; all things show me death.]

The speech contains many echoes of Euripides and Apollonius Rhodius; these too help to distance it, by making it so much more 'literary' and self-conscious.[42] At its climax Ariadne declares that her complaints are forced from her by the violence of a crazed and burning rage (196f.): the claim is hardly plausible, nor is it meant to be. Finally, Catullus himself undermines the potential tragedy of Ariadne by revealing that the embroidery is not, after all, a scene of sorrow, for it depicts her on the point of receiving that supreme privilege which Peleus too will receive when he sleeps beneath it: the love of a god. 'Where am I to go?' Ariadne has asked. 'What hope is left to me? Where can I find love?' (177, 182, etc.). These rhetorically despairing questions are to get a surprisingly quick and easy answer. In the poem we have to wait a little while to learn what that answer is; but *on the coverlet*, and in the experience of the Thessalian spectators, it is given at the very moment of utterance.

It is also significant that Ariadne's laments and reproaches are addressed to a man who cannot possibly hear her; they are in fact designed for her own gratification, or, as we half feel, the gratification of us, the readers. Virgil's Dido, by contrast, is engaged in a desperate struggle to keep her lover, and even Ovid's letter-writing heroines despatch their epistles with the notional purpose of wounding or persuading or in some way acting upon the men whom they address. But

[40] Virgil did, however, use the phrase 'sole. sub rupe' at *Ecl.* 10. 14. On the style of this poem see below, p. 122.

[41] The weary lengthening of the last syllable of the second 'nulla' is effective. Cf. Hopkins in similar mood: 'What hours, o what black hoûrs have we spent . . .' The bleak monosyllable 'spes' and the stark asyndeton after it add to the sense of dull hopelessness.

[42] It may be objected that the *Aeneid* draws continually upon literary reminiscence, and yet distancing is not intended: we are not meant to be any the less involved in Dido's suffering because her words and situation recall Homer, Apollonius and Attic tragedy. But if Virgil does succeed in combining literary echoes with emotional immediacy (and it may perhaps be doubted whether even so great a poet as he has entirely succeeded), the puzzle is how he manages so strange a feat. The problem, in other words, is one for the critic of Virgil, not for the critic of Catullus.

Ariadne knows with absolute certainty that her words to Theseus are
futile; in mood her lament is less close to Dido's speeches than to the
self-conscious musicality with which Virgil – the neoteric Virgil –
makes Gallus apostrophise his absent Lycoris in the tenth Eclogue:

> *tu procul a patria (nec sit mihi credere tantum)*
> *Alpinas, a! dura nives et frigora Rheni*
> *me sine sola vides. a, te ne frigora laedant!*
> *a, tibi ne teneras glacies secet aspera plantas!*
> *ibo et Chalcidico quae sunt mihi condita versu*   50
> *carmina pastoris Siculi modulabor avena.*

[You far from your homeland (would that I did not have to believe such
a thing) are looking (ah, hardened girl) upon Alpine snows and the
frost-bound Rhine, alone and without me. Ah, may the frosts not harm
you! Ah, may the jagged ice not cut your tender feet! I will be gone, and
play the songs that I composed in Chalcidian verse on a Sicilian shepherd's
oaten pipe.]

The lines are suffused with an exquisite egoism; it would be a naive
reader who thought that Gallus' first concern was for the condition of
his lady's feet.

4

I have shown that Catullus is at pains to bring out the pictorial quality
of Ariadne on the tapestry, but it is even clearer that most of the time
he is not describing a picture at all. He makes this dramatically
obvious at the point where he returns to the wedding of Peleus and
Thetis. We have seen that when he introduces Iacchus he carefully
reminds us that he is dealing with a static scene; but immediately
after the three lines beginning with 'pars' he brings in the idea of
sound – 'orgia quae frustra cupiunt *audire* profani' – and the next four
lines (261–4) form a crescendo of noise brilliantly realised by a battery
of onomatopoeic effects:

> *plangebant alii proceris tympana palmis,*
> *aut tereti tenuis tinnitus aere ciebant;*
> *multis raucisonos efflabant cornua bombos*
> *barbaraque horribili stridebat tibia cantu.*

[Others were banging tambourines with outstretched palms or making
thin ringing sounds with cymbals of rounded bronze; many blew on horns
with harshly sounding booming, and the barbarian flute shrilled with
thrilling music.]

The first of these lines is as much visual as auditory in its effect – a picture of the hands stretched flat to beat against the tambourine forms a characteristic detail – but eventually sound comes to dominate over sight entirely. As we reach the climax of barbarian ferocity, the Ariadne episode, which has lasted for over two hundred lines, comes with startling abruptness to an end. 'Talibus . . .,' Catullus begins the next line: 'with such . . .' – what? We have to wait to the end of the line to discover that the noun is 'figuris', echoing the 'figuris' which closed the very first line of the Ariadne section, but clashing grotesquely with the immediately preceding lines and above all with their last word, 'cantu'.

Most commentators strangely ignore this striking disharmony, but it is clearly calculated and important.[43] In part it is a reflection of the formal structure of the poem, which cultivates surprise and disproportion. But it is much more than this, for here as elsewhere in the work form and content are one. If one looks at ancient descriptions of works of art, one finds again and again that what they are praised for is their realism; to say that a statue or picture was so lifelike that it seemed to be breathing was a cliché of approbation. Throughout history many artists and many poets (though not Catullus in this piece) have sought to create the illusion of reality, to involve the reader or spectator to such an extent that he feels himself to be actually present and caught up in the actions and emotions that are displayed to him. Yet art and reality are distinct; ultimately the illusion must always fail. The paradox of art – that it seems to heighten and intensify reality, and yet can never be more than an imitation of reality – is exposed by the way in which Catullus constructs his poem. The embroidered Bacchants are so vividly realised that it seems one can hear them banging and crashing, but in an instant the poet can shatter the illusion. So it is with Ariadne herself: she 'comes to life' as though she were a real person, but in the end she can never escape from her frame. The poem itself, which is a conscious 'work of art', a conscious 'masterpiece', mimics this pictorial character. 'Sed quid ego a primo digressus carmine plura/commemorem . . .' (116f.) ('But why should I, digressing from my original song, tell further . . .?'). The oddly prosaic character of this question is inexplicable until we realise that Catullus is drawing to our notice the tension between narrative and static description. This tension imparts a splendid élan to the poem: Ariadne acquires so strong an autonomy that she threatens to burst from her frame; similarly, Catullus makes as though he cannot keep to a straight description of the embroidery but must constantly digress, flashing back to Ariadne's childhood or forward to Aegeus in Athens,

[43] Friedländer saw that it was significant (p. 16). Boucher remarks on it, but sees it merely as an awkwardness caused by the poet's enthusiasm for the details of sense impressions (p. 199).

or plunging his heroine into a lamentation of disproportionate length. The complexity and incompleteness of this method of narration have their own fascination – they are part of the neoteric manner that Catullus adopted and to an unknown extent created – but in this poem at least they are also the expression of an exuberant fertility and vitality of imagination. Such liveliness is hardly compatible with tragedy in the true sense of that much debased word; rather, the mood is one of nostalgic enchantment and romantic pathos.

After a single reading of the work the account of Ariadne is what most people recall most clearly, and although poets are not always in perfect control of the effects which they produce (a fact that critics too often forget), I believe that in this case Catullus had calculated the extent to which she would dominate; after all, he devoted half the poem to her story. At first we are led to suppose that Peleus and Thetis will be the principal personalities, but this is one of Catullus' deceptions; in the event they turn out to be very shadowy characters. We see Theseus a little more clearly, but even so the claim that the coverlet shows forth the noble deeds of heroes ('heroum . . . virtutes indicat') proves to be something of a feint, for in the end, as we look back over the account of Ariadne, we realise that we have seen him only through her eyes; Brooks Otis (p. 100) is right to see in Catullus' treatment of her an example of that empathetic style which Virgil was later to perfect.

The only two characters who at any time form a clear focus for the reader's sympathies are Ariadne, a figure on an embroidery, and Aegeus, who in a sense is even further distanced from immediacy, since he is merely a digression within the description of the embroidery. To him, indeed, belong perhaps the most poignant words in the poem, and one of its few moments of real psychological penetration:

> *gnate mihi longa iucundior unice vita,*   215
> *gnate, ego quem in dubios cogor dimittere casus,*
> *reddite in extrema nuper mihi fine senectae,*
> *quandoquidem fortuna mea ac tua fervida virtus*
> *eripit invito mihi te, cui languida nondum*
> *lumina sunt gnati cara saturata figura . . .*   220

[My only son, dearer to me than my long life, my son, whom I am compelled to send out to face uncertain hazards, son newly restored to me at the extreme limit of my old age, since my fortune and your zealous courage snatch you from me against my will, although my feeble eyes are not yet satiated with the dear form of my own son . . .]

The old king, accustomed for so long to believing himself to be childless, cannot resist repeating the unfamiliar name of 'son'. Even here Catullus has taken care to distance him from the reader: we are told not that Aegeus said these words but that he is said to have said them ('ferunt . . . dedisse', lines 212–14); and the archaic form 'gnatus' for 'natus' adds a touch of the grand, operatic manner.[44] Hardly less affecting are his final words (237): 'cum te reducem aetas prospera sistet' ('When a happy season shall set you back at home again'). Forgetful for a moment of his anxious prayers for Theseus' safety, he allows his imagination to leap forward into the future, and he looks upon his son's return as a certainty.

The emotional importance given to *formally* subsidiary characters is paradoxical: the poem is like a magic box that turns itself inside out, so that the innermost parts are exposed most conspicuously on the surface. Besides, the visual artist who seeks to depict Theseus sailing away from Ariadne can hardly give an equal prominence to both protagonists, as the poet can, if he so wishes; one of the two must occupy the foreground. Catullus shows us Ariadne's processes of thought in a way that no visual artist can ever do; but he makes this subjective way of telling his story grow naturally out of the way in which she is visually depicted. Here is another paradox, one that much later Petronius was to reveal again when he made Encolpius describe the work of Apelles (*Satyricon* 83): 'tanta enim subtilitate *extremitates imaginum* erant ad similitudinem praecisae, ut crederes *etiam animorum* esse picturam' ('For the outlines of his figures were defined with such subtle accuracy, that you would have declared that he had painted their souls as well') (tr. M. Heseltine (Loeb)).

The equivocation between art and reality begins in the very first line describing Ariadne (52), with the word 'fluentisono'. Epic in formation, light and luxurious in sound, the adjective has a stylistic function, but at the same time, by appealing simultaneously to the senses of sight and hearing, it has an expressive purpose; right from the beginning the picture is struggling to become more than a picture, pressing against the frame that encloses it. The most subtle use of the equivocation comes in the lines:

quem procul ex alga maestis Minois ocellis,　　　　　　　　　　60
saxea ut effigies bacchantis, prospicit, eheu,
prospicit et magnis curarum fluctuat undis . . .

[Like a stone statue of a Bacchant, the daughter of Minos with sorrowful eyes gazes forth at him from the seaweed, ah, gazes forth, and is tossed by great waves of emotion . . .]

Ariadne is like a stone statue of a Bacchant. When we come to the arrival of Bacchus and his rout, we shall find a new significance in

---

[44] It is Aegeus, indeed, who at line 228 refers to Minerva as 'incola Itoni' ('she who dwells at Itonus'); Fordyce comments, 'To make a king of Athens, the chief seat of the goddess, use this description of her is an absurd piece of Alexandrian erudition.'

this phrase; for the time being we see in it a fine piece of observation. She is like an 'effigies' because although her emotions are wild within her she is externally motionless; there is an instant after the revelation of a great joy or grief during which the mind is shaken to the core but the body is momentarily paralysed – a space of dry-eyed horror or amazement before the tears begin to flow. Catullus indicates that he is focusing upon this tiny morsel of time in line 55: 'necdum etiam sese quae visit visere credit' ('nor does she yet believe that she sees what she sees'). But Ariadne is also like a woman of stone in that she is part of the picture and therefore cannot ever move. The anaphora in line 61f. – 'prospicit, eheu,/prospicit' – contributes to the same effect; it is pathetic and elegant, certainly, but it also stresses that the artist has captured a moment and frozen it. 'She gazes forth'; the word is repeated because the embroidered Ariadne will be gazing in the same pose for ever.[45] Although the two poets are so different, and so far apart in time, Catullus has a hold upon the idea that Keats was to explore in his *Ode on a Grecian Urn.* The lovers on Keats's vase are just about to kiss; their lips (we surmise) are moving together and almost touching – almost but not quite. The fascination of the scene lies in the fact that the artist has caught not just any moment but one that of its nature is exceptionally transitory. In Catullus we do not find Keats's moving reflections about the value and meaning of art, but the surface effect is the same: the artist has taken Ariadne at the terrible moment of discovery and, like the lepidopterist with his pin, transfixed her.

The idea of transitoriness connects with the idea of motion. Theseus is moving away from Ariadne even as she looks: 'Thesea cedentem ... tuetur' (53) – the present participle is precise. At line 59 we are again shown the hero escaping in haste: 'immemor at iuvenis fugiens pellit vada remis' ('But the youth, forgetful, drives the waters with his oars in his flight'). As the commentators suggest, the odd rhythm, with the clash of ictus against accent carried right through into the fifth foot, seems to convey the hurried energy with which the oars are driven into the sea. Taken by themselves, these indications of movement would not be significant; for how else is one to describe a picture? But indeed it is a part of Catullus' artistry that in developing his paradoxes he has started from a type of description that seems quite natural, though it is strictly speaking illogical. The wind, which in a sense is among the least possible of all physical things for an embroidery to represent, since by definition it is both invisible and in motion, blows right through the account of Theseus and Ariadne; we are shown it directly, indirectly (for example in the description of the waves

---

[45] Meaning and verbal beauty are both enhanced by the position of the line division: 'She gazes, ah,' – the suspicion of a pause – 'she gazes ...'

playing), and metaphorically. Catullus is already revealing the fascination of blending metaphor and actuality at line 59: 'irrita ventosae
linquens promissa procellae' ('abandoning his promises, unfulfilled, to
the stormy winds'). It is literally true that Theseus is breaking his
promise in leaving Ariadne, and literally true that the wind is blowing
as he departs (and indeed assisting his escape, since the implication
is presumably that he is using sail as well as oars); but the casting of
promises to the wind is of course figurative. It is the mark of a poetic
mind to be able to compress the actual and the imaginative into one,
and that in a line of no difficulty or obscurity, but of easy grace.

Theseus is borne to Crete by gentle breezes (line 84); Aegeus en-
trusts his departing son to the winds (line 213); when Theseus returns,
his father's injunctions slip from his memory like clouds driven by the
winds from a snowy mountain-top (line 239f.). By its recurrence this
theme helps to bind together the diverse vignettes that make up the
inner section of the poem; it has an obvious connection with the other
recurrent themes of sea and ships and sailing, and it is also associated
with the theme of forgetting both at line 58f. and at 238ff. All of these
themes, except the last, form a further link between the inner section
and the first thirty lines of the piece. In short, the repeated references
to wind and water have a structural function; but here, once again,
structure and meaning are indissolubly joined. We have found nature
lavishly personified at places in the poem; conversely, human feelings
and experiences are described in natural terms. While the waves of
the sea are literally toying with her clothing (line 66f.), Ariadne
herself at the very same moment is tossed about by great waves of
emotion ('fluctuat undis', line 62; the Latin, with waves in both the
noun and the verb, is more emphatic than any translation can be). At
line 140ff. Ariadne declares,

> *non haec miserae sperare iubebas,*   140
> *sed conubia laeta, sed optatos hymenaeos,*
> *quae cuncta aerii discerpunt irrita venti.*

[Alas for me, you bade me hope, not for this, but for joyful marriage, for
the wedding that I longed for, but all these things the winds of heaven
tear into useless shreds.]

Though the last of these lines is metaphorical, the metaphor is very
close to reality, for the winds are indeed destroying her hopes by
impelling Theseus away from her. A little later she assails his ingra-
titude by asking him what sea spewed him forth, what Syrtis, Scylla
or Charybdis – places, real or mythological, where sailors were notoriously in danger from the treacherous combination of wind and waves.
At line 149 she describes Theseus in Crete as 'in medio versantem
turbine leti' ('tossed in the midst of a whirlwind of death'); at line 167

she describes him as he is now: 'prope iam mediis versatur in undis' ('He is now being tossed almost in the midst of the waves'). In the first of these lines the weather is metaphorical, in the second literal; the marked similarity of language between the two passages indicates that human emotions and natural forces are virtually merged into one. But with what effect? The fuzziness, the blurring of man and nature, of inner and outer sections – these spread over the whole poem a luxurious indistinctness; elements which in the hands of another poet might well be discrete, become ingredients of a blend which is intentionally rich, almost voluptuous. Here once more is the correspondence of style and content; the sumptuous pathos of the poet's narrative matches the self-conscious melodiousness of his verse.

To Bramble (p. 40) line 264 seems 'uneasy, almost hysterical'. So perhaps it might be, if taken entirely on its own; but read in context, it forms part of an almost ostentatious demonstration of control, since, as we have seen, Catullus instantly shuts off the noise (and the hysteria, if there is any), observing, with unruffled urbanity, that the Bacchants were merely shapes in a picture. This kind of emotional deflation is not unique to Catullus, nor is it necessarily a product of cool detachment. Other writers have used demonstrations of control as a vigorous, even passionate form of poetic argument. Milton was especially fond of this technique. In the fourth book of *Paradise Regained* Satan baits the Saviour with one of his subtlest temptations: urging him to master the learning of the pagans, he evokes the glory that was Greece in a passage of celebrated eloquence. An idyllic account of the sights and sounds and climate of Athens is followed by a roll-call of Greek genius; Homer, 'Whose poem Phoebus challenged for his own', the 'lofty grave tragedians ... teachers best of moral prudence', the famous orators whose 'resistless eloquence' fulminated against the dynasts of Macedon and Persia; and Socrates, the modest inhabitant of a humble home, 'Whom well inspired the oracle pronounced Wisest of men.' The Saviour sagely replies,

> Think not but that I know these things, or think
> I know them not; not therefore am I short
> Of knowing what I ought: he who receives
> Light from above, from the fountain of light,
> No other doctrine needs, though granted true;   290
> But these are false, or little else but dreams,
> Conjectures, fancies, built on nothing firm.

The praise of Greece has been put into the mouth of the fiend, but that is not to say that it is simply false, or persuasive only to those of depraved taste. On the contrary, the beauties of Attica, the poetry of Homer, the democratic defiance of royal tyranny, and the wisdom and humility of Socrates were things that Milton himself deeply loved and valued. The authentic beauty of Satan's discourse is essential to Milton's rhetorical method: he demonstrates the strength of his own and his Saviour's faith by putting the case that he is to repudiate in language of apparently irresistible charm, only to reject it with a few words of simple dismissal. The demonstration of calm control, in fact, is necessary to the expression of an intense conviction: the assertion of Christian faith.

Milton uses a similar technique in part of the first book of *Paradise Lost*. The account of Mulciber's fall from heaven is modelled on Milton's great exemplar Homer (*Il.* 1.591–5):

> Nor was his name unheard or unadored
> In ancient Greece; and in Ausonian land
> Men called him Mulciber; and how he fell   740
> From heaven, they fabled, thrown by angry Jove
> Sheer o'er the crystal battlements; from morn
> To noon he fell, from noon to dewy eve,
> A summer's day; and with the setting sun
> Dropped from the zenith like a falling star,   745
> On Lemnos the Aegaean isle: . . .

Here, superbly realised, is the remote and magical beauty of Greek mythology. These lines have often been quoted on their own, but their function is transformed by Milton's continuation:

> > thus they relate
> Erring; . . .

With a single brilliantly positioned word the poet coolly crushes his own lovely creation.

This example is of particular interest for our present purpose, because Milton had derived his effect from Lucretius 1.391–3:

> *quod si forte aliquis, cum corpora dissiluere,*
> *tum putat id fieri quia se condenseat aer,*
> *errat;* . . .

> [If anyone happens to think that this comes to pass when bodies have leapt apart because the air condenses, he goes astray; . . .]

I find it hard to doubt that Milton thought he found in Lucretius the method which he was to make his own, or that he was right in his perception; for here, I believe, lies the explanation of the so-called anti-Lucretius in Lucretius. The Epicurean poet shapes his argument so as to demonstrate his self-command, not only within the individual sentence but on a larger scale also. When he declares in Book 5 that it is hard to look up at the stars in the heavens or to contemplate the sun and moon in their courses without being tempted to believe in the

existence of the gods, he is not inadvertently allowing his own hesi-
tations to seep into his work; rather, he is with calculated purpose
demonstrating the strength of his philosophic faith.[46] Bailey suspects
in Lucretius a 'lurking affection' for the forms of Roman ritual, and
he may be right (Commentary, vol. 3, p. 1515); but the stronger the
emotional pull of ancestral tradition, the more impressive is the poet's
assertion that reason overcomes it.

In the later part of Book 3, where Lucretius is seeking to dispel the
fear of death, this method of persuasion is seen at the full height of its
power. The words in which he imagines men lamenting the sorrow of
parting from wife and children are among the most famous in Latin
literature; they are followed by two lines of cool rebuttal (3.894ff.).[47]
Twice more unphilosophic man is permitted to voice his griefs and
anxieties; and twice more he is answered by the philosopher poet. No
one should imagine that Lucretius has lost control of his feelings; but
it is no less mistaken to suppose that he is merely caricaturing his
adversaries, or trying to disguise their arguments as Aunt Sallys.[48]
The emotional tension, the awareness of the risk that the poet is
running, are at the heart of his meaning. Some readers may feel that
Lucretius has wound up the tension to such a pitch that the cord has
snapped, that the eloquence which he allows to his opponents is so
great that his replies to them seem inadequate; but that is another
matter. We must not suppose that an intention is absent just because
it has not been fully achieved.

There are many similarities of language between Lucretius and
Peleus and Thetis, too many to attribute to coincidence. The question
is therefore: who was imitating whom? *Prima facie* one would suppose
that the learned and eclectic Catullus would be more likely to use
Lucretius than the sternly independent Lucretius to draw upon a poet
of a fashionably decadent school; and this presumption is fortified by
certain other considerations. In the first place, we have seen that
Catullus used epic and archaic language as a means of creating a
particular kind of atmosphere. He therefore had a motive for soaking

[46] I refer to the poet's conscious intention. Of course, it is open to anyone to suppose
that behind his deliberate adoption of a particular method lie unconscious motivations
of an opposing kind; but this brings us to the borders of psychohistory, for which our
pathetically small knowledge of Lucretius' life and character affords no adequate data.

[47] An analogous case would be the second and third chapters of the *Wisdom of
Solomon*, which were written with the specific purpose of combating the disbelief in
immortality expressed by the author of *Ecclesiastes*. For twenty verses the deluded are
allowed to plead for their philosophy of pessimistic hedonism in sentences of admirable
force and beauty; whereupon the writer continues quietly, 'Such things they did
imagine, and were deceived ... But the souls of the righteous are in the hand of
God ...'

[48] It is true, however, that Lucretius allows the note of irony to grow more evident as
the argument proceeds. This ironic element is well brought out by D. A. West (p. 28ff.);
but he seems to miss the emotional complexity of the passage.

himself in Lucretius, and it thus becomes easy to understand why Lucretius' influence on him was virtually confined to this one poem. Moreover, the similarities between *Peleus and Thetis* and Lucretius are restricted to the poem's inner section (and Bramble has further noted that they are concentrated between lines 124 and 250); it is easy to imagine Catullus being especially under the spell of Lucretius at one stage in the composition of his piece, but hard to suppose that Lucretius was so impressed by one section of one poem by Catullus that its influence may be found dispersed throughout his great work. These arguments confirm and are confirmed by my interpretation of line 261ff., where the echoes of Lucretius are more blatant and more sustained than in any other place. In his second book Lucretius describes the rites of Cybele:

> *tympana tenta tonant palmis et cymbala circum*
> *concava, raucisonoque minantur cornua cantu,*
> *et Phrygio stimulat numero cava tibia mentis* . . .   620

[Taut tambourines thunder beneath their hands, and hollow cymbals all around, and horns menace with harshly sounding music, and the hollow flute goads their minds with the Phrygian mode . . .]

The alliterations are the same as those in Catullus; even the four musical instruments are the same. Now these lines come from one of those passages in which Lucretius uses the rhetorical technique described above to most powerful effect.[49] For some forty lines he depicts the worship of the goddess, bringing to brilliant life its excitement and beauty, only to conclude that the rites are 'far removed from the truth', however admirable the justifications for them offered by learned men; and he goes on to condemn them as an example of 'shabby superstition'. The lines that so closely resemble those of Catullus describe the noisy procession of the eunuch priests.

From this jigsaw of evidence a picture begins to emerge: Catullus, like Milton, found in Lucretius a distinctive and elaborately developed technique of poetical argument, and saw that he could adapt it to his own very different purpose. Even the contrast between din and silence he found in his model, for Lucretius follows the raucous music of the priests with a picture of the goddess passing silently through great cities. It is not surprising that Catullus was struck by the passage: line 625, in which Lucretius describes Cybele's unvoiced salutation –

---

[49] Milton probably had this passage in mind, along with the others already mentioned, when he wrote his description of the fall of Mulciber. Lucretius begins his account of the worship of Cybele at line 600, 'hanc veteres Graium docti cecinere poetae' ('The learned ancient poets of Greece sang that she . . .'); cf. *Paradise Lost* 1. 738ff.: 'Nor was his name unheard or unadored *In ancient Greece*; and in Ausonian land Men called him Mulciber; and how he fell From heaven, *they fabled*, . . .'

'munificat tacita mortalis muta salute' ('silently she blesses mankind with an unspoken salutation') – is among the most beautiful in all Latin poetry and would have slipped gratefully into a sensitive neoteric ear.

My argument has been this: we detect in Lucretius a certain technique; and we find confirmation of its existence when we discover that it has been used (with variations) by at least two other poets of genius in places where they can be shown to have been under Lucretius' influence. But it is clear that in using this technique Catullus directed it to new ends. Lucretius, and Milton after him, used it as a means of argument and persuasion, but the *novus poeta* is not concerned to proclaim a message or enforce a belief. Earnestness and moral energy (or the pretence of them) appear towards the end of the poem, but no qualities could be more alien to this part of it. Nor have we to do with Wordsworth's idea of 'emotion recollected in tranquillity', since Catullus gives no sign of 'powerful feelings' that he has needed to reduce to poetic order.[50] Puck's breaking of the illusion at the end of *A Midsummer Night's Dream* is nearer –

> If we shadows have offended,
> Think but this and all is mended,
> That you have but slumbered here,
> While these visions did appear,
> And this weak and idle theme,
> No more yielding but a dream,
> Gentles do not reprehend.

– but even here the comparison is not close, for it is one thing to lift the spell at the very end of the work (thus in a sense proving the power of the enchantment), another to keep resisting the reader's will to suspend his disbelief during the course of it.

Analogy is a tricky business, but in this case it may help us to understand the way in which Catullus' poem works. As it so happens the scene of Ariadne's desertion by Theseus has several times been taken as a type or symbol of high art; art, that is, presented with a degree of formality or elevation sufficient to mark emphatically its distinctness from the conditions of real life. Propertius (partly inspired, I would suppose, by Catullus) begins one of his best known poems (1.3) by comparing the sleeping Cynthia to Ariadne asleep as Theseus' ship departs, then to Andromeda and an exhausted Maenad. For several lines the world of myth is evoked, beauteous and still (we

[50] I am not at all persuaded by the notion that *Peleus and Thetis* is 'really' about Catullus and Lesbia; but even those who hold this opinion must allow that the poem does not fit Wordsworth's phrase in the way that (for instance) Poem 101 does, where manifestly deep feelings are contained within the framework of a calm and carefully wrought composition.

are probably meant to think of paintings or statuary), and then the picture of art and elegance is abruptly shattered as the poet reels in, drunk and eager for sex. Nineteen hundred years later T. S. Eliot took up the theme again in *Sweeney Erect*:

> *Paint* me a cavernous waste shore
>   Cast in the unstilled Cyclades,
> *Paint* me the bold anfractuous rocks
>   Faced by the snarled and yelping seas.

> *Display* me Aeolus above
>   Reviewing the insurgent gales
> Which tangle Ariadne's hair
>   And swell with haste the perjured sails.

This romantic world of art – and specifically of pictorial art – is sharply contrasted with the coarse Sweeney waking between the steamy sheets and Doris padding in from the bathroom with brandy and sal volatile.

Some thirty years before Eliot, John Davidson wrote his play *Scaramouch in Naxos*, a 'pantomime' in which the lush lyricism of Bacchus and Ariadne is set against the *commedia dell'arte* figures of Columbine and Harlequin and their employer, the English showman Scaramouch, with his talk of policemen and railways, and his lively interest in money. This work curiously anticipates Strauss's opera *Ariadne auf Naxos*, to a libretto by Hugo von Hofmannsthal. The opera opens with a prologue; this is set in the seventeenth or eighteenth century in the house of a rich Viennese parvenu, who has commissioned a young composer to write an *opera seria* on the subject of Ariadne for the entertainment of his guests. The composer is appalled to learn that a second company has also been hired; his beautiful music is to be followed by a vulgar harlequinade, 'Zerbinetta and her Four Lovers'. Worse is to come: the parvenu has changed his mind and he now requires the two companies to combine in a single entertainment so that the fireworks may start promptly at nine o'clock. With intense reluctance the composer consents to the mutilation of his masterpiece, and the rest of Strauss's opera consists of the performance of the fictitious composer's Ariadne in the new form demanded by his patron. Thus Strauss's Ariadne is 'framed', just like the Ariadne of Catullus, and presented not directly but as a work of art. Moreover, the librettist emphasises the artificiality: in the prologue Zerbinetta and her associates laugh at serious opera for being boring and stuffy, while the composer, for his part, is proud to think that his created world is remote from real life: 'The comedy to follow! To lead them back to everyday grossness! This unthinkably uncultured mob seeks a way forsooth from my ideal sphere, to its material life! . . . Ariadne on Naxos, Sir, she is the symbol of Mankind in Solitude' (tr. A. Kalisch).

Within the 'performance' itself, Strauss and Hofmannsthal, in this too like Catullus, remind the audience from time to time that the world of art is only illusion. Ariadne's declamatory lamentations are superbly melodious and powerfully affecting; but every so often they are interrupted by the *commedia dell'arte* characters, whose down-to-earth attitude to sexual passion is in marked contrast to her exalted ideality. Ariadne longs for death; Zerbinetta assures her that her grief for Theseus is excessive: another man will be along soon, and every new lover seems like a god to a girl when he first makes his appearance. Enter Bacchus; Ariadne welcomes him in the belief that he is the god of Death, and the music ascends into a sumptuous *Liebesstod*; but even in this last lush scene Zerbinetta is allowed to insert the deflating comment that things have turned out just as she had predicted.

Sed quid ego a primo digressus carmine . . . ? I have drawn out these parallels at some length, and for two reasons. We have seen that Ariadne on Naxos has repeatedly been used as a symbol of art as artifice; if we combine this observation with the striking fact that no writer in antiquity, so far as we know, ever used Ariadne as the subject for an epic or tragedy, a picture begins to form. There has been a tradition by which the story of Ariadne is regarded as the vehicle not of tragedy but of a kind of gorgeous pathos; and though such matters are not susceptible of proof, it seems a likely inference that Catullus played some part in transmitting or shaping this conception, even though the later heirs of the tradition may not all have known what they owed to him. But more particularly I draw attention to Strauss and Hofmannsthal's treatment of the theme for the simple reason that it seems to be comparatively unproblematical; by starting from a work of art that we can readily comprehend, or at least accept, we may gain insight into art of a kind that is more alien from us. *Ariadne auf Naxos* holds the stage, and audiences do not seem to be too greatly puzzled by the juxtaposition of deserted heroine and irreverent commentary. A straightforward appeal to experience suggests that we do not find Ariadne the less moving when her artificiality is forced upon our attention; her music works upon our emotions, triumphing, as it is intended to, over the comedy that seeks to undermine it. We may say easily enough, therefore, that art *can* work in this way; it is harder to explain why. Part of the answer lies in the marvellousness of art itself; man is able of himself to create beauty, and it can be affecting merely to contemplate this astonishing fact. Wonder and pity are sometimes closely allied; our sympathy for Ariadne, whether in Strauss or in Catullus, may even be enhanced by the obtruded reminder that she is merely the creation of a human mind.

The paradox that music, the most artificial and rule-bound of all arts, has an immediate hold over the emotions as strong, if not stronger, than that of any other art form, is familiar to us all; more people are made to weep or tingle or grow weak in the pit of the stomach by music than by paintings or poetry. But the paradox is also to be found in visual art, as may be seen from the popularity of (for example) Michelangelo's *Pietà*; our dazzlement at its technical virtuosity and our response to its manifest pathos are not discrete reactions but inseparable elements of a single experience. There is no reason in principle why the same paradox may not operate in the art of words also (though it is less familiar to us in this form), especially in a poem that explicitly tries to assimilate itself to the character of pictorial representation. But there is a difference between literature and the other arts. The question of the creator's 'sincerity', so troubling in the case of literature, is far less pressing in the visual arts, and less still in music. In the latter cases the mastery of a difficult technique is so obviously necessary that we take the enjoyment of its display as a natural and proper part of the aesthetic experience, even in works of the highest seriousness (it is significant that Strauss needs *words* to suggest to us that there is anything about his manifest use of *musical* artifice worthy of comment). In the case of literature, however, we are constantly under the temptation to imagine that the author is merely warbling his native wood-notes wild; the reader will probably not think of enjoying the sheer artifice of a work unless the author carefully draws it to his attention. Catullus therefore uses virtuosity in a manner more self-conscious, more narcissistic even, than is customary with the painter or the composer.

Moreover, fragility itself can be a source of beauty: the creator confidently holds the loveliness that he has made in the palm of his big hand, showing to us that he can crush it at will. Alternatively – or even simultaneously – the beauty of fragility may work upon us in an opposite way. We may be uncertain whether the artist can pull off the trick, and the tension that results from our uncertainty may be both exciting and touching; the pathos of Ariadne in both Strauss and Catullus is the greater because it is a triumph of daring, a success against the odds. Such words as wonder, magic, amazement may get us closer to the tone and mood of *Peleus and Thetis* than the more conventional terms of the critical vocabulary. Men enjoy being deceived, as we learn in childhood the first time that we see a conjuror at work; but part of the thrill of the display lies in the element of risk, the ever present possibility that the conjuror may fail. Puritans may not be at ease with the concept of the artist as prestidigitator; but then Catullus was not a puritan. *Peleus and Thetis* is in a way a very self-indulgent poem; but it is saved from sloppiness by Catullus' extraordinary command of both technique and emotional control. Once again, the combination of discipline and sensuousness finds its paradigm in music, and that analogy may help us to see why in Catullus too it is so beautiful, and so moving.

Proust remarked in *The Captive* that the greatest writers of the nineteenth century, 'watching themselves at work as though they were at once author and critic, have derived from this self-contemplation a novel beauty' (vol 1, p. 211, tr. C. K. Scott Moncrieff). This subtle perception can be applied to the literature of other self-conscious periods. The supreme example of self-consciousness in antiquity is Virgil; his works are in part poems about poetry, explorations of the problems and possibilities of writing verse in his own time and circumstances. He is for ever indicating to us that he is what we would now call a secondary writer; he is constantly establishing and adjusting his own position in relation to his great predecessors, Greek and Latin; by these methods he manages to put his own personality into even the traditionally objective art of epic, so that when Dante made himself a central character in an epic poem, he was no more than making explicit and external what had been implicit in his master's work so many centuries before.[51] The self-conscious element in Virgil's art was inherited and developed from the neoterics of Catullus' generation; where he differed from them was in strangely combining it with an Augustan *gravitas* and an epic monumentality. Virgil's strangeness in this respect needs to be remembered; self-conscious art naturally tends to be inward-looking, even self-regarding, and to avoid 'statement'. It is not true that all art aspires towards the condition of music, but it is true that some does; significantly, it was a prophet of aestheticism who coined that aphorism. By its virtual elimination of narrative, its elaborately melodious diction, its refusal to be about any one subject, to make a statement or proclaim a message, *Peleus and Thetis* belongs to the musical class of literature; and in a special and specific sense one half of it aspires to the condition of visual art as well.

We tend to approach music and the visual arts in a different way from literature; we are far less inclined to ask what a string quartet means or what a still life is about than we are to apply such questions to prose and poetry. This is natural enough: 'meaning' and 'statement' and so on are words about words, and only by some form of metaphor or transference are they applicable to other forms of expression. Conversely, since poetry is made up of words, it must always have some content and meaning; it can never attain to the fully abstract nature of music or even to the state of self-contained completeness that we

---

[51] It is a remarkable but surely indisputable fact that we know Virgil's personality better than we know those of Catullus, Propertius and Ovid. And yet Virgil was never, like the others, a 'personal' poet.

find in many pictures and statues. Any aspiration which it may have towards the condition of music or visual art will ultimately remain just that: an aspiration. The necessary incompleteness of such aspiration is dramatised in Catullus' poem by the tension between the pictorial Ariadne and the Ariadne who moves and weeps and utters. Certainly, there is meaning in *Peleus and Thetis* and even some vestiges of narrative, for all its lyricism; none the less, it belongs to that class of poetry which strives not so much to *say* as to *be*. We could almost say of most of it, as Pater said of the Venus de Milo, 'That is in no sense a symbol, a suggestion of anything beyond its own victorious fairness' (*Studies in the History of the Renaissance*, 'Winckelmann').

5

> *quae postquam cupide spectando Thessala pubes*
> *expleta est, sanctis coepit decedere divis.*
> *hic, qualis flatu placidum mare matutino*
> *horrificans Zephyrus proclivas incitat undas,*   270
> *Aurora exoriente vagi sub limina Solis,*
> *quae tarde primum clementi flamine pulsae*
> *procedunt leviterque sonant plangore cachinni,*
> *post vento crescente magis magis increbescunt,*
> *purpureaque procul nantes ab luce refulgent:*   275
> *sic tum vestibuli linquentes regia tecta*
> *ad se quisque vago passim pede discedebant.*

[After the people of Thessaly had taken their fill of eagerly gazing on these things, they began to give place to the holy gods. It was as when Zephyr ruffles the calm sea with his morning breath and urges on the tumbling waves, as Dawn rises to the threshold of the journeying Sun; at first the waves, driven by the kindly breeze, advance slowly, and the cry of their laughter sounds lightly, but after, as the wind gets up, they crowd onwards more and more, and as they float, they shine afar, reflecting the radiant light. So now the people left the royal halls, and their feet variously dispersing here and there, each man departed to his own home.]

Some of the qualities of the Ariadne episode seem to linger on after it has ended in the long simile of lines 269–75; this is another example of the technique of making contrasts and then blurring them. Here once more are wind, waves and brilliant light. The delicate line 273 returns to the spirit of line 67. There are winds were playing, here they are laughing; those motifs of joy and the personification of nature are both still with us. There is a suggestion of oxymoron in the words 'plangore cachinni', since in the time of Catullus 'plangor' was coming to be applied specifically to sounds of lamentation. Catullus' phrase is beautifully evocative of the sea's melancholy enchantment; the mood of romantic nostalgia is not yet dispelled. In line 274 the forward pressure of the rhythm across the weak caesura in the third foot and the lengthening out of *cresc-* into *-crebesc-* (an effect enhanced by the spondaic fifth foot) admirably suggest the growing power of wind and waves. In line 275 both 'purpurea' and 'refulgent' combine radiance with an implication of high ceremony, while 'nantes' adds a hint of buoyant gaiety, like 'nasse' in line 2. The wayward rhythm of line 277, an alternation of spondees and dactyls, agreeably mimics the 'wandering feet' of the Thessalians, while the spondaic ending 'discedebant' conveys the slow dissevering as the crowded mass of spectators gradually unravels, each man going to his own home.

Not until the men have gone do the gods arrive. This, I think, adds to the glamour of their feast: it is as though the grown-ups have sent the children to bed and can now get on with the mysterious dignities of adult life.[52] But in what direction is the poem to go now? Clearly Catullus cannot allow the spirit of the Ariadne episode to linger much longer without risk of repetitiousness. Part of his problem is that the married lives of Peleus and Thetis do not have much 'story' attached to them; with Hercules or Ulysses or Agamemnon the case would be very different. A late development of the myth did indeed add dramatic incident to their wedding, by making it the occasion on which the three goddesses quarrelled over the apple of discord, but we do not know whether this story had yet been invented at the time that Catullus wrote.

Another problem is created by the work's odd proportions. If we examine those other examples of poems within poems, Theocritus' first and eleventh Idylls, Virgil's story of Aristaeus and Catullus' own *Vesper adest*, we find that in each of them the first outer section is significantly longer than the second. This is as we should expect: a poem is, ideally at least, a continuous experience in time, and in those forms of art which necessarily require the passage of time it seems to be a general aesthetic principle that the element of variety or contrast should be introduced nearer to the end than the beginning; this is when the reader or auditor is liable to flag and will most welcome a change. Musicians will note this principle in (for instance) ternary form, and in the usual system of repeats in sonata form, minuets and trios, and so on. Catullus has chosen, however, to avoid the natural proportions: he needs to extend his poem for at least another hundred lines if the story of Peleus is not to seem merely a frame for the story of Ariadne, but at the same time he must avoid a sense of anticlimax.

---

[52] There may also be, as some critics suggest, a foreshadowing of the separation of gods and men lamented at the end of the poem. But there is no justification for the view that the Thessalians leave reluctantly: on the contrary, we are told that they have satiated their desire of gazing at the bridal bed ('expleta est', line 268).

Here we enter again upon controversial ground: G. Giangrande has vigorously contested the claim that the account of the heroic age is equivocal, and to come to an understanding of Catullus' poetic purpose we shall need to consider the main issues in dispute. In what follows I shall try to be objective, in so far as that is possible in a literary argument, and so it may be as well to add a subjective comment here. The later parts of the poem, rich in beauties though they are, do not seem to me quite to attain to the astonishing inventiveness and imaginative power of the first two hundred and fifty lines. Some of the difficulties that they present derive, I suspect, from Catullus' handling of his material being less perfectly lucid and assured here.

1. The first question is whether Catullus means to imply in the early part of his poem that the Argonauts were impious or that Peleus' wealth was reprehensible? To this question I have already answered no. The most I should be willing to concede is that the reader, looking back from the end of the poem to the beginning, may reflect that the voyage of the Argo *might* have been handled in a more unfriendly spirit.

2. At line 51 Catullus announces that the tapestry shows 'heroum virtutes', the valiant deeds of heroes, and then goes on to describe Theseus' desertion of Ariadne; is this meant to be a bitter irony? It is hard to doubt that the reader will be rather surprised at the heavy weight laid upon Ariadne's misery after what he has been led to expect, or that Catullus means the blighted love of Theseus and Ariadne to contrast with the fulfilled love of Peleus and Thetis.[53] On the other hand, we eventually discover that what the tapestry actually depicts is a kind of divine comedy, with Bacchus about to bring the happy ending. Furthermore, Giangrande has argued (p. 127) that Catullus is following, in the allusive manner of a Hellenistic poet, the version of the myth whereby Theseus was the victim of involuntary amnesia. Lenchantin, Kroll and Granarolo, with no polemical axe to grind, had already reached the same conclusion, and it is almost certainly right;[54] it can hardly be coincidence that all the criticisms of Theseus are put into Ariadne's mouth, whereas Catullus in his own person speaks warmly of his heroism and self-sacrifice at lines 81ff. and 101f. To take her words as objective truth is to ignore Catullus' subjective or empathetic style; and indeed there is an elegant irony in

[53] Giangrande recalls Kroll's statement that 'indicat' in line 51 shows that the coverlet does not set forth 'heroum virtutes' but merely reminds us of them (p. 127). This seems strained. He is no doubt right to suppose that strict logic can reconcile line 51 to what follows; but the sensitive reader will still feel an emotional dissonance.

[54] Granarolo, p. 153n. (He has argued the point at greater length in 'L'infidèle Thésée', AFL Nice 1967, 2, 15–20.) Giangrande gives the other references (p. 127).

her using the word 'immemor' in the metaphorical sense of 'ungrateful', not knowing that Theseus is 'forgetful' in a strictly literal sense.
We cannot say, therefore, that Catullus is covertly attacking the heroic
age. Nor should we suppose that the Thessalians are disturbed to see
the grieving Ariadne displayed upon the bridal bed;[55] that would be
a way of crudely severing literature from life. The Valmarana thought
that Angelica in chains, Iphigenia sacrificed and Briseis led sorrowfully from the tent of Achilles were charming decorations for their
Vicentine villa; Queen Victoria breakfasted unconcernedly in the
Heaven Room at Burghley, with pagan nudities and adulteries on the
walls and ceiling around and above her; and the various Campanian
gentlemen who commissioned mural paintings of Ariadne for the man-
sions of Pompeii and Herculaneum showed that the Romans were
capable of a similar dissociation.[56]

3. Various ambivalences have been detected between lines 278 and
302. The last of the trees that Penios bears into the house is the
cypress (line 291), a tree associated with death. Among the wedding-
guests is Prometheus, and three lines (295–7) are devoted to recalling
the tortures of which he still bears the traces. Next Catullus tells us
that Apollo and Diana are absent, scorning Peleus and refusing to
celebrate the marriage of Thetis. This seems to add a disagreeable
note; and are we also reminded that Apollo was to kill the one child
of the marriage? Without claiming to any feeling of certainty, I would
suppose that some shadow of uneasiness passes over the festivities at
this point, and perhaps elsewhere in this section of the poem.

4. Previous poets had given the wedding song for Peleus and Thetis
either to Apollo or to the Muses; against all precedent Catullus puts
it into the mouth of the Parcae or Fates. It seems hard to doubt that
this adds a dissonant note. His account of the goddesses continues to
blend verbal ingenuity with a fixity of visual interest in the way
characteristic of this poem (it is significant that he devotes some
fifteen lines to describing their appearance), but these qualities become slightly disturbing in their new context.

. . . cum interea infirmo quatientes corpora motu   305
veridicos Parcae coeperunt edere cantus.
his corpus tremulum complectens undique vestis
candida purpurea talos incinxerat ora,
at roseae niveo residebant vertice vittae . . .

[And meanwhile the Fates, their bodies shaking with a feeble motion,

[55] In fact the tapestry holds them rapt: 'cupide spectando', line 267.
[56] Giangrande observes, reasonably enough, that it is hard to imagine what the
coverlet was doing on the bed in the first place, if it was really so ominous (p. 127).
The only answer which I can think of – that it is placed there for 'literary' reasons
in defiance of plausibility – is hardly complimentary to Catullus.

began to utter their truthful chant. Their white clothing, embracing their
trembling bodies on every side, girt their ankles with a crimson border;
rosy ribbons rested on their snowy heads . . .]

When Catullus introduces the Fates at line 305, he tells us at once
that their bodies are shaking with infirmity, and he repeats this idea
in line 307, as he describes how their robes embrace their bodies. We
have had earth embraced by Ocean at line 30, Theseus embraced by
his loving father at line 213, the bridal couch embraced by the tapestry
at line 265f. (in language strikingly similar to that here at line 307),
Ariadne embraced by her mother at line 88, and again by both mother
and sister at line 118. All these embracements contribute to the atmosphere of luxury and enjoyment, but in this one place there is an
element of unpleasantness, of sexual disgust even, in the embrace not
of a lovely young girl but of quivering crones.[57] The details in the
description – the tightness with which the robes fit round the aged
bodies ('undique', line 307), the white cloth with its red or purple
border wrapping the ankles – compel our eyes towards the Fates'
physical appearance. Having introduced the opposition between white
and red, Catullus dwells upon it in the next line, even though his eye
has now abandoned the old women's feet and travelled upwards; the
Fates wear rosy ribbons upon their snowy heads. In both line 308 and
line 309 the pairs of adjectives are placed together at the beginning
of the line to bring out the force of the contrast. The mixture of red
(or pink) and white is a stock theme in descriptions of a girl's complexion; we find it in Virgil, Propertius, Lygdamus, and in Catullus'
own wedding song for Torquatus and Junia.[58] So once more there is a
disharmony in the application to old women of language that more
naturally suggests youth and beauty.[59] This point should not be ov-
erstressed. Catullus' picture of the old women is at least as much
pathetic as repulsive; the wheedling diminutives of 'aridulis . . . la-
bellis' in line 316 ('their poor old dry lips,' as Fordyce translates) may
remind us of the sentimental realism often found in Hellenistic sculpture. If his eye is fastened upon the Fates, it is not with horror or awe

[57] We may perhaps compare the way in which Aeschylus uses the language of youth
and love to bring out the disgustingness of his Furies (*Eum.* 68–70): *hai kataptustoi
korai,/graiai palaiai paides, hais ou meignutai/theōn tis oud'anthrōpos oude thēr pote.*
('Maidens to be spat upon, aged ancient children, with whom none of the gods ever
mingles [this is the word so often used of sexual intercourse] nor any man nor even
beast'). Of course these lines are charged with a sexual horror far more overt and
powerful than Catullus desires.

[58] Cat. 61. 186–8; Virgil *Aen.* 12. 67–9; Propertius 2. 3. 11f.; [Tibullus] 3. 4. 30–4.

[59] In line 311 Catullus draws attention to the whiteness of the wool spun by the Fates,
in line 318 to its whiteness and softness. Here again he surely means a contrast of
textures, in the former line with the left hand that holds the wool, in the latter with
the feet before which the wool falls. Catullus gives no epithet to hands or feet here, but
he can expect our imaginations to supply the wrinkles.

but rather with that fascinated absorption in the material world which suffuses the whole poem. He enjoys distinguishing the actions of the left hand from the right (311ff.), setting the soft mass of wool on the distaff (311) against the slender threads that are drawn off it (312), watching first the fingers turned up to shape the strands (312f.), and then the thumb pressed down to twirl the spindle (313f.). He likes to watch the tufts of wool clinging to the old women's lips (316), and to bring to life the thread snapping against their teeth with the mono-syllabic 'dens' at the end of the line.[60] At the same time he is creating opportunities for elegance of expression; for him part of the attraction in the contrasts of white and red is the chiasmus that allows him to place white before red in the first line, pink before white in the second. Nor should we underestimate his delight in sheer incongruity. Like the Ariadne episode, the song of the Fates springs out of its surprising context with an unexpected vitality, and one of Catullus' reasons for lengthily describing the Fates as poor old women is to startle us when they suddenly begin to pour forth divine song with loud voice (320ff.). Virgil surely remembered this passage when he put the story of Orpheus and Eurydice into the mouth of Proteus. The Fates are not grim or horrific, but their combination of power and decrepitude is a little uncanny, and their introduction into the wedding feast is troubling, not deeply but none the less perceptibly.

5. After celebrating the love between Peleus and Thetis, the Fates declare that a son Achilles will be born to them, and go on to prophesy his career. I fully agree with those who insist that a sinister note now enters the poem. Catullus makes the transition skilfully: the first four lines devoted to Achilles (338ff.) applaud the prowess of a heroic warrior in traditional terms, but from line 343 onwards his deeds are described in a way calculated to stress their more repugnant side. The Phrygian plains are drenched in Trojan blood at line 344, and the city devastated at line 346; it is in keeping with the new mood that in the latter line Agamemnon should be alluded to as 'the third heir of perjured Pelops'. At line 348 the Fates begin a new section of their song:

illius egregias virtutes claraque facta
saepe fatebuntur gnatorum in funere matres,
cum incultum cano solvent a vertice crinem,   350
putridaque infirmis variabunt pectora palmis.

[His surpassing achievements and famous deeds mothers shall often own at the funerals of their sons, as they loose their dishevelled hair from their hoary heads and mottle their withered breasts with feeble hands.]

---

[60] The only other place at which Catullus ends a line with a stressed monosyllable is 68. 19, where again he is aiming for a special effect. See above, p. 89f.

Catullus exploits the ambiguity of the epithets in the first of these lines: 'egregius' commonly means 'excellent' and 'clarus' 'glorious', and that is how we will naturally take the words as we first read them, but then we get a sharp jolt. This apparent praise of Achilles proves to be the reluctant tribute ('fatebuntur', line 349) of the mothers whose sons he has slaughtered. 'Egregius' need mean no more than 'outstanding' or 'remarkable', 'clarus' no more than 'famous', and by the end of the sentence we are forced to understand the words in these less flattering senses. As the women beat themselves with shaking hands, patches of colour break out on their withered dugs; Catullus' visual imagination is as sharp and original as ever, but it is now used to create a scene at once grotesque and pathetic; the verb 'variabunt', implying that the women's battered breasts display a decorative *poikilia*, is savagely ironical.

Lines 359–60 are extravagantly gruesome: the river Scamander is choked by the heaps of corpses, and its waters grow warm with the blood that stains them; then the 'denique' of line 362 announces that we are approaching a climax. Catullus now makes his Parcae devote eight whole lines to the most repulsive feature of the Achilles legend, the sacrifice of the maiden Polyxena to his shade. We are forced to contemplate the hideous details: the snow-pale limbs of the corpse, the burial mound soused in blood, and finally the body kneeling – without a head. After this last grisly detail, it is and must be shocking that the Fates continue with a bland 'quare' – '*Wherefore* come, unite in the love that your hearts desire.' It is obvious that Catullus did not have to present Achilles in this manner, and his reason for doing so must surely be to excite our distaste.[61] Giangrande has denied this (p. 138ff.), arguing that Catullus is polemically engaged against Apollonius Rhodius in favour of an alternative Alexandrian tradition represented by Rhianus, who modelled Aristomenes, the hero of his *Messeniaca*, upon Achilles, and made pitilessness one of his characteristics. I cannot see any evidence for this odd (and surely unattractive) idea. In any case Giangrande is mistaken in thinking that the reasons for believing Catullus to be unsympathetic to the Fates' account of Achilles are based on inference from Alexandrian literary history; they are founded, as we have seen, on the text of the poem, and the way in which Catullus himself has chosen to select and shape his material. More importantly, Giangrande is oblivious to the subtlety of Catullus' subjective style: the Fates themselves look forward to Achilles' career of slaughter with a grim enjoyment, but their song has been composed in such a way as to suggest that the poet's own view is different.

---

[61] Catullus intends this distaste to be directed against the way in which the Parcae describe Achilles' career, not against Achilles himself. See below, p. 146.

No less than three times Catullus affirms the infallible truth of the Fates' prophecies (lines 306, 322, 326); this solemn emphasis imports a serious tone alien to the early parts of the poem, but at the same time it shows us that while we are at liberty to reject the attitudes that the Fates express, the facts which they give us must be accepted. From this it is clear that Catullus does not mean to criticise Peleus and Thetis themselves, since one of the facts that the Fates stress is that there has never been a love so close and harmonious as theirs:

> *nulla domus tales umquam contexit amores,*
> *nullus amor tali coniunxit foedere amantes,*   335
> *qualis adest Thetidi, qualis concordia Peleo.*

[No house ever sheltered such love, and no love ever joined lovers in an alliance to equal the harmony enjoyed by Thetis, and by Peleus.]

We do not find an elegant use of chiasmus here; the many repeated words occur each time in the same part of the clause or line. There is a certain heaviness in the construction of the verses, appropriate to a formal occasion. But mingled with the solemnity there is also a note of jubilation, expressed not in the form but in the content of the sentence. In each of the three lines a unity and harmony between Peleus and Thetis is brought out by the use of a *con-* compound – 'contexit', 'coniunxit', 'concordia' – and each of these words is a little more general, more abstract, than the one preceding it. In line 334 the house literally covers the married pair, and in the context, after lines 330ff., we are bound to think of it covering them and sheltering them for the act of sexual union;[62] in line 335 the idea of physical union is still present, 'coniunxit' echoing the 'coniungere' in line 331, but it is now subordinate to the idea of the 'foedus', which is both the ceremony of marriage and the more informal 'contract' of love and affection between the two; the 'concordia' of line 336, the unanimity of their domestic life, is purely abstract.

For their full effect to be appreciated, these lines need to be taken in context with those that precede them. With self-conscious ingenuity Catullus turns the song of the Fates into a combination of epithalamium and prophetic chant:[63] the latter element predominates in the Fates' first sentence, but at line 328 the emphasis changes:

---

[62] I suspect that this feeling is reinforced by the close similarity between the words 'contexit' ('covered') and 'contexuit' ('wove together' or 'bound together'). The thought of the latter word is especially liable to suggest itself to the reader after 'subtegmina' ('woof-threads'), another word formed from the root *tex-*, in line 333.

[63] This was a kind of ingenuity that attracted the young Virgil. In his fourth Eclogue, a poem whose debt to *Peleus and Thetis* he acknowledges at line 46f. by adapting the refrain of the song of the Fates, he blends elements of Sibylline prophecy, wedding song and genethliacon (birthday song).

adveniet tibi iam portans optata maritis
Hesperus, adveniet fausto cum sidere coniunx,
quae tibi flexanimo mentem perfundat amore,   330
languidulosque paret tecum coniungere somnos,
levia substernens robusto brachia collo.

[Soon you will find Hesperus come, bearing what the married desire; your wife will come with the star of good omen, to steep your spirit in soul-charming love, and to prepare to unite in languorous sleep with you, laying her smooth arms beneath your manly neck.]

The rising of the Evening Star is a conventional feature of wedding songs; Catullus adds a vivid touch by presenting Hesperus as though he were a guest bearing gifts, rather like Chiron and Penios earlier in the poem; indeed line 279 – '*advenit* Chiron *portans* silvestria dona' ('Chiron came, bearing sylvan gifts') – is markedly similar to line 328. Then in line 329 'adveniet' is repeated, but in a moment we realise that its significance has changed from metaphor to fact. Thetis will come; and the sudden shift from figurative to literal meaning gives her physical presence a special immediacy.

In each of the next three lines the language grows more concrete and more precise. In line 330 it is Peleus' mind that Thetis will soak in love, but already a strongly sensuous atmosphere is created by the powerfully luxurious verb 'perfundat' and the epithet 'flexanimo'. This adjective, as the commentators tell us, is equivalent to the Greek *thelxiphrōn*, 'soul-charming', but the idea of bending in 'flex-' is distinctive to the Latin word. The bending of the mind is of course metaphorical, but in the context we shall surely think of the delicious relaxation of the body too.[64] This notion is reinforced by 'languidulos' in the next line, the only diminutive in the whole of the Fates' song, and a touch of tender simplicity amid the voluptuousness. The languor here is the languor that follows coition; this idea, and the suggestion in 'coniungere', prepare the way for the superb line 332, in which we see with our own eyes the two bodies conjoined. The contrast of textures between the smooth arms of Thetis and Peleus' virile neck is enhanced by the word order: the intertwining of limbs is evoked by the intertwining of 'levia brachia' with 'robusto collo'. After this high point of visual clarity and physical intimacy the Fates interpose their refrain, and the next lines, as we have seen, move back towards the abstract. Taken as a whole, the passage finely presents the corporeal union of the married pair as the core and centre of a larger experience: man and wife living together in concord.

After the Fates have ended their song, Catullus states in his own person that the gods delighted to visit the chaste homes of the heroes,

---

[64] Cf. line 303, 'postquam niveis flexerunt sedibus artus' ('After they had bent their limbs on snow-white seats'). The verb, finely chosen, indicates the gods' stately comfort.

and to show themselves openly to mortals, in the old days before piety was scorned. All this is clear and explicit, and it would not need to be stated if it had not been doubted. Peleus is a hero, he is pious and his home is chaste; otherwise the gods would not have so signally honoured him. From the concluding part of the poem it is scarcely less evident that Catullus means to represent the whole of the heroic age, not just Peleus and Thetis, in the same favourable light. He gives three examples of how the gods showed their favour by appearing among men; these examples are not chosen at random, for each one recalls some earlier part of the poem. Jupiter used to be present at the great festivals in his honour (387ff.); and we recall that Jupiter came to Peleus' wedding (298f.); he is called 'pater divum' in both places. Bacchus used to lead his revellers in person (390ff.); he does so, of course, when he comes for Ariadne. Lastly, the gods – Mars, Minerva or Diana – used to come and urge men on in battle. The classic instance of this is the Trojan War, and we are bound to think back to Achilles. He too is of the privileged race of heroes, and if the Parcae choose to dwell upon the grimmer parts of his story, he is apparently not be blamed himself.

Similarly, some at least of Catullus' examples of later depravity are chosen to contrast with his account of the age of heroes.[65] The son who fails to mourn his dead parents contrasts with the grief that Theseus feels at his father's suicide (compare 'luctum', line 247, with 'lugere', line 400); the father who longs for his son's early extinction contrasts with the heartbroken Aegeus. The mother's impious incest with her son is the very opposite of the virtuous union between Peleus and Thetis (the repetition of 'substernens' from line 332 at line 403 is striking); she outrages the gods of her household, whereas they can welcome the favouring gods to their chaste home.[66]

6

Our analysis has indicated that Catullus is not concerned to undermine his idealised picture of the legendary past, but that there are none the less patches of darker colour in his poem. If we take these

[65] I am unsure what to make of the fratricide in line 399; there is no obvious point of comparison or contrast with the rest of the poem. At line 181 Ariadne calls Theseus' killing of *her* brother 'fraterna caede'; are we meant to contrast her apparent regret at a brother's death with the fratricide of a later generation? If so, Catullus left his meaning somewhat obscure. (There is, incidentally, no comfort here for those who think that Catullus is out to attack Theseus. The killing of the Minotaur is not represented as an impious act; indeed, how could it be?)

[66] The contrast between wicked and virtuous homes depends on 'penates' at the end of line 404. The mss. read 'parentes', but the correction seems probable, 'parentes' having crept in from line 400.

two conclusions together, we can see just how remarkable *Peleus and Thetis* is simply as a technical achievement. Catullus set himself to write a long poem in which the age of heroes would be viewed with a romantic nostalgia; it would be difficult in any circumstances to sustain this atmosphere without insipidity, and he made his task even harder by adopting a method of verse construction that because of its general avoidance of enjambement was peculiarly liable to monotony, and by his decision to introduce his principal element of variety, the story of Ariadne, so early on in his account of Peleus and Thetis. The last of these problems was to some degree eased by the creation of a second inner section, the song of the Parcae, and the problems of style and content by a fertility of imagination and invention that can be demonstrated only by detailed examination of the text, but a large part of the solution is reached through the dynamic structure of the poem. Catullus creates a sense of development and continued vividness by changing and darkening the tone of the poem as it proceeds, not steadily, for that would compromise the deliberate unpredictability of the work, but from time to time.[67] First come Ariadne's operatic lamentations, contrasting with the happiness of Peleus and Thetis; but it must be emphasised that it is only the tone which is darkened, for Ariadne's story has a happy ending. Catullus' account dwells upon her short moment of unhappiness, but this need not seem such a very unusual procedure; the heroes and heroines of most love comedies and comedies of manners are seen largely in distress and anxiety, and yet no one doubts that such comedies are meant to be delightful and enjoyable. Catullus differs from the usual pattern chiefly in that by a stroke of genius he cuts short his story just before it reaches its natural climax and consummation. With the return to the theme of Peleus and Thetis, the idyllic mood is re-established, though perhaps with one or two suggestions of unease. With the song of the Fates the darker colour reappears, but with a difference; the Ariadne section retained much of the rococo brilliance of the opening, but the effect is now grimmer. Grimmer still is the final account of later mankind, an unrelieved catalogue of appalling crime.

The sombreness of the close is thus in a sense prepared; though it comes as a surprise, the surprise is one that does not, in retrospect, seem wholly unconnected with what has gone before. Yet all critics of the poem are agreed, I think, that its ending is distinctly different from the rest of it. Catullus' conception was impressive: for almost all its length the poem would be a brilliant display of technical mastery,

---

[67] Bramble sees a pattern of alternate light and dark (his scheme is more elaborate in detail). He may be right; but if a structure of this kind exists, it will only become evident to the reader when he has finished the poem. As he reads, he is conscious only of an unpredictable variety.

but there should finally come a point at which the elegance, detachment and subjectivity are dropped and the poet speaks out openly and directly. We must awake from the dream of fair women and brave men, shrug off the enchantments of the realm of art, and face the bleak reality of the real world. But though the conception is fine, the execution is less felicitous. Lines 387–404 are really one enormous sentence; the first part of it is vigorously constructed, but towards the end it becomes oddly vague and slack. The feebly scandalised note struck by the repeated 'impia' in line 403f. is especially disappointing, when we recall how brilliantly Catullus has used anaphora earlier on.[68] But the wrongness is more than a matter of style; the nice balance between variety and continuity that Catullus has so finely maintained for so long is disrupted. It is not change of mood or subject in itself that is to blame, for such changes have been the poem's lifeblood; and in any case we have seen that Catullus is at pains to make connections here with the rest of the poem. Other people have claimed to find yet more connections, which I have questioned, but the trouble is one which no number of such connections can overcome: Catullus' problem lies in the particular mood that he has chosen to adopt at this moment. The nature of the poem has been such that the question of sincerity has not arisen hitherto, but now it becomes insistent; the sudden tone of stern condemnation is acceptable only if we sense a genuine pressure of feeling behind it. This judgment is as much aesthetic as moral: the reader asks to be gripped, and Catullus' grip starts to slacken here; his imagination ceases to be active, and he slips instead into easy clichés about degeneracy.

Ovid designed his *Ars Amatoria* to be a work of monumental flippancy, but when he wrote in it that despite other people's preference for the past he was glad to be living in the present age, now that rusticity had given way to refinement (3.121–8), he displayed a clear-sightedness that deserves to be called, in literary terms, a kind of integrity. *Peleus and Thetis* is, by contrast, a poem of profound and curious beauty, with which Ovid's piece cannot begin to compare; in a superficial sense Catullus avoids seriousness until near the end, and yet when he turns to denounce the crimes of latter-day humanity he is in a deeper sense less serious than in any other part of the work. We know from the rest of Catullus' poetry that he too held rusticity in scorn, and even if *Peleus and Thetis* had been his only work to survive, we might still have inferred as much; he ought to have had the self-knowledge to say with Ovid, 'haec aetas moribus apta meis'

---

[68] Nisbet, suspecting corruption on other grounds, tentatively suggests 'improba' in place of the first 'impia' (p. 104). This does not seem to me to improve the poetry. Reeve, tentatively again, offers 'substernens impia nato ilia'; which would certainly be more vigorous (p. 183).

('the present age suits my style of life'). If this criticism seems hard, it may be said in his defence that he is in part the victim of his own brilliance; the lack of focus at the end would be less visible but for the life, originality and vivid detail of the rest. Fortunately, our final impression is not to be one of disappointment, for the last two lines are superbly evocative:

quare nec talis dignantur visere coetus,
nec se contingi patiuntur lumine claro.

[Wherefore they do not deign to visit such gatherings, nor suffer themselves to be touched by the bright light of day.]

The idea of the gods themselves going into the dimness and losing the light of the sun seems to belong with Heine and the cultivated neo-Hellenism of the nineteenth century, not to the Roman world; I hesitate to attribute it to Catullus, and yet I cannot resist the impression that it is there in the Latin.

Wilamowitz (1924; 2.298) began his discussion of *Peleus and Thetis*, 'This poem is the work in which Catullus wanted to write his masterpiece.' This is a suggestive comment, for what are our grounds for believing it to be true? Surely the evidence of the poem itself. We have already seen that it is a work which presents itself to us as a masterpiece, not just in the sense in which every great work may be said to do, but as a part of its intended meaning; and we should not leave it without reflecting what a tricky tightrope Catullus chose to walk. It is a familiar thought that a writer working in a highly developed literary tradition faces a peculiar difficulty in composing a long poem, because the increased refinement of culture demands the kind of continuous intensity characteristic of lyric verse, whereas a long poem must contain passages of less concentrated quality. This is an idea that T. S. Eliot has impressed upon our own century, but Horace said something not unlike it in the first book of his Satires. In *Peleus and Thetis* Catullus aims for a continuous brilliance over a length of four hundred lines; and the extent of his success is astonishing. Virgil, in the next generation, was to compose a whole epic in which virtually every line, in defiance of the laws of poetic nature, seems to aspire to the detail and concentration of the shorter poem; here the conflict between two aspirations – the grand sweep of the whole, and the loading of every rift with subtle ore – becomes a significant part of the poet's statement. Catullus was working on a far smaller scale, but in one respect his task was even harder. 'Tantae molis erat' . . . Virgil makes us feel the effort involved not only in founding the Roman race but in creating the *Aeneid*: Catullus' conception, on the other hand, permits no sense of strain to appear. The work might be long in the making, like Cinna's *Zmyrna*, but the final result must be one of poise and polish. What we are given is a series of 'shining pictures'; the phrase is again from Wilamowitz (p. 303), and once again it suggests an instinctive appreciation of the work's character. The poem is made up of pictures in that it is a gallery of tableaux or set-pieces; it aims to dazzle metaphorically and almost literally, so full is it of light and colour and precious substances. Narrative is pared to a minimum, so that the poem almost seems to be a succession of high points – pictures without the frames, as it were. The Ariadne section, the recreation of a consummate work of art, is appropriately the core and centre of such a conception. Here for once a poet's intention and execution correspond; Catullus' art is at its most exquisite and original just where the logic of his structure demands an effect of the rarest beauty. Ariadne is merely a lovely figure on a tapestry, and yet by a mysterious paradox she is the more moving for being viewed by the poet with detachment and from afar. I use the word 'mysterious' advisedly, for there is surely a feeling of something strange – uncanny would be too strong a word – in this luminous evocation of a remote and radiant world, though the feeling is not one that can be justified by the quotation of any particular lines or phrases. For all its aspirations to the classic status of a masterpiece, this remains a strongly idiosyncratic poem. We can say with some confidence that its most distinctive qualities were not derived from those Hellenistic poets to whom Catullus paid tribute; and if his contemporaries were producing works of a like subtlety and invention, Rome was more richly endowed with poetic talent in the last years of the republic than we commonly dare to imagine.

Part Three

Juvenal the Poet

When H. W. Garrod introduced his *Oxford Book of Latin Verse* to the world in 1912, he explained that he had left out satire altogether. For the omission of Horace's *Satires* and *Epistles* he evidently felt some twinge of regret: 'By their large temper and by their complete freedom from cant they have achieved a place in the regard of men from which they are not likely to be dislodged by any changes of literary fashion or any fury of the enemies of humane studies. I am content to leave them in this secure position, and not to intrude them into a Collection where Horace himself would have known them to be out of place. Indeed, he has himself said upon this subject all that needs to be said.' The later satirists got shorter shrift: 'Persius similarly, in the Prologue to his *Satires*, excluded himself from the company of the great poets. Nor can I believe that Juvenal has any place among them. In the rhetoric of rancour he is a distinguished practitioner. But he wants two qualities essential to great poetry – truth and humanity. I say this because there are critics who speak of Juvenal as though he were Isaiah.'

There are two disparaging judgments here: a general one about the value of satiric verse, and a more particular one (superfluous, one might suppose, if it be an article of faith that a satirist cannot write great poetry) about Juvenal. The first of these judgments is, upon a closer inspection, curiously confused. An anthology that finds a place for Valerius Aedituus and Porcius Licinus, for Lygdamus, Pentadius and Reposianus, cannot convincingly claim to have excluded Juvenal and the hexameter verse of Horace for having failed to meet a standard of quality. What Garrod really felt, surely, was that satire was not Poetry at all, that it was out of place in a Collection (note the capital letter) dignified with the authoritative status of *The Oxford Book* . . . In this view he was following the taste of his time. When he wrote, the standard anthologies of English poetry were Palgrave's *Golden Treasury*, first published in 1861 but still immensely popular, and Quiller-Couch's recent *Oxford Book of English Verse* (1910), both restricted to lyric pieces; Dame Helen Gardner's *New Oxford Book of English Verse* (1972) is in this respect markedly different. Until quite

recently many English children, otherwise well educated in the hu-
manities, grew up virtually unaware of the rich tradition of satiric
and didactic poetry that their native literature possesses.

The value of these more discursive or informal types of poetry is
now better appreciated, and yet the feeling that poetry is something
grand and lofty or at last apart from mere verse is deeply rooted in
our consciousness; as Garrod was able to point out, it goes back to
Horace. And indeed this feeling does correspond to a reality. When
Pope writes in his *Essay on Man* (*Epistle* 1. 193f.),

> Why has not Man a microscopic eye?
> For this plain reason, Man is not a Fly.

he produces an effect which is unobtainable in prose. The wit of the
words depends on the adroit use of rhyme and metre. The very method
of persuasion derives from the same resource; the tartness, the neatness, the apparent justness of the sentiment depend upon the organ-
isation of the verse form. Here is a type of rhetoric which so far from
being inimical to verse is possible in verse alone. When, a few lines
later (209f.), he contemplates the creation with the words

> Mark how it mounts, to Man's imperial race,
> From the green myriads in the peopled grass   210

we become aware of a different order of thought and feeling. The
evocative compression of the second line, the sensibility that can turn
the grass into a jungle teeming with bizarre inhabitants, the imagination that can seize upon the adjective 'peopled', so that we perceive
the scene from an insect's eye view and enter into a world as busy and
important in its own estimation as that of imperial Man himself –
these are all qualities that we commonly describe, even when we meet
them in prose, as 'poetic'. In practice there is no hard and fast division
between these two types of poetry, and I shall seek to show that
Juvenal possesses a command of the Latin hexameter which it is not
sensible to set apart from the techniques that we unhesitatingly call
poetic in the works of other writers; but I shall also claim – and here
we come back to Garrod's more particular criticism – that Juvenal's
work has a literary character unlike that of the other writers of Roman
satura, and that he deserves to be recognised as a great 'poet' even by
those who use the word in its more exalted sense. Certainly, Virgil
was the poet who exercised the profoundest influence over him, an
influence deeper than that of Horace, Lucilius or even Martial.

We can begin to get an idea of the character and quality of Juvenal's
sensibility if we compare him with other poets. One of Virgil's most
original achievements was his way of describing the natural scene.
The surface appearance is evoked as vividly as ever before, if not more

so, but behind the observed reality we are also made aware of a 'spiritual landscape', a penumbra of emotional associations. Sometimes we are given an atmosphere of numinousness, sometimes a quality subtler still, a sense of history, patriotism, tradition or moral values, or a mixture of all these things. In some of Virgil's greatest passages – above all in *Georgics* 2 and *Aeneid* 7 and 8 – he persuades us that the spiritual landscape is not just a romantic decoration of the physical landscape (which is perhaps the impression we get from parts of the *Eclogues*), but inseparable from what is seen by the outer eye. Ruskin says somewhere of a view in Europe that no landscape in America could conceivably be so beautiful, because it would be scenery merely, and nothing more; the man who can see what Ruskin is driving at, whether or not he agrees with him, is on the way to receiving Virgil's meaning. Virgil's perception of the natural scene is both elusive and complex; it has not yet been adequately described, and can only be grasped through a close study of his text, for which this is not the place. For our purposes it is enough to note that other poets tried to imitate Virgil's accounts of landscape, and found it very difficult. We find Ovid at the beginning of his third book of *Amores* (3.1.1–8) using the Virgilian furniture in a rather mechanical way before dissolving the solemnity into a joke:

> *Stat vetus et multos incaedua silva per annos;*
> *credibile est illo numen inesse loco.*
> *fons sacer in medio speluncaque pumice pendens,*
> *et latere ex omni dulce queruntur aves.*
> *hic ego dum spatior tectus nemoralibus umbris,*   5
> *quod mea, quaerebam, Musa moveret, opus;*
> *venit odoratos Elegia nexa capillos,*
> *et, puto, pes illi longior alter erat.*

[There stands an ancient wood, untouched by the axe over many years; you can believe that there is a deity in the place. In the midst is a sacred spring and a cave with overhanging rock, and on every side the birds complain sweetly. While I walked here, covered by the shade of the trees, I sought a subject for my Muse to work upon; Elegy came, her hair scented and bound up, and, I think, one of her feet was longer than the other.]

Here are the aged, inviolate wood, the sense of the numinous, the sacred spring, the romantic grot; but the goddess who appears to the poet is not some ancient Italic deity, but a literary personification. And then comes the throwaway joke; the goddess of the elegiac couplet, with one leg longer than the other, advances from the gloom with a limp.

Since Ovid's intention here is deliberately facetious, it may be unfair to complain of the flatness of his opening description; but several passages in the *Metamorphoses* where he attempts a set piece about the beauties of nature suggest that he had not the capacity to penetrate beyond the surface of the Virgilian manner. For example (5.388–92):

> *silva coronat aquas cingens latus omne suisque*
> *frondibus ut velo Phoebeos submovet ictus.*
> *frigora dant rami, Tyrios humus umida flores:*   390
> *perpetuum ver est. quo dum Proserpina luco*
> *ludit et aut violas aut candida lilia carpit . . .*

[A wood encircles the waters on every side like a crown and keeps off the rays of the sun with its leaves as with an awning. The branches afford coolness, the moist earth affords richly coloured flowers; spring is everlasting. While Proserpine was sporting in this grove and gathering violets or white lilies . . .]

Virgil had the power to invest wood or riverside in Italy with a magical quality, but when Ovid tries to describe a magically beautiful place, the magic remains purely literal and external. Spring is perpetual in his Sicilian valley; he loses contact with reality in a way that Virgil hardly ever does. The passage tinkles prettily enough, but there is no authentic imagination in it. Another set piece is his depiction of Narcissus' place of refuge (3.407–14):

> *fons erat inlimis, nitidis argenteus undis,*
> *quem neque pastores neque pastae monte capellae*
> *contigerant aliudve pecus, quem nulla volucris*
> *nec fera turbarat nec lapsus ab arbore ramus;*   410
> *gramen erat circa, quod proximus umor alebat,*
> *silvaque sole locum passura tepescere nullo.*
> *hic puer et studio venandi lassus et aestu*
> *procubuit faciemque loci fontemque secutus . . .*

[There was a clear spring, with sparkling silvery waters, which neither shepherds nor the goats that feed on the mountain nor any cattle had ever touched, which no bird or beast or branch falling from a tree had ever disturbed; there was grass around it, nourished by the water nearby, and a wood which never allowed the sun to warm the place. Here the boy, tired by his eager hunting and by the heat, lay down, drawn by the appearance of the place and by the spring . . .]

Ovid makes the place into a secret, inviolate ground, where no shepherd ever treads; but we get no sense, as we would from Virgil, of a mysterious sanctity. We are shown a pleasant secluded spot for a picnic, or for admiring one's own reflection; the absence of people is merely agreeable. But whereas Ovid goes through the right motions only, Juvenal has a genuine sensitivity to the spiritual quality of landscape. In his third satire he describes the valley of Egeria:

> *hic, ubi nocturnae Numa constituebat amicae*

(nunc sacri fontis nemus et delubra locantur
Iudaeis, quorum cophinus fenumque supellex;
omnis enim populo mercedem pendere iussa est 15
arbor et eiectis mendicat silva Camenis),
in vallem Egeriae descendimus et speluncas
dissimiles veris. quanto praesentius esset
numen aquis, viridi si margine cluderet undas
herba nec ingenuum violarent marmora tofum. 20

[Here, where Numa held his assignations by night with his lady-friend (now the grove and shrine by the sacred spring are let out to Jews, who have a basket and some hay for their furniture; for every tree has been ordered to pay rent to the people, the Camenae have been thrown out and the wood goes begging), we go down to the valley of Egeria and to caves unlike nature. How much more present would the divinity be to the waters, if grass enclosed the pool with a green border and marble did not violate the native tufa.]

In the *Amores* we saw Ovid moving from nature to fantasy; here Juvenal reverses the process. After a pleasantly ironical phrase about good King Numa's assignations with his high-minded lady-friend, he declares that the shrine, grove and sacred spring have been spoiled by the arrival of Jewish beggars: 'Iudaeis' is placed with scornful emphasis at the start of a new line. The racial sneer is important, for he now goes on to say that this foreign invasion has driven out the Camenae, the native goddesses of the old Italy. In *Aeneid* 12 the Trojans, effeminate orientals in the eyes of their Italian adversaries, have torn up an olive tree sacred to Faunus. Turnus prays for aid to Faunus and to his native Earth, and his prayer is for a moment answered, but Venus, a deity of the new order, is able to override the old Italian gods (766–87). Juvenal's lines can be seen as a sort of satirical version of this idea. And as with Virgil, the idea is caught up with the physical landscape. Juvenal's account of Egeria's pool and caves is extraordinary; indeed, I know of nothing in ancient literature quite like it. There is no Latin word equivalent to 'unspoilt', and Juvenal is perhaps the only Latin poet who might have wanted to use it; in effect he is talking about the 'atmosphere' of the spot, in a fashion that is almost Betjemanic. Modern zeal for improvement has smartened the place up with marble, but the charm has gone with the disappearance of the green banks and tufa, and the divine seems less present; the attitude is half aesthetic, half historical–cum–religious.[1] However, though part of the feeling is aesthetic, it is not so in simple sense, for tufa is not an attractive stone to look at, and marble is; but like the adult Wordsworth, Juvenal cannot rest in

[1] I do not imply that Juvenal in any strong sense believed in traditional religion. A man whose beliefs are vestigial or non-existent may enjoy imagining a kind of religious emotion.

a feeling and a love,
That had no need of a remoter charm,
By thought supplied, nor any interest
Unborrowed from the eye.[2]

He too is conscious of something 'more deeply interfused', though it is of course a very different something from what Wordsworth found. Would Horace have objected to seeing the banks of the Bandusian spring edged with marble, or even Virgil? There is no reason to suppose so. As for Ovid (*Met.* 2.155–62):

> *vallis erat piceis et acuta densa cupressu,*   155
> *nomine Gargaphie, succinctae sacra Dianae,*
> *cuius in extremo est antrum nemorale recessu*
> *arte laboratum nulla: simulaverat artem*
> *ingenio natura suo; nam pumice vivo*
> *et levibus tofis nativum duxerat arcum.*   160
> *fons sonat a dextra tenui perlucidus unda,*
> *margine gramineo patulos succinctus hiatus.*

[There was a valley named Gargaphie, thick with pine and pointed cypress, sacred to girt Diana. In its furthest recess was a woody cave, wrought by no art: nature by her own genius had mimicked art; for she had led across a natural arch of living rock and light tufa. The thin waters of a clear spring sounded on the right, and where the pool spread out more widely it was girt with a grassy bank.]

Here again are the native tufa and the artistic caverns, and yet the difference is enormous. Ovid is pleased by the notion that a natural cave should seem to have been made by the hand of man; Juvenal, however, dislikes those artificial grottos: 'dissimiles veris' comes starkly and contemptuously at the start of the new line after the sentence seemed complete in the line before.[3] Juvenal has a sense that art is one thing, nature another, and that they ought to look different; the attitude is not unusual today, but found at the end of the first century A.D., it reveals a mind both poetic and original.

A similar spirit reappears in the eleventh satire (111, 155f.):

> *templorum quoque maiestas praesentior . . .*
> *hanc rebus Latiis curam praestare solebat*
> *fictilis et nullo violatus Iuppiter auro.*

[The majesty of the temples too was then nearer to help . . . Such was the care that Jupiter was wont to show for the fortunes of Latium, while he was made of clay and undefiled by any gold].

---

[2] *Lines composed a few miles above Tintern Abbey . . . 80–3.*
[3] Juvenal's writing is quietly skilful here. The rhythm of the verse and the shape of the clauses invite us to stress 'numen' and 'herba' in the next sentence, words which a speaker would naturally want to emphasise.

Consciously or unconsciously Juvenal must have had a passage of Lucan in mind (9.517-21):

quamvis Aethiopum populis Arabumque beatis
gentibus atque Indis unus sit Iuppiter Hammon,
pauper adhuc deus est, nullis violata per aevum
divitiis delubra tenens, morumque priorum   520
numen Romano templum defendit ab auro.

[Although for the Ethiopian people and the wealthy tribes of Arabia and the Indians there is one Jupiter Hammon, he is still a poor god, and as a deity of the old kind he defends his temple from Roman gold.]

The differences between the two poets here are instructive. Lucan is doing little more than producing a variant on the commonplace that poverty encourages virtue and wealth corrupts. This thought is still present in Juvenal, but he has added something more. He particularises the idea by fixing his eye upon a statue of Jupiter, and he suggests that gilding the old image (or perhaps replacing it with a golden statue) has spoiled it; once more there is a union of aesthetic with religious or moral feeling. Lucan's impecunious god is an amusing idea, but it goes no further; Juvenal has the power of imaginative compression to give us simultaneously a picture, a mood, and a moral idea. And again the sensibility is distinctive, as can be seen from a comparison with Horace's more conventional view (*Carm.* 2.15.13f., 17ff.):

privatus illis census erat brevis,
commune magnum . . .

nec fortuitum spernere caespitem
leges sinebant, oppida publico
  sumptu iubentes et deorum
    templa novo decorare saxo.   20

[Their private wealth was small, their public resources great . . . Nor did the laws permit them to scorn the turf that lay to hand, but commanded them to build towns at public cost and to adorn the gods' temples with newly quarried stone.]

There was no lack of brand new stone, in fact, but it was used for temples. Despite those humble turves, there is no trace of the idea that too much could be spent on the gods.

Dryden believed that Virgil would have been the sharpest of Roman satirists, had he chosen to turn his hand to that genre. This was a superficial judgment: Dryden was thinking only in terms of technical capacity, forgetting that an appropriate temperament is also a vital ingredient for poetic success in any style. Juvenal obviously possessed the technique and the personality required by a satirist, so that we might have expected him to turn to satire whatever the circumstances of his life and times; yet we may also detect in him instincts that point in a different direction. When Dr Johnson passed Dryden's translation in review, he observed, 'The peculiarity of Juvenal is a mixture of gaiety and stateliness, of pointed sentences and declamatory grandeur.' This is a very just assessment, and as it implies, the grand element in Juvenal goes beyond a command of the hexameter; it is no less a part of his character as a writer than his bitterness or his wit. We may well feel that he would have made a far finer epic poet than Statius, Silius or Valerius Flaccus.

There are signs that Juvenal himself was conscious of an urge towards nobler and grander genres. When he wrote his sixth satire it was surely his deliberate intention to produce a poem much larger and of coarser grain than anything he had written before. Towards the end of it he invites us to consider whether he has not gone beyond the proper bounds of his genre:

> *fingimus haec altum satura sumente coturnum*
> *scilicet, et finem egressi legemque priorum*   635
> *grande Sophocleo carmen bacchamur hiatu . . .*

[You may think that satire is putting on the tragic buskin; that I am inventing these things, going beyond the limits and rules of my predecessors, and crying out a grand song with the wide-open mouth of a Sophocles.]

It should be obvious enough (though critics often forget this) that *Satire* 6 is rather different from the rest of Juvenal's work; but we are surely not tempted to think that his departures from the proper character of *satura*, if there are any, go in the direction of tragedy. Juvenal neither confirms nor denies his suggestion; but he has left it in our heads. The significance of the passage is that he is thinking about high tragedy even in a place where we ourselves would hardly have suspected it.

He was not a reflective man, and in any case those satires in which he may be saying something about poetry contain so much shadow-boxing that it is hard to know what he really thought.

> *si natura negat, facit indignatio versum*
> *qualemcumque potest, quales ego vel Cluvienus.*   80

[If nature refuses, indignation makes such verses as it can – such as I write or Cluvienus.]

The second of these two famous lines (1.79f.) is one of Juvenal's characteristically abrupt deflations, and perhaps it is no more than an aside, to be thrown away. But for what it may be worth, the lines as they stand seem to express not exuberant anger but a self-contemptuous pessimism: the sort of verse that 'indignatio' produces is mean stuff. The writer of satura conventionally alludes to the lowness of his muse, but here we have neither Horace's studied modesty nor Persius' gay burlesque of epic convention; instead, there is a sullen chafing at the bit.

'Difficile est saturam non scribere' (1.30) ('it is hard not to write satire'); these words too can be interpreted along the same lines. Juvenal may be saying that if one lives in a world of ugly vulgarity, it is hard to resist exposing its folly. But it is more natural to take the words another way, with the stress on 'satura': under such conditions it is hard to write in any genre but this. In other words this satirist, unlike Horace, is forced to his task. The two ideas are not incompatible, and both meanings are probably present. A brief passage in *Satire* 4 suggests a comparable moral:

> *incipe, Calliope. licet et considere: non est*
> *cantandum, res vera agitur. narrate, puellae*   35
> *Pierides, prosit mihi vos dixisse puellas.*

[Begin, Calliope. We may sit down: this is not a grand poem, a true story is being told. Tell it, you girls of Pieria, and may it benefit me that I have called you girls.]

The muses are now elderly ladies; the art of poetry is old and tired. There seems also to be a contrast between the subjects of high poetry ('cantandum') and the reality ('res vera') with which the satirist deals.

Statius, parodied in *Satire* 4, receives a somewhat ambiguous treatment in *Satire* 7. In this later poem Juvenal seems to include himself among the rabble of ineffective poets, ambitious to write but unable to plough anything but infertile soil:

> *nos tamen hoc agimus tenuique in pulvere sulcos*
> *ducimus et litus sterili versamus aratro.*
> *nam si discedas, laqueo tenet ambitiosum*   50
> *scribendi cacoethes et aegro in corde senescit.*
> *sed vatem egregium, cui non sit publica vena,*
> *qui nihil expositum soleat deducere, nec qui*
> *communi feriat carmen triviale moneta,*
> *hunc, qualem nequeo monstrare et sentio tantum,*   55
> *anxietate carens animus facit . . .*

[Still, we work away; we draw furrows in the thin dust and turn over the shore with useless plough. For should you try to give it up, the ambitious itch to write holds you in a noose and grows inveterate in your diseased heart. But a great poet, with a vein all his own, who would not weave hackneyed verse or strike the coin of everyday poetry from the common

mint – such a man, whom I cannot point to but only imagine, is produced
by a spirit free from worry . . .]

It is interesting that whereas Horace in contrasting his own pedestrian
Muse with grander poetry thinks in terms of theme and diction, Juvenal is concerned, more shrewdly, with originality; that is what he
looks for in the true poet, and that is what he cannot find in contemporary verse. The particular subject of this satire, patronage, leads
him to stress the importance of leisure and freedom from petty care;
but we need not dismiss this point as inspired purely by the convenience of the moment. Virgil, a notoriously slow composer, could
certainly not have written the *Aeneid* without the leisure and security
provided for him by Maecenas; it seems clear that Juvenal, too, wrote
very laboriously: a rate of one poem a year may be too high an esti-
mate. For a fastidious craftsman here was another serious obstacle to
work on a large scale.

Horace's well known plumpness adds an extra touch of comedy to
Juvenal's illustration of his topic (7.59–62):

> *neque enim cantare sub antro*
> *Pierio thyrsumque potest contingere maesta*   60
> *paupertas atque aeris inops, quo nocte dieque*
> *corpus eget: satur est cum dicit Horatius 'euhoe.'*

[Poverty, sad and short of the money that the body needs night and day,
cannot sing in the Pierian cave or touch the thyrsus: Horace's belly was
full when he cried 'Euhoe.']

But at the same time this is a brilliant display of Juvenal's sensitivity
as a reader, for he has seized upon an example of Horace at his most
tiresomely bogus: *Odes* 2.19, a work of laboured correctitude in which
the poet claims to be carried away by bacchic frenzy.[4] When Juvenal
moves on to Virgil, the wit seems less penetrating, perhaps because
he admired him too much.[5] The number and variety of his allusions
to Virgil show how well he knew him.[6] When he invites a friend to
dinner, the entertainment is to be recitation from Homer and Virgil
– poetry, and epic poetry at that (11.180f.); Horace, in an equivalent
passage, imagined himself and his friends discussing questions of
moral philosophy. Juvenal's phrase for Virgil here, 'Maronis altisoni'

[4] Horace's insistence that we should believe what he says ('credite, posteri') is particularly offensive. I do not think that his credit is to be saved by supposing the poem
to be ironic: that merely turns it into bad wit.
[5] The main joke here seems to be at Virgil's luxurious style of life (see Rudd, p. 98).
The passage to which Juvenal alludes, *Aen.* 7.445ff., may be felt to display the efficiency
of Virgil's art at its most mechanical, but I doubt whether anything is to be made of
this.
[6] See Gehlen (though various of the echoes that he claims to find are implausible).

('lofty-toned Maro'), is not without irony; sometimes the satiric tone is more marked (12.70–4):

tum gratus Iulo   70
atque novercali sedes praelata Lavino
conspicitur sublimis apex, cui candida nomen
scrofa dedit, laetis Phrygibus mirabile sumen
et numquam visis triginta clara mamillis.

[Then they catch sight of the lofty height dear to Iulus and preferred by him as a home to his stepmother's Lavinum – that height which got its name from the white breed-sow whose belly was marvelled at by the delighted Phrygians and which was famous for its thirty nipples, a sight never seen before.]

The story of the miraculous sow in *Aeneid* 8 is neatly punctured by the word 'scrofa' (breed-sow), well positioned at the start of a line, and the idea of Iulus founding Alba Longa to get away from father's new wife makes a pleasant joke. But it must be recognised that this kind of humour is affectionate; we do not suppose Miss Anna Russell hostile to Wagner when she remarks that it is small wonder Siegfried deserted Brünnhilde for Gutrune so briskly, since the only woman he had seen before was his aunt. Indeed, some of his 'parodies' clearly use Virgil as a yardstick against which the modern world is measured and found to fail. There is an unsubtle example of this at *Satire* 2.99f.: 'ille tenet speculum, pathici gestamen Othonis,/Actoris Aurunci spolium' ('another man holds a mirror, once carried by the effeminate Otho, a spoil taken from Actor of Aurunca'). The last three words of line 99 are adapted from *Aeneid* 3.286, 'aere cavo clipeum, magni gestamen Abantis' ('a shield of convex bronze, once carried by great Abas'); the first three words of line 100 are quoted from *Aeneid* 12.94. The heroic world is recalled in order to show up the degeneracy of modern times.[7]

The great diatribe of Umbricius, which occupies all but the first twenty lines of *Satire* 3, ends, rather unexpectedly, in a quiet fashion (316): 'sed iumenta vocant,' Umbricius says, 'et sol inclinat. eundum est . . .' ('But the animals summon and the sun is descending. I must go'). As Charles Witke has observed, this echoes the closing motifs of Virgil's *Eclogues*, no less than four of which end at dusk: the sun is going down and it is time to go home. But in its new context the motif has acquired a new force. The natural life of the countryside – 'early to bed and early to rise' – stands in contrast to the frenetic and artificial existence of Rome, described in the main body of the poem. And whereas the true countryman goes home to rest at dusk, Umbricius must go because he is starting a long journey. In due course he

---

[7] It is typical of Juvenal that his parody is in part visual. The bronze shield of Abas and the homosexual's bronze mirror look so similar, and yet are so different.

will become a real countryman – he will cross the frozen fields 'caligatus', in thick boots – but this is not for him, as it was for Virgil's Corydon, a source of embarrassment, but a matter of pride and relief. Juvenal has echoed Virgil in order to transform him.

Juvenal again uses the *Eclogues* for ironical contrast with contemporary reality in *Satire* 9 (102–4):

> *o Corydon, Corydon, secretum divitis ullum*
> *esse putas? servi ut taceant, iumenta loquentur*
> *et canis et postes et marmora.*

[O Corydon, Corydon, do you think a rich man has any secrets? Though the slaves may keep quiet, the beasts of burden will talk, the dog, the doorposts, the marble.]

Here there is an obvious echo of *Eclogue* 2.69: 'a, Corydon, Corydon, quae te dementia cepit!' ('Ah Corydon, Corydon, what madness has seized you!'). Juvenal quotes from the naive soliloquy of a rustic lover in a sarcastic address to an urban parasite, the sodomite Naevolus. Corydon's passion is homosexual, and yet curiously innocent: besides, the homosexual element in this eclogue owes much to Greek literary tradition, although Virgil's main source, Theocritus' eleventh Idyll, is heterosexual. Naevolus, on the other hand, is totally corrupted, and his vices are explicitly described. Juvenal warns him that no rich man can keep any of his doings secret; Virgil's Corydon, on the other hand, is guarded by rural solitude and modesty of means.

A side of Juvenal which is barely if at all satiric can be seen in his pictures of the Italian countryside and its life. This is a theme which can easily lead to insipidity and falseness; for the most part Juvenal handles it in a genuinely poetic way, with a clarity and integrity of perception. In *Satire* 3 the picture of a small-town theatrical entertainment has charmed many readers (lines 172–9). Even here, as it happens, Juvenal has taken inspiration from epic: when he described the country child ('rusticus infans') shrinking against its mother at the sight of the actor's pale, gaping mask, he surely remembered the famous scene in *Iliad* 6 where Hector's baby is frightened by the plume on his father's helmet. The 'rusticus infans' reappears briefly in *Satire* 9, 'cum matre et casulis et conlusore catello' ('with his mother and the cottage and the puppy, his playmate', line 31). Since this line is given to the self-indulgent Naevolus, it would not matter if it were sentimental; but it is in any case saved from this charge by the distinctiveness of the last two words. Very briefly we see the boy and his little dog playing together, as companions (this a truly child's-eye view); the scene is both sharpened and made touching by the contrast between the pretentious 'conlusore' and the colloquial diminutive 'catello'.

It is a sort of sensible clear-sightedness that makes the picture of primitive man at the beginning of *Satire* 6 effective:

Credo Pudicitiam Saturno rege moratam
in terris visamque diu, cum frigida parvas
praeberet spelunca domos ignemque laremque
et pecus et dominos communi clauderet umbra,
silvestrem montana torum cum sterneret uxor   5
frondibus et culmo vicinarumque ferarum
pellibus, haut similis tibi, Cynthia, nec tibi, cuius
turbavit nitidos extinctus passer ocellos,
sed potanda ferens infantibus ubera magnis
et saepe horridior glandem ructante marito.   10

[When Saturn reigned, Shamefastness, I believe, for long remained and was seen upon the earth, when a cold cave provided a small home, and a single shelter enclosed hearth and household gods, cattle and their masters; when a mountain wife laid her woodland couch with leaves, straw and the skins of beasts, her neighbours, a wife not like you, Cynthia, or like you, whose bright eyes were clouded by the death of a sparrow, but with breasts for her big babies to drink from, and often more unkempt than her acorn-belching husband.]

This huge sentence, at once monumental and informal, affords a good example of Juvenal's unspectacular craftsmanship. 'Credo,' he begins, almost casually; and as the sentence unwinds, he has room for a touch of humour in 'vicinarum': primitive man sleeps on pelts made out of his next-door neighbours. The direct address to Propertius' and Catullus' mistresses in line 7f. may have been inspired by metrical necessity, but the declaimer's accusatory 'tibi ... tibi ...' adds a usefully satiric edge to the poetic texture before we return to primitive man again. Wisely, Juvenal does not idealize our ancestors; Beaumont and Fletcher caught the tone in the words they gave to Philaster:

Oh, that I had been nourished in these woods
With milk of goats and acorns ...
And then had taken me some mountain-girl,
Beaten with winds, chaste as the hardened rocks
Where on she dwelt, that might have strewed my bed
With leaves and reeds, and with the skins of beasts,
Our neighbours, and have borne at her big breasts
My large coarse issue! This had been a life
Free from vexation   (*Philaster*, act 4, sc. 2.)

The prince envies the simple life, but he cannot altogether lose his courtliness and sophistication; it is appropriate that his sense of irony should be preserved.

In *Eclogue* 4 Virgil envisages the return to the golden age not as a sudden miracle but as a gradual process: a second Achilles must fight, a second Argo sail before the return to paradise can be complete. When he celebrates the blessings of the farmer's life in *Georgics* 2, he does not say that justice still abides in the country; rather, this is the last place where Justice left traces when she abandoned the earth. In both places 'vestigia' is a key word.

> *te duce, si qua manent sceleris* vestigia *nostri,*
> *inrita perpetua solvent formidine terras . . .*
> pauca *tamen suberunt* priscae vestigia *fraudis . . .*

(Eclogue 4.13f., 31)

[In your time of leadership, if any traces of our crime remain, they will be nullified and free the earth from its perpetual fear . . . However, a few traces of former sin shall lurk . . .]

> extrema *per illos*
> Iustitia excedens terris vestigia *fecit.*

(Georgics 2.473f.)

[When she quitted the earth, Justice left her last footprints among them.]

Virgil's subtle sense of process and his delicate awareness of imperfection are not equalled by any other Latin poet, but Juvenal has something of the same feeling, and this gives more depth and verity to his picture of the past (6.14–16, 19, 21–4).

> *multa Pudicitiae* veteris vestigia *forsan*
> *aut aliqua exstiterint et sub Iove, sed Iove* nondum   15
> *barbato . . .*
> paulatim *deinde ad superos Astraea recessit . . .*
> anticum et vetus *est alienum, Postume, lectum*
> *concutere et sacri genium contemnere fulcri.*
> *omne* aliud *crimen* mox *ferrea protulit aetas;*
> *viderunt* primos *argentea saecula moechos.*

[Maybe a good many traces of the old Shamefastness, or some at least, survived even under Jupiter's rule, but only while Jupiter had not yet grown his beard. . . . Then gradually Astraea withdrew to heaven . . . It is an old, old custom, Postumus, to rattle another man's bed and scorn the genius of the sacred head of the couch. The age of iron brought forth every other crime in due course; the silver age saw the first adulterers.]

In *Satire* 11 (60–2, 65f.) Juvenal recalls Evander's entertainment of Hercules and Aeneas, evidently a specific allusion to *Aeneid* 8; the reference to a kid from Tibur a few lines later may be a bow in the direction of Horace. The theme of simple country fare is common enough in Latin poetry; part of Horace's *Satires* 2.2 and 2.6, the meal of Philemon and Baucis in Ovid's *Metamorphoses* 8, and the anonymous *Moretum* may stand as examples. It may seem rash to challenge comparison with Horace's *Hoc erat in votis*, but in one respect Juvenal is more sophisticated than his model. We do not feel that beans and greasy greens are what Horace really enjoyed dining upon; this is picturesquely coarse fare which he condescends, *de haut en bas*, to consume (*Serm*. 2.6.63f.). Juvenal is more like Elizabeth David writing about French country cooking; his view is that the best country food is genuinely delicious, and he devotes fourteen lines to a loving account of it (the apples especially are described in the tones of a connoisseur). Then he adds (77–81):

haec olim nostri iam luxuriosa senatus
cena fuit. Curius parvo quae legerat horto
ipse focis brevibus ponebat holuscula, quae nunc
squalidus in magna fastidit conpede fossor, 80
qui meminit calidae sapiat quid volva popinae.

[Such was once the dinner, already quite luxurious, of our senate. Curius himself would put on his small hearth the modest vegetables he had picked in his little garden, though they are now scorned by the dirty ditcher in his heavy chains, who remembers the taste of the haggis in the steamy cookshop.]

The ditcher despises such a plain dinner, but the ditcher is wrong; Juvenal understands the true culinary refinement. This is the kind of liking for what the country can offer that we would expect a city dweller genuinely to feel. Juvenal's attitude is both more sophisticated than Horace's and more honest; the great respect in which Horace's poem is held should not blind us to the notes of falsity that it contains. By contrast, Juvenal's most relaxed and tolerant satire breathes a spirit of modest country-gentlemanliness that does indeed recall *Aeneid* 8.

In the same satire (11.86–9) an evocation of ancient simplicity is created poetically, through the shape of the verse.

cognatorum aliquis titulo ter consulis atque
castrorum imperiis et dictatoris honore
functus ad has epulas solito maturius ibat
erectum domito referens a monte ligonem.

[A kinsman who had thrice borne the title of consul, who had commanded the army and held the office of dictator would come home to such a feast earlier than usual, bringing back his spade erect from the conquered hill.]

The sonorous amplitude of line 87 is matched by the culminating line, 89, held, in the grand manner, between a noun and its epithet. The sense of the two lines also corresponds: just as the farmer has once been a general and a dictator, so now he is 'conquering' the mountain and holding his spade majestically like a spear or standard. The dignity of labour is rather splendidly brought out by the 'noble' verse construction.

'Nunc modus hic agri nostro non sufficit horto' ('now this portion of ground is not enough for our garden'), Juvenal writes in his fourteenth satire (172), echoing the sentiments of Horace's *Satire* 2.6 and the language of its first line:[8] 'Hoc erat in votis: *modus agri* non ita magnus/*hortus* ubi ...' ('This was what I prayed for: a portion of ground, not so very big, where a garden ...'). This suggestion of the Horatian mood gives a sort of glow to Juvenal's tone. Here his picture of country simplicity skirts the edges of sentimentality, but perhaps just avoids it (14.166–71):

> saturabat glebula talis
> patrem ipsum turbamque casae, qua feta iacebat
> uxor et infantes ludebant quattuor, unus
> vernula, tres domini; sed magnis fratribus horum
> a scrobe vel sulco redeuntibus altera cena   170
> amplior et grandes fumabant pultibus ollae.

[A little plot like this used to feed the father himself and the crowd in his cottage, where his wife would be lying pregnant and four children playing, one slave, three free; but when their big brothers came back from ditch or furrow, there would be another, larger dinner for them, and great pots steaming with porridge.]

'Turbamque casae' prevents idealisation, suggesting the crowdedness and maybe too the noisiness of the family home. The lines that follow are exceedingly plain and factual. A touch of irony enters, however, when Juvenal calls infants 'domini'; perhaps he is already beginning to look at the household from a child's-eye view, as he does in the next two and a half lines. '*Magnis* fratribus', '*grandes* ... ollae' – these things are big and splendid only from an infantine viewpoint; and the slight shift of tone is nicely and economically achieved.

A little further on Juvenal exhibits a control of tone on a larger scale. First we hear the voice of the rustic past:

> 'vivite contenti casulis et collibus istis,
> o pueri,' Marsus dicebat et Hernicus olim   180
> Vestinusque senex, 'panem quaeramus aratro,
> qui satis est mensis: laudant hoc numina ruris,
> quorum ope et auxilio gratae post munus aristae
> contingunt homini veteris fastidia quercus.'

['Live content with these cottages and hills, my lads,' the Marsian, Hernican or Vestinian patriarch used once to say; 'let us seek by the plough

[8] Cf. *Sat.* 14. 140ff., on coveting your neighbour's land, the subject of Horace's *Serm.* 2.6.8ff.

bread to suffice our board. This the country gods approve, through whose
aid and support, since the welcome gift of corn, man is able to look down
upon the acorn, once his food.']

Juvenal is simultaneously evoking both a rural and a poetic past, for
we have here the spirit of Horace and Virgil. The Augustan poets
loved to praise the dour peoples of the Apennines, the tough backbone
of the old Italy; the Marsians were a particular favourite. *Georgics* 2,
for instance (167–9):[9]

haec genus acre virum, Marsos pubemque Sabellam
adsuetumque malo Ligurem Volscosque verutos
extulit

[Italy has brought forth a vigorous race of men, Marsians, the Sabine
stock, the Ligurians accustomed to hardship and the Volscians with their
pikes.]

Juvenal's old man speaks with a sort of quiet exaltation; we may note
the 'o' in the vocative 'o pueri',[10] and another Virgilian touch, the
'numina ruris'. The old man tells us, as Virgil tells us at the beginning
of the *Georgics*, that the gods have taught us to disdain the primitive
life of acorn eating.[11] As in *Satire* 11, a kind of country-gentlemanliness is the ideal; the noble simplicity with which the old man speaks
is, as it were, the voice of the Horatian sermo at its best; which is not
a primitive voice.

Then comes the contrast (14.189–93):

haec illi veteres praecepta minoribus; at nunc
post finem autumni media de nocte supinum   190
clamosus iuvenem pater excitat: 'accipe ceras,
scribe, puer, vigila, causas age, perlege rubras
maiorum leges . . .'

[These were the precepts which those men of old gave their descendants;
but now, when autumn is over, the clamouring father rouses his sleeping
son after midnight: 'Get your tablets, write, boy, stay awake, work at
your cases, read well the red-lettered laws of our ancestors . . .']

A couple of brusque monosyllables at the end of line 189 jerk us back

---

[9] Cf. Horace *Carm.* 3. 5. 9: 'Marsus et Apulus' as types of the good old Italian. Virgil
Geo. 2. 167 is echoed by Juvenal at *Sat.* 3. 169.

[10] There is a hint of oxymoron in the juxtaposition of the grand 'o' and the modest
'pueri', but it is an oxymoron without satire in it. The delicate blend of the stately and
the simple, a kind of pastoral majesty, is not far from the tone we catch occasionally in
the *Eclogues*; e.g. 'pascite ut ante boves, pueri; summittite tauros' ('Feed your oxen as
before, lads; put your bulls to the yoke') (1.45); 'claudite iam rivos, pueri; sat prata
biberunt' ('Close the channels now, lads; the meadows have drunk enough') (3. 111).

[11] Evander's speech at *Aen.* 8. 314ff. carries a similar messgae.

to a satiric from almost an epic tone. In line 190f. the rhythm moves from spondaic to dactylic, then from heterodyne to homodyne; and when the modern father speaks, it is in a series of small sharp commands. Juvenal is deliberately aiming for drabness here: an unadorned 'puer' (the very word one would use to address a slave) replaces the countryman's 'o pueri', and whereas the countryman's language was rounded out with several relative clauses, the modern father uses no subordinate clause of any kind until line 197. Apart from the grand and generalised 'vivite' with which he begins, the countryman uses no imperatives at all, and his 'quaeramus' breathes a spirit of cooperation and mutual effort; the modern father's speech seems at first to be nothing but imperatives. The countryman's address is unspecific; he speaks as the voice of ancestral wisdom, and he advises rather than commands; the modern father nags and frets at a particular luckless individual. This is not one of the high points of Juvenal's poetry, but what should strike us – and what few other Roman poets can rival – is such assured and intelligent control in a fairly ordinary passage of verse. And Juvenal's work is full of such minor pleasures.

2

The lines which Dryden quoted to show that Virgil could have been a sharper satirist than Horace or Juvenal are these (*Ecl.* 3.26f.):

> *non tu, in triviis, indocte, solebas,*
> *stridenti, miserum, stipula, disperdere, carmen?*

[Ignorant fellow, used you not at the crossroads to murder a wretched tune on a squeaking straw?]

The curious punctuation is Dryden's own, to show that Virgil 'has given almost as many lashes, as he has written Syllables'. Milton's imitation of Virgil (*Lycidas* 123f.) –

> their lean and flashy songs
> Grate on their scrannel pipes of wretched straw

– reproduces the harsh, mean sounds of his model, but what Dryden admires in the Latin lines is more than mere sound; those seven commas bring out the intensity, the concentration with which Virgil writes. We are in the area where technique goes beyond simple competence or experience and shades into what (for want of a better word) we may call inspiration. Expressive sound and verbal concentration – these are qualities which seem to be at the very heart of poetry; and these are qualities, Dryden judges, which Juvenal supplies, while in

Horace they are manifestly deficient: 'We cannot deny, that *Juvenal* was the greater poet, I mean in Satire.'

Juvenal sometimes uses sound and metrical speed to reinforce his satiric message (6.272f.):

testiculos, postquam coeperunt esse bilibres,
tōnsōris tāntūm dāmnō răpĭt Hēlĭŏdōrŭs.

[After the testicles have begun to weigh two pounds, Heliodorus whips them off, and only the barber loses.]

The doctor's sudden snip is conveyed by the sudden movement from spondees to dactyls. Another passage (15.77–9) reverses this pattern:

labitur hic quidam nimia formidine cursum
prāēcĭpĭtāns căpĭturque. ast illum in plurima sectum
frusta et particulas . . .

[Hereupon one man, rushing to get away with an excess of fear, slips and is caught. He is cut up into a great many bits and pieces . . .]

The speed of the dactyls is enhanced by the echo '-cipit- . . . capit'. We shall find other examples of Juvenal using monumental or elegant sonorities for certain particular purposes. But far more commonly his mastery of the hexameter exhibits itself in a distribution of words in relation to both the line and the sentence structure, so that an important word, a paraprosdokian, an aside or a new idea is placed where it is most effective. Constantly the verse form is exploited to convey the feeling of a speaking voice, urgent, vigorous, witty, cogent, bitter. Boissier's description of the nature of declamation – 'the habit of writing as if one were speaking and being heard' (p. 233) – is especially true of Juvenal. It is often remarked that Juvenal is much less forthcoming about himself than the other Roman satirists, but this, though true, can be misleading. What he does give us, through his distinctive voice and manner, is a forceful sense of personality as outwardly perceived. And that, after all, is how we perceive most people, especially perhaps those who make the most immediately vivid impression upon us: we see the external character, not the inner man.

To demonstrate the range and flexibility of Juvenal's use of the hexameter would require much space. Perhaps it may be sufficient to suggest that even the most famous Juvenalian tags gain from being read in metre and in context. For example (6.347f. (O.31f.)):

'pone seram, cohibe.' sed quis custodiet ipsos
custodes?

['Bar the doors, keep her inside.' But who shall guard the guards themselves?]

The change of voice after the first three words is marked by the change from dactyls to spondees, and from brusque imperatives to a more flowing sentence. Juvenal cuts in quietly, as it were; and he also delays the climactic word 'custodes' until the start of the new line, where it will fall with most force. Similarly in *Satire* 10:

> *nam qui dabat olim*
> *imperium, fasces, legiones, omnia, nunc se*
> *continet atque duas tantum res anxius optat,*   80
> *panem et circenses. 'perituros audio multos.'*
> *'nil dubium, magna est fornacula.' 'pallidulus mi*
> *Bruttidius meus ad Martis fuit obvius aram;*
> *quam timeo, victus ne poenas exigat Aiax*
> *ut male defensus: curramus praecipites et,*   85
> *dum iacet in ripa, calcemus Caesaris hostem.*
> *sed videant servi . . .*

[The people, who once gave power, authority, legions, everything, now restrict themselves and long eagerly for just two things, bread and games. 'I hear many will die.' 'Sure to; the furnace is a big one.' 'At the altar of Mars I came upon my friend Bruttidius looking a little pale; I am afraid that the defeated Ajax may take vengeance for being badly defended. Let us run in haste and trample on Caesar's enemy, while he lies on the bank. But make sure the slaves see . . .']

The famous 'panem et circenses' is delayed to the end of a long sentence, its simple concrete completeness contrasted with the abstract, incomplete list that precedes it, 'imperium, fasces, legiones, omnia'. Then comes a change of tone; the sentences become short and furtive, their informal, colloquial character stressed by the juxtaposed diminutives 'fornacula' and 'pallidulus' (the understatement in 'pallidulus' is superbly sinister). 'Calcemus Caesaris hostem' is expressed with vigour, almost with grandeur; but ironically so, for the two gentlemen kick with the vigour of cowardice. The phrase marks a minor climax, and Juvenal might have made the speaker end with it; accordingly, there is a sly air of afterthought when he adds a new idea, 'sed videant servi', a brilliantly humiliating reversal of the more natural theme of 'not in front of the servants'.[12]

Especially interesting from our point of view are those places where satiric, declamatory effect shades most obviously into the 'poetic', in the old-fashioned sense of that word. Many Latin poets saw the effectiveness of occasionally placing a sharp stop immediately after the first word of a new line; we have already examined two examples of this device.[13] Both Catullus and Lucretius exploit its rhetorical force, but it is to Juvenal, the satirist, that we must look to see it used

---

[12] Cf. *Sat.* 9. 102ff.
[13] Catullus 68. 20; Lucretius 1. 393. See above, pp. 89f., 129.

'poetically' in the creation of a visual picture. His lines on the death of Hannibal are famous (10.163–6):

finem animae, quae res humanas miscuit olim,
non gladii, non saxa dabunt nec tela, sed ille
Cannarum vindex et tanti sanguinis ultor   165
anulus.

[Not swords, not stones or spears shall put an end to the life of this man who once threw human affairs into confusion, but that punisher for Cannae and avenger of so much blood, a little ring.]

The diminutive 'anulus' and the sudden isolated dactylic word after all those monumental spondees impress upon us the physical littleness of the ring; to think, Juvenal is saying, that so small an object could end so great a life. Less rhetorically splendid, perhaps, but still more effective visually is a metrically very similar passage in *Satire* 11:

        hic tamen idem   25
ignorat quantum ferrata distet ab arca
sacculus.

[Yet this same man does not know how different from an iron chest is a purse.]

The change of metrical movement emphasises the difference between the great iron-bound chest and the little purse (a diminutive again).[14] The similarity between these two passages extends even to the little conjunctions and pronouns ('sed ille', 'hic tamen idem'); the poet seems to be momentarily marking time, or pausing to gather breath, before the big spondaic line is declaimed.

Juvenal had a fondness for ending sentences with a fourth-foot dactyl, commonly placing upon the last word an indignant or scornful emphasis (7.90, 13.191f.):

quod non dant proceres, dabit histrio.   90

[What noblemen do not give, an actor will give.]

        vindicta
nemo magis gaudet quam femina.

[No one enjoys vengeance more than a woman.]

He will even do this in two consecutive lines (15.159–61):

---

[14] The effect of *Sat.* 10. 166 is, so to speak, distributed between two passages in *Sat.* 11, for at 11.42f. we read, 'talibus a dominis post cuncta novissimus exit/anulus, . . .' ('With such possessors the last thing to go, after everything, is the ring'). Here 'everything' and the little ring form a contrast.

parcit

cognatis maculis similis fera. quando leoni   160
fortior eripuit vitam leo?

[One beast spares another with spots like its own. When has a stronger
lion ever taken the life of the weaker?]

The effect may simultaneously be one of climax and of paraprosdokian
(6.50f.):

paucae adeo Cereris vittae contingere dignae,   50
quarum non timeat pater oscula.

[So few women are there worthy to touch Ceres' fillets, or whose kisses
their fathers would not fear.]

Or the fourth-foot dactyl may be part of some larger effect (6.185–7):

nam quid rancidius quam quod se non putat ulla   185
formosam nisi quae de Tusca Graecula facta est,
de Sulmonensi mera Cecropis?

[For what could be more disgusting than the fact that no woman thinks
herself handsome unless she has turned from a Tuscan into a Greekling,
from a woman of Sulmo into a pure Cecropid?]

In the second of these lines Italy and Greece are juxtaposed: spondee
against dactyl; 'Tuscus', an adjective with ancient, honourable associations, against the contemptuous diminutive 'Graeculus'. The pattern
is then repeated on a larger scale in the next line: the slow syllables
of 'Sulmonensi' contrast with the thin, trivial sound of 'mera Cecropis',
made still thinner by the rising note of the declaimer's querulous
question. We recall that Sulmo was the place of which Ovid wrote
with such affection: his 'patria', his home. 'Sulmonensi', then, res-
onates with warm, sentimental patriotic associations; 'Cecropis',
meaning 'Attic', is on the other hand a piece of fancy diction, Cecrops
being a mythological king of Athens. Thus metre, diction and word
order work together in the service of the satiric message.

Sometimes Juvenal fills that fourth foot with a trisyllable; sometimes he ends with a shorter word: 'fructus amicitiae magnae cibus'
(5.14) ('The reward for your grand friendship is food'). The littleness
of the word 'cibus' contrasts with the ironically asserted greatness of
the friendship; the contrast is an abstract one on both sides, for it is
the paltriness of food as a reward rather than the smallness of the
portion that is at issue here, but the abstract idea seems to be straining, as it were, towards a concrete realisation. In *Satire* 13 the little
dissyllable accompanies a picture that is fully concrete and particular.
Now Juvenal has an idiosyncratic taste for bizarre or grotesque

vignettes which intrude into his satire with a delightful incongruity: the great fish fattening beneath the ice of Maeotis and emerging torpid into the Pontic Sea; the elephant shedding his precious tooth in a Nabataean glade,[15] or fetched from among dusky tribes and grazing amid those Italian trees and fields which Turnus and his Rutulians had once known; the wrinkled mother monkey with pendulous cheeks, where Numidia spreads its shadowy forests; sea-monsters and mermen.[16] In *Satire* 13 it is the pygmy's turn:

> *ad subitas Thracum volucres nubemque sonoram*
> *Pygmaeus parvis currit bellator in armis,*
> *mox inpar hosti raptusque per aera curvis*
> *unguibus a saeva fertur grue.*   170

[The Pygmy warrior rushes out in his little arms to meet the sudden onset and noisy cloud of Thracian birds, but soon, unequal to his foe, he is snatched up by curved talons and borne through the air by the savage crane.]

The small squeaky word 'grue' is, as ever, part of the declamatory effect, but it also emphasises, by its form and position, the modest size of the birds and thus the tiny scale of the whole scene. Sir Walter Raleigh saw the force of concluding an orotund sentence with 'narrow words' when he ended his famous apostrophe of Death, 'Thou hast drawn together the far-fetched greatness, all the pride, cruelty, and ambition of man, and covered it all over with these two narrow words, *Hic jacet.*' As declamation this is superb; but it is to Juvenal that we must look to see this technique serving a pictorial imagination and a lively, idiosyncratic fantasy.

'Aspice', 'respice' ('look') – such words are frequent in Juvenal. As de Decker demonstrated, these imperatives form a part of declamatory technique and help to shape the structure of the argument. 'Accipe', 'cognosce', 'primo fige loco'; in such ways Juvenal introduces the rhetorical figure of 'propositio'. But a word like 'aspice' goes further than this; it is his constant habit to think in pictures. More exactly, he likes to extract one or two details out of the picture, and give us these. Just how rooted a habit this is with him can be seen from some comparatively dull passages, when he is just, as it were, ticking over. Instead of saying 'women wrestlers' he seizes upon two items of their equipment (6.246f.): 'endromidas Tyrias et femineum ceroma/quis nescit ... ?' ('Who does not know of athletes' cloaks of purple and wrestlers' oil used by women?'). Instead of simply telling us that women pay to copulate with actors, he watches the actor's pin being undone

---

[15] 'Et quos [sc. dentes] deposuit Nabataeo belua saltu', a line of remote and evocative sound.
[16] *Sat.* 4. 42–4; 11. 126; 12. 103–5; 10. 192–6; 14. 283.

(6.73): 'solvitur his magno comoedi fibula' ('They pay well, and the actor's pin is undone for them'). Or (a finer line) instead of writing 'if you are reluctant', he gives us (14.325), 'haec quoque si rugam trahit extenditque labellum' ('If this too draws a furrow on your brow and pushes out your lip').

This method of presentation, then, is almost a matter of routine with him; it is a technique that we could well imagine another satirist adopting. Yet his use of it is outstandingly imaginative and inventive; again and again he zooms in like a camera upon some odd, revealing patch of reality that we feel nobody but he would have noticed (6.457–9).

> *nil non permittit mulier sibi, turpe putat nil,*
> *cum viridis gemmas collo circumdedit et cum*
> *auribus extentis magnos commisit elenchos.*

[There is nothing a woman does not allow herself, nothing she thinks shameful, when she has surrounded her neck with green jewels and attached great pendants to her stretched ears.]

The lines are characteristically dynamic – the women does not *wear* jewels, she *surrounds* her neck with them and *commits* them to her ears – but the brilliance is above all in the word 'extentis': we see the flesh of the lobe pulled downwards by the weight of the pearl attached to it. The accuracy, the minuteness of Juvenal's vision are in themselves deeply impressive; but his mastery lies not in visual awareness alone, but in the selection of the significant and penetrative detail. The distortion of the lobes exposes the futility of the woman's pretension: her ostentation is, to a clear-headed spectator, quite literally 'turpis', ugly. The kind of vision that we might expect from a novelist or a poet is not, when we encounter it in Juvenal, something distinct and different from the satirist's eye, but identical with it.

He focuses again on a woman's ear in *Satire* 11. 186–9, though this time with a different purpose:

> *nec, prima si luce egressa reverti*
> *nocte solet, tacito bilem tibi contrahat uxor*
> *umida suspectis referens multicia rugis*
> *vexatasque comas et voltum auremque calentem.*

[And do not let your wife arouse your silent rage, if she is wont to leave at dawn and return at night, coming back with her fine clothes damp and suspiciously wrinkled, her hair disturbed and her face and ear hot.]

Most of the evidences of guilt – the dishevelled hair, the damp and crumpled clothing – though vivid, are obvious enough;[17] who but Ju-

---

[17] But the hint of personification in 'vexatas' ('her troubled hair') is clever.

venal, though, would have thought of ending with 'aurem calentem'? And here too the detail is not only minute but penetrative; it gets us under the skin of the cuckolded husband, whose agonised suspicions direct him to every telltale sign, however tiny. In *Satire* 6. 572–4, the poet warns against superstitious women:

illius occursus etiam vitare memento,
in cuius manibus ceu pinguia sucina tritas
cernis ephemeridas . . .

[Remember too to avoid meeting the woman in whose hands you see worn almanacs, like balls of resinous amber.]

'Cernis', 'you see'; once more we encounter the investigative eye, which notices not just the almanacs, but how worn they are: the obsessive woman has been neurotically fiddling with them, like more conventional ladies with their balls of amber. The speed with which another woman changes husbands is not directly asserted but demonstrated to us by two pictures: her wedding veil is worn out; and when she returns to the home that she has earlier forsaken, the bed still bears the imprint of her body. The exaggeration is gross, perhaps intolerably so; yet it is to some extent compensated for by the urgency of imagination that gives us that still dented bed. And the economy of expression is remarkable:

permutatque domos et flammea conterit: inde   225
avolat et spreti repetit vestigia lecti.

[She changes houses and wears out her bridal veil: then she flies off, and makes again for her own imprint on the bed she has scorned.]

Sometimes Juvenal's pictorial details seem to serve no satiric purpose, and to be simply the outcome of an alert enjoyment of the external world: the new-born baby, for instance, wailing and 'adhuc a matre rubentem' ('still red from the womb', 6.196); or the rope tightening as the bullock resists his handler (12.5); at other times the picture acquires a force that we might be tempted to call symbolic, were this not too portentous and systematic a word for Juvenal's method. Persicus is told not to expect the displays of dancing girls when he comes to dine; such things may be left to the man 'qui Lacedaemonium pytismate lubricat orbem' (11.175) ('who makes circles of Laconian marble slippery by spitting wine upon them'). A whole way of life, expensive and vulgar, is summoned up in a single image by the ironic collocation of imported marble and spewed out wine; an irony admirably reinforced by the pompous and pretentious diction.

Despite his habit of fastening upon details, Juvenal is also expert

at envisaging a complete scene. His picture of the lady musician is
sparkling in a double sense (6.380–4):

> *organa semper*   380
> *in manibus, densi radiant testudine tota*
> *sardonyches, crispo numerantur pectine chordae*
> *quo tener Hedymeles operas dedit: hunc tenet, hoc se*
> *solatur gratoque indulget basia plectro.*

[Musical instruments are always in her hands, her sardonyx rings glitter
thickly all over the sounding-board, the strings are struck by the quivering quill with which soft Hedymeles has performed: she clings to it,
consoles herself with it, and lavishes kisses on the dear plectrum.]

Besides their visual inventiveness the lines are splendidly alive in
their depiction of arty gesture and behaviour; the scene is worthy of
Jane Austen. Indeed, Juvenal's talent for high comedy has perhaps
been underrated. In *Satire* 2 he displays to us a group of effeminates,
each posturing in a different attitude, one regarding himself in a
mirror, another swearing by Juno, a third enclosing his long locks in
a golden hairnet and drinking from a vessel shaped like a male organ,
while yet another makes himself up:

> *ille supercilium madida fuligine tinctum*
> *obliqua producit acu pingitque trementis*
> *attollens oculos; vitreo bibit ille priapo . . .*   95

[One man, with needle slantwise, extends the line of his eyebrow with
damp soot and raising his fluttering eyes, paints them; another drinks
from a glass phallus . . .]

The feeling for detail is still there – the lifted eyes, the slanting
movement of the needle; so too is the feel for significance. The pose in
which the transvestite is caught and the words that Juvenal uses –
'supercilium, 'tinctum', 'obliqua', 'trementis' – all work towards an
impression of feeble, fluttering affectation. This poem, indeed, is much
concerned with appearances, true and false. 'Frontis nulla fides,' he
has said (2.8) ('There is no trusting a man's face'); but now, behind
closed doors, man is indeed as he appears. In a later poem Juvenal
gives through the mouth of Naevolus a more sinister picture of an
effeminate (9.95): 'nam res mortifera est inimicus pumice levis' ('For
an enemy smoothed with pumice is a death-bearing thing'). To regard
'pumice levis' as merely a periphrastic way of saying 'homosexual'
would be to misunderstand the nature of Juvenal's sensibility: it is by
the man's smooth, scraped flesh that we know his vengefulness.

Juvenal's wonderful eye for detail, for focusing upon precise and yet
expressive actuality, is combined in his poetry with fantasy which, as

we shall see again later, is not contradictory to his literalism but the reverse side of the same coin. It is because the experience of his senses is so vivid that he can momentarily make us see or smell what is not there. 'My whole page smells of man,' says Martial (10.4.10), and we enjoy the vigorous, picturesque turn of speech; but when Juvenal uses the same metaphor, we sense a poetic power of a wholly different order. In *Satire* 14 the modern father urges his son to devote himself to money making, and adds,

> nec te fastidia mercis
> ullius subeant ablegandae Tiberim ultra,
> neu credas ponendum aliquid discriminis inter
> unguenta et corium: lucri bonus est odor ex re
> qualibet. 205

[Let no distaste come upon you for a trade that must be banished to the far side of the Tiber, and do not suppose that any distinction should be made between unguents and hides: the smell of profit is good whatever it comes off].

In such a context we can almost begin to believe that profit has its own odour and that we can smell it clinging to the merchant's garments.

In *Satire* 10. 92–4 Juvenal asks the reader whether he would like to have Sejanus' powers of patronage, and

> tutor haberi
> principis angusta Caprearum in rupe sedentis
> cum grege Chaldaeo . . .

[to be regarded as the guardian of an emperor sitting on the narrow crag of Capri with a herd of astrologers]

Juvenal gives an impression that reminds one of those photographs of gannets crammed on to the cliffs of the Orkneys: a great gaggle of astrologers squeezed on to a rock that has barely enough space to hold them. This is a wild hyperbole, and yet it should be effective to anyone who has seen the extraordinarily narrow and precipitous promontory upon which Tiberius built his palace at the eastern extremity of Capri.[18] Juvenal's fantastic picture seems for an instant persuasive because, for all its preposterousness, it is inseparable from an animated perception of the real world.

Satire 6 includes a brilliantly rhetorical paragraph denouncing the tiresome Hellenism affected by some women. They pour forth all their joys and sorrows and secrets in Greek; they even copulate in a Greek

[18] The picture is inspired by a play upon words, Capri being, according to its name, the island of goats.

style. And suppose we allow young girls their sillinesses; what of the woman who is still talking in Greek at the age of eighty-five?[19]

> non est hic sermo pudicus
> in vetula. quotiens lascivum intervenit illud
> ζωὴ καὶ ψυχή, modo sub lodice relictis   195
> uteris in turba. quod enim non excitat inguen
> vox blanda et nequam? digitos habet.

[This language is not decent in an old woman's mouth. Whenever that lascivious 'my life and soul' slips in, you are using in public words that have just been left under the counterpane. What groin does not an alluring, dissolute voice stimulate? It has fingers.]

The power of these lines can only be fully appreciated in the context of the massive rhetorical momentum that has been built up from the opening of the paragraph. 'Graecula . . . Graece . . . Graece . . . Graece . . .' – these repetitions have accumulated such a weight of scorn and indignation that three words of the hated tongue are forced on to the page. Their appearance is the more remarkable when we remember that Horace had condemned the use of Greek phrases in satura; and Persius had of course followed Horace. In their setting these words – simple enough words, though their odiously cooing vowels are well chosen – have such impetus that they acquire a solid, physical presence: they should have been left under the bedclothes. A seductive voice can give a man an erection, Juvenal continues, and again that voice springs into physical solidity, for he adds two words which give his sentence an appalling concreteness. 'Digitos habet'; and we suddenly see those fingers playing with the man's genitals. The shocking fantasy that makes a mere voice accessible to the senses of sight and touch is not the product of a mind half detached from reality. On the contrary: we sense the tremendous impetus needed to thrust what is impalpable into physical embodiment; which is to give to the visible and tactile world a great weight and importance.

Sometimes Juvenal flashes momentarily across our consciousness an absurd or irrelevant picture which is perhaps the more memorable for being nonsensical. In *Satire* 7, 226f. he refers to the boys in school,

> cum totus decolor esset
> Flaccus et haereret nigro fuligo Maroni.

[with Horace discoloured all over and soot clinging to a blackened Virgil.]

What he means, in prosaic terms, is that the boys' copies of the school

---

[19] *Sat.* 6. 193–7. 'Relictis' looks corrupt, but emendation is not likely to affect the essentials of my argument.

classics are grimy with use and the smoke of the lamps; but his way
of putting it is such that for a second we see Virgil and Horace
themselves, those noble Augustans, discoloured and covered with
smuts. Friedlaender's suggestion that Juvenal was thinking of busts
of these great men set up in the schoolroom spoils the joke and misses
the fantastic and yet particularising character of this poet's imagination. In *Satire* 13 he ironically describes the blessings of the Golden
Age: there was no grim Pluto in the underworld, no wheel of Ixion, no
vulture feeding upon Tityos, 'sed infernis hilares sine regibus umbrae'
(52) ('but the shades were merry, with no kings in the underworld').
The extraordinary epithet 'hilares' gives us for an instant a grotesque
picture of the shades having a merry old time down there in the gloom,
and this picture by its very incongruity reinforces our awareness of
the underworld's proper bleakness. Juvenal perhaps recalled Charon's
sombre understatement in *Aeneid* 6. 392f. –

nec vero Alciden me sum laetatus euntem
accepisse lacu

[nor indeed did I rejoice to take Hercules as a passenger on the lake]

– where again the powerfully incongruous 'laetatus' emphasises the
ferryman's dourness. The technique may call to mind the signs one
sees on leaving French and German towns, which give the name of
the place with a diagonal stroke through it; for whatever reason, the
name is more forcefully impressed upon us when we see it crossed out
then when we see it undefaced.

Juvenal's imagination is perhaps at its highest when he unites
fantasy and literal clarity in a single phrase or image. This combination of powers blazes out in the middle of a long sentence in *Satire*
4, where he describes the gathering of Domitian's councillors:

Montani quoque venter adest abdomine tardus,
et matutino sudans Crispinus amomo
quantum vix redolent duo funera, saevior illo
Pompeius tenui iugulos aperire susurro,   110
et qui vulturibus servabat viscera Dacis
Fuscus marmorea meditatus proelia villa,
et cum mortifero prudens Veiiento Catullo . . .

[That great paunch Montanus came, slowed by his belly, and Crispinus
reeking of balsam, in the morning, almost as strongly as the perfume of
two funerals, and Pompeius, more savage than he at slitting throats with
a thin whisper, and Fuscus who thought over battles in his marble villa
and was keeping his guts safe for the vultures of Dacia, and careful
Veiiento along with deadly Catullus . . .]

As a whole, these lines are richly and variously inventive. 'Montani venter' is a pleasant parody of epic metonymy which has the additional advantage of focusing our view upon the feature of the man that is at once most outwardly conspicuous and most revealing of his inner character. The oozy scent of Crispinus is well conveyed by the slow spondees of the second line, while in the third line the quickening of the rhythm presses forward to a climax in the unexpected word 'funera', with the emphasis and irony resting on Juvenal's favourite fourth-foot dactyl. The idea is as gripping as the expression: on a literal level the poet is alluding to the custom of perfuming corpses and their pyres, but in the sardonic context it is difficult to avoid the darkly paradoxical implication that the sweet, sticky smell of Crispinus is itself the smell of death:

> A little sickness in the air
> From too much fragrance everywhere.

The two nobly constructed lines devoted to Fuscus splendidly contrast contemplation with action, home with a distant land, death and squalor with cool luxury ('marmorea' is a finely suggestive word). In view of the calculating self-preservation of this gang of sycophants, the irony in 'servabat' is superb; while in the last of the lines quoted the collocation of the two adjectives 'mortifero prudens' is brilliantly sinister. But the master stroke is in line 109f. The sound is marvellously suggestive, matching the horrid idea that the whisper of the informer – quiet, penetrating – is like the thin edge of the razor cutting through flesh. But indeed to say that the one thing 'is like' the other is a prosaic paraphrase, for in Juvenal's sentence the whisper and the razor are assimilated to one another and it is the whisper itself that slits the veins. We receive a memorably lifelike impression of Pompeius and his voice, but it is produced by a conception which is itself imaginative and fantastic.

Juvenal's procession of councillors was a parody of an equivalent catalogue in Statius' *Bellum Germanicum*. By chance a fragment of it has come down to us:

> *lumina; Nestorei mitis prudentia Crispi*
> *et Fabius Veiento; potentem signat utrumque*
> *purpura, ter memores implerunt nomina fastos;*
> *et prope Caesareae confinis Acilius aulae.*

> [. . . lights; the mild wisdom of Nestor-like Crispus, and Fabius Veiento (the purple marks each of them as important; thrice their names have filled the recording annals), and Acilius, close neighbour to Caesar's palace.]

Juvenal's lines are finer poetry than this, by any definition of poetry whatever, and we may well suspect that he could have outstripped

Statius in any genre that he had chosen to attempt. Nonetheless, we may be able to understand why so resourceful and imaginative a poet restricted himself to satura if we now turn to look at him in relation to his time.

3

The history of Roman poetry can almost be described as a perpetual struggle against having nothing to say. From one point of view it went in the republican period through a development similar to that of Greek literature, but in a shorter time: first come the epic poets, then an age of drama, then the deliberate Alexandrianism of Catullus' time. But from another viewpoint Latin literature originates in an age of decadence, when most poetic seams appeared to have been already worked out. In cultural terms as in political, the expansion of Rome meant her entry into the Hellenic sphere. Ennius himself – 'father Ennius' – emerges from his minor works as a Hellenistic man of letters, translator of the obscene epigrams of Sotades, adapter of the gastronomic poetry of Archestratus, and in his *Euhemerus* rationaliser of traditional religion. Nor is this surprising: born and bred in Calabria, speaking Greek as well as Latin and Oscan, Ennius was a native of greater Hellas. Macedon, Epirus, Egypt, even Judaea, were all hellenized sooner or later; how could Rome have escaped? Hellenic Italy stretched as far north as Naples; one hundred miles south of Rome, Greece began.

So while the first century and a half of Latin literature may look in one way like a roll-call of distinguished (if sometimes shadowy) names, one can also see it in another light, observing a succession of Greek genres being imported into Italy and failing to take lasting root. Certainly, that view of literary history which sees the Latin writers of the first century B.C. steadily and confidently colonising one Greek territory after another is, in the field of poetry at least, substantially misleading. When Accius, last of the tragedians, died in the seventies, the future of Latin poetry cannot have looked bright: an erudite elegance was all that was left. The neoteric style can again be viewed in two ways: as a self-conscious assumption of the Alexandrian manner, and as the emergence of the natural condition of poetry in a sophisticated Graeco-Roman society. Earlier Latin poets had been engaged in more or less artificial attempts to revive dead forms; the neoterics could claim to be working along the same lines as their Greek-speaking contemporaries.

The Augustan miracle could not have been predicted. But in the event Lucretius, the most eccentric figure in the history of Latin literature, showed Virgil, by first instinct a miniaturiser, the possibility of writing didactic poetry grander and yet subtler than the Greeks had ever achieved; and the experience of writing the *Georgics* gradually revealed the way to the 'civilised' epic poetry of the *Aeneid*.[20] Horace discovered in archaic lyric a new source for the Roman adapter, and found that Alcaeus at least could be beaten at his own game. Latin elegy transcended its Greek models and found new ways of talking about love. But the Augustan equilibrium was very fragile. Indeed, our talk of the 'Augustan age' is half a misnomer, since for the last quarter-century of Augustus' reign there was no poet of substance still active except Ovid, who was to be reminded in the bluntest way possible that he had stayed around too long.[21] Both Virgil and Horace were exceptionally unnatural writers (if that epithet may be used without disparagement); the sophisticated magnificence of the *Aeneid* is a *tour de force*, a virtual contradiction in terms which no one but Virgil could have brought off; and though Horace's *Odes* have been regarded by posterity as the classic embodiment of Augustan art, they are of all Augustan works perhaps the most untypical of their time. Horace laments the public indifference to his odes; Ovid exults in his own popularity. Lyric poetry did not 'belong' in Rome, and when Quintilian was looking for a second Roman lyricist to compare with the Greeks, he could think of no one except Caesius Bassus, for whom small enthusiasm was possible. And besides, the Augustan poets carried every genre they attempted to the point of technical perfection, epic, elegy, lyric, epistle. In Ovid the mechanics of the verse have reached such a degree of ease and smoothness that they almost dominate and become the subject of the poetry; elegy is already half on the way to self-parody. How could anyone solemnly lay claim to the passion of a Catullus or a Propertius after the *Amores*? How could anyone follow in the footsteps of Virgil or Horace without producing a feeble pastiche? The current of poetry seemed to have run into the sand.

In the forty years after the death of Ovid, a remarkably barren period for verse, we might expect to find literary men taking stock and

---

[20] The oddity of the *De Rerum Natura* is not widely enough realised. This is the first *genuinely* didactic poem since the fifth century; Aratus and his ilk no more intended to be practically useful as instructors than did Virgil. Lucretius sincerely desired to inform and expound, and the measure of his strangeness is that though his philosophical argument is far more impressive than Cicero's (or Seneca's), no Roman writer ever thought to cite him as a philosophical source. In its primary intention this great work was a total failure.

[21] Compare the 'Elizabethan age'. We too easily forget that the greater part of the queen's reign was one of the blankest periods for literature in all our history, and that Shakespeare in his greatest phase was at least as much a Jacobean as an Elizabethan. It was by political propaganda expressed through poetry that both Augustus and Elizabeth imposed upon posterity the idea of themselves as presiding geniuses of a culminating age. In this respect poets are indeed the unacknowledged legislators of the world.

asking themselves what the conditions might be for the production of great poetry. And so they did – or at least Velleius Paterculus did, and he is not a man whom we naturally regard as exceptional in originality or profundity of thought. He maintains that the greatest achievements in any one branch of literature have usually fallen within a small space of time. It was so in Greece, and the same holds true for Rome: the great period of Roman tragedy was around the time of Accius, of comedy in the age of Caecilius and Terence; with minor exceptions, the best historians, orators and poets were active within a single period of no longer than eighty years. If we look at painters, sculptors and grammarians, Velleius adds, we shall find the same pattern. Why should this be? Velleius' answer deserves quotation, because however great or small its truth, it is the view of a fairly ordinary literary gentleman of the time:

> Genius is fostered by emulation, and it is now envy, now admiration, which enkindles imitation, and, in the nature of things, that which is cultivated with the highest zeal advances to the highest perfection; but it is difficult to continue at the point of perfection, and naturally that which cannot advance must recede. And as in the beginning we are fired with the ambition to overtake those whom we regard as leaders, so when we have despaired of being able either to surpass or even to equal them, our zeal wanes with our hope; it ceases to follow what it cannot overtake, and abandoning the old field as though preempted, it seeks a new one. Passing over that in which we cannot be preeminent, we seek for some new object of our effort. (1.17, tr. F. W. Shipley (Loeb))

New forms of poetic expression were needed; but the Roman muse remained static and numb. 'Omnia iam vulgata,' Virgil complains in the *Georgics*; all the old mythological themes are trite (3.4–6):

> *quis aut Eurysthea durum*
> *aut inlaudati nescit Busiridis aras?* 5
> *cui non dictus Hylas puer . . . ?*

[Who does not know of unrelenting Eurystheus or the altars of unadmired Busiris? who has not told of the boy Hylas . . . ?]

A century later Martial is still making the same complaint (10.4.1–3):

> *Qui legis Oedipoden caligantemque Thyesten,*
> *Colchidas et Scyllas, quid nisi monstra legis?*
> *quid tibi raptus Hylas . . . ?*

[If you read of Oedipus and Thyestes in the darkness, of Colchian women and Scyllas, what are you reading but prodigies? What is the rape of Hylas to you . . .?]

However, epics, mythological or historical, were still ground out; and as the surviving examples show, competence was the most that could be expected in this genre. It is very striking that Statius should end his *Thebaid* by asking whether his work will endure and by noting its inferiority to the *Aeneid*. The pastoralist was expected, with a studied and ambivalent humility, to remark the slenderness of his verse, the satirist to speak self-deprecatingly of his 'Musa pedestris'; but the grander poet was required to project a confidence and pride to match the elevation of his style. Horace rounded off his third book of *Odes* by declaring that he had erected a monument loftier than the pyramids and more durable than bronze; Ovid concluded the *Metamorphoses* on a similar note. Virgil, writing under the shadow of Homer himself, allows the *Aeneid* to betray no hint that it may be unequal to its great models. He may have been privately tormented by self-doubt, and indeed he was, if we are to believe the anecdotes preserved in the ancient lives; but publicly he expects his account of Nisus and Euryalus to last as long as the Capitol; that is, for ever. Statius, however, with a modesty that more than a thousand years later was to inspire Dante to one of the most memorable moments in all the *Divine Comedy*, feels himself unequal to the epic pose; the burden of the past has become too great.

Martial contrasts the frigid artificiality of high poetry with the liveliness of his own humbler art (10.4.7–10):

> *quid te vana iuvant miserae ludibria chartae?*
>   *hoc lege, quod possit dicere vita 'meum est.'*
> *non hic Centauros, non Gorgonas Harpyiasque*
>   *invenies: hominem pagina nostra sapit.*   10

[Why does the empty nonsense of a wretched page please you? Read this, of which life could say, 'It is mine.' You will not find centaurs, gorgons or harpies here: my page smells of man.]

As he says elsewhere (4.49.3ff. and 10), the mythological writer is really more frivolous ('magis ludit') than the epigrammatist; and besides, he is unread. Pompous tragedies and epic battles smell of the schoolroom, where they spread despondency among boys and girls, but Martial's own poetry is sprinkled with 'Roman salt' (8.3.13ff.); it springs naturally from the Roman soil.

Martial's verse, for all its wit and occasional charm, is smallish beer; what hope for the more ambitious poet? The same question was to be asked again, and Velleius' analysis often quoted, in the eighteenth century, another period much exercised, as the Augustan and silver Latin ages had been, by the burden of the past and the difficulty of finding anything worth saying when so much had already been so consummately achieved by the great writers of earlier times.[22]

---

[22] On Velleius in the eighteenth century see W. J. Bate, p. 82f.

Eighteenth-century critics were particularly concerned about epic; as Dr Johnson said, this was by general consent the highest kind of poetry, and yet it was a form in which success, it seemed, was no longer possible of attainment. Or was it? Byron, whose literary attitudes make him in some respects the last of the eighteenth-century poets, was to produce his *Don Juan*, 'after *Paradise Lost* our second English epic' in Quiller-Couch's opinion; but this was of course an anti-epic, an 'epic Satire', in the poet's own words, which made fun of the old conventions (1.200f.).

> My poem's epic, and is meant to be
>   Divided in twelve books; each book containing,
> With love, and war, a heavy gale at sea,
>   A list of ships, and captains, and kings reigning,
> New characters; the episodes are three:
>   A panoramic view of hell's in training,
> After the style of Virgil and of Homer,
> So that my name of epic's no misnomer. . .
>
> I've got new mythological machinery,
> And very handsome supernatural scenery.

Here at last was something new in the epic line, but the poem's newness consisted in a parody of the genre to which it purported to belong.

If we look back again to Latin literature, do we not find a comparable process? It seems almost to be a literary law, once genres get worn out, that like the legendary serpent they turn round and devour themselves. Ovid's love poetry is half burlesque of love poetry; his *Metamorphoses* resist tidy categorisation, but here is certainly a mythological poem the aim of which is not to ennoble but to entertain, and the form of which shatters traditional epic unity into a dazzle of fragments. After Virgil there is only one epic poem (unless the *Metamorphoses* can be so described) of real conviction and imaginative power, Lucan's *Pharsalia*. This, like *Don Juan*, was the work of a romantic, cynical young man with the gift of exceptional speed and wit in the art of putting verses together; and it resembles *Don Juan* in this too, that it mounts an assault on the old epic assumptions – not indeed with Byron's ebullience but with a sort of sardonic remorselessness. His first lines announce his intention. 'Bella. . .,' he begins (Virgil had begun, 'Arma'); war is the epic poet's theme. But at once we receive a shock, for Lucan's war is not heroic but criminal: 'Bella per Emathios plus quam civilia campos/iusque datum sceleri. . .' ('Wars more than civil on the plains of Thessaly and legality granted to crime. . .'). Right at the start he announces to the reader that this is to be a work of bitter wit, for the first line contains the poem's first epigram: the war is 'more than civil' because it is fought between kinsmen, Pompey having been Caesar's son-in-law. This is also to be an epic without gods – no 'mythological machinery' – and without heroes: in the great battle of Book 7 there will not be a single *aristeia*. Like Byron, he might claim to have no stomach for 'the blaze Of conquest and its consequences, which Make epic poesy so rare and rich' (*Don Juan* 8.90).

Subsequent epic poets, writing on as though Lucan had never written, fell into a fatal falsity. But Lucan's own epic must be judged a failure as a whole. He is often cheap, often crude, sometimes absurd; but even purged of these vices, narrative poetry that is relentlessly bleak and ironic over thousands of lines could not fail to be wearisome. And yet Lucan seems at times close to Juvenal; many of his passages of moral denunciation could be mistaken for the work of his greater successor. To take one example almost at random (4. 373–8):

> o prodiga rerum
> luxuries numquam parvo contenta paratis
> et quaesitorum terra pelagoque ciborum   375
> ambitiosa fames et lautae gloria mensae,
> discite quam parvo liceat producere vitam
> et quantum natura petat.

[O luxury, prodigal of wealth, never content with what comes cheaply, and ambitious hunger for foods sought over land and sea, and pride in a smart table, learn how cheaply life may be maintained, and how little nature asks for.]

The two poets' use of *sententia* is sometimes similar. Here, from Lucan, is the end of Lentulus' speech pressing upon the defeated Pompey and his followers the fatal advice to rely upon Egypt (8. 452–5):

> 'nil pudet adsuetos sceptris: mitissima sors est
> regnorum sub rege novo.' non plura locutus
> inpulit huc animos. quantum, spes ultima rerum,
> libertatis habes! victa est sententia Magni.   455

['Those used to the sceptre shrink at nothing; the lot of kingdoms is easiest under a new king.' Without saying more he drove their spirits in this direction. O final hope of success, how great a freedom you have! Pompey's plan was defeated.]

And here, from Juvenal, is Montanus advising Domitian on his turbot (4. 134–6):

> 'argillam atque rotam citius properate, sed ex hoc
> tempore iam, Caesar, figuli tua castra sequantur.'   135
> vicit digna viro sententia.

['Hurry and bring clay and wheel; but from henceforth, Caesar, let potters accompany your camp.' The proposal, worthy of the man, won the day.]

In both cases a grandiose speech comes to an end, and there is an abrupt change of tone and pace as the poet rams home his epigrammatic comment behind it.

If Lucan has a satiric streak, Juvenal may conversely have an epic streak. That he owed something to Lucan is evident from a number of verbal echoes, but unlike the earlier poet, he did not make the error of trying to marry satiric tone to epic shape and scale. His achievement may appear all the more impressive if we see it as a remarkably brilliant solution to the problem of how to write poetry in an unpropitious age. Juvenal takes from Lucan his strange combination of grandeur and bitterness and pours it into a more suitable mould; at the same time he invents a new kind of satura that is not, like Persius', shackled to the memory of Horace. It has often been observed that Juvenal is in some respects the child of his time – that, for example, his rhetorical cast of thought and language is inevitable in a Roman of the imperial age – but it is equally important to realise that his poetry is strikingly different from anything that his contemporaries were producing. Paradoxically, he was unlike his time because he was the one man, apart from Martial, who understood what the times required of the would-be poet. We do not know, of course, that Juvenal's mind worked consciously along these lines; his escape from the silver poet's dilemma may have been instinctive. He himself advances two objections to writing a more glorious kind of poetry: the lack of the leisure and comfort needed for composition on the grandest scale, and the corruption of the times. Neither of these objections need be lightly dismissed. The exhaustion of the genres called for a new kind of poetry; the vices of Rome called for satire; Juvenal found a voice that answered to both the literary and the social circumstances of his age. Like Martial he might claim that his is a truly Roman poetry, with the smell of real life to it; and yet of his contemporaries the writer who comes closest to him is perhaps Tacitus. 'Nobis in arto et inglorius labor,' Tacitus says; the imperial historian's theme is constricted, his tale shabby. And yet Tacitus is the most poetic of historians (the debt to Virgil is obvious and unconcealed); and at the same time, by his dogged concentration on his grim subject-matter, he creates a kind of magnificent bleakness, an austere grandeur.[23] That grandeur is not attained in despite of the drabness and narrowness; the drabness and narrowness *are* the grandeur. In Juvenal too the grandiloquence is not at odds with the satire, or even separable from it; his is a kind of satire that is essentially grand both in style

---

[23] That, at least, is the effect intended. But it may be felt that Tacitus occasionally enjoys himself a little too much. And the same may be said of Juvenal.

and content. It is not simple accident that the two great writers working in the first half of the second century A.D. both chose to be nobly
ignoble; both realised their genius through a capacity to respond to
the necessities of their time.

The Victorian belief that the good artist must be a good man has
provoked a sharp reaction in this century, and it is often maintained
today that a writer's moral character has no bearing whatever on the
value of his work as literature. This view is as facile as the Victorian
one, and probably not much less false. Can a man be at once a great
poet, even in satire, and a mean spirit? The question is difficult; but
in the case of Juvenal the issue can be side-stepped, for it is not true,
as some critics suppose, that he is usually indifferent to all sufferings
except the shabby-genteel frustrations experienced by himself and his
class. A virtue of his grand style is that it enables him to achieve, as
one of his characteristic tones, a kind of magniloquent and scornful
pity. This tone is perhaps easier to illustrate than to define; its great
merit lies in its allowing him to express a restrained sympathy without
losing that certain hardness which is felt in his best poetry. Accordingly, this quality does not lie on the surface, and has been missed by
many readers, predisposed perhaps to regard Juvenal as a splendid
brute; but such lack of explicitness can be paralleled in other satiric
writing. Swift's *Modest Proposal* is rightly praised for 'its anger and
its compassion',[24] but the tone is one of relaxed callousness from end
to end, and the compassion is the more powerful for being unexpressed.
A similar moral can be applied to Juvenal; his pity is often most
effective when kept in check. *Satire* 15, on the other hand, with its
solemn headshaking over the cruelty of mankind, whom nature has
designed to be gentle in heart, aims obviously at a lofty moralism; but
the nobility rings hollow.[25]

In *Satire* 7 (27–9) Juvenal's attitude to poets is satirical, but not
straightforwardly so.

> *frange miser calamum vigilataque proelia dele,*
> *qui facis in parva sublimia carmina cella,*
> *ut dignus venias hederis et imagine macra.*

[Break your pen, poor creature, and destroy the battles that have kept
you awake, you who compose lofty strains in a small chamber, in the hope
of ending up worthy of ivy and a scrawny bust.]

In between the agitation of the first of these lines and the jeer of the
last comes a line of great beauty both in thought and sound. Its fine

---

[24] The phrase is from K. Williams's introduction to the Everyman edition of *A Tale
of a Tub and other Satires*, p. xxi.

[25] Much of the trouble lies in the subject-matter: cannibalism in Egypt is no doubt
deplorable, but Juvenal has chosen a theme that seems at once too easy and too far-
fetched. We feel that he has bought his moral superiority at a cheap rate.

simplicity after the restless dactyls that have preceded it creates a moment of stillness; we rest upon it briefly before the declamatory voice returns. Some readers may be reminded of Marlowe's Jew of Malta and his 'Infinite riches in a little room'. The English poet too was in a sense satirical; at least he put these words into the mouth of an evil and avaricious man. But there is a sort of splendour that remains, that escapes from the immediate context; someone who finds the words strongly evocative is not merely negligent of the setting in which they are placed. And Juvenal is constantly doing this. Often, it is true, the lines will allow some variation of emphasis. To take the present case, the reader may on one occasion believe in the quality of the neglected poet, while on another he may give an ironic inflection to the epithet 'sublimia' (perhaps even detect a pun, if we may imagine the man writing away in a garret); but it is a sign of largeness that there is room for some legitimate difference of interpretation. The important thing is the *possibility* of the words.

Sometimes the effect may be complicated by echoes of other poets (4.72–5).

> *vocantur*
> *ergo in consilium proceres, quos oderat ille,*
> *in quorum facie miserae magnaeque sedebat*
> *pallor amicitiae* 75

[So the chief men are summoned to advise, men whom he [i.e. Domitian] hated, and in whose faces abode the pallor of that wretched and great friendship.]

We cannot tell how much *Satire* 4 owes to Statius' *Bellum Germanicum*, but surely, even if these lines correspond to a similar scene in that poem, we cannot dismiss them simply as parody. These words have an authentic magnificence; indeed, coming with a special force after the smart, conversational manner of the lines preceding them, they exemplify Juvenal's command of tone. The alliteration of 'miserae magnaeque' has an epic feel to it; we are reminded for an instant of Ennius or Lucretius. Most poets would have written 'magnae miseraeque'; the reversal of the expected word order is obscurely powerful, somehow suggesting that wretchedness is not just a common consequence of high station but an inevitable part of it. 'Sedebat' is a telling verb: their fear does not come or go but is a perpetual companion. The climax comes with the splendid oxymoron of 'pallor amicitiae', admirably delayed to the end of the sentence and the start of a new line. And characteristically the *bon mot* is united to a sudden flash of visual clarity: it is those faces, pale amid the grandeur, that reveal the truth. It would be too much to say that Juvenal feels sympathy for Domitian's courtiers; but his sonorous language does surround them with a kind of pomp and circumstance. He is depicting a sort of scene in which

Lucan delighted; and Lucan, however fiercely he hated his characters, did at least expand them to an epic magnitude.

Virgil's famous description of Theseus in Tartarus, 'sedet aeternumque sedebit', (*Aen.* 6.617) was recalled by Juvenal at a surprising moment in *Satire* 10:

> *nam coitus iam longa oblivio, vel si*
> *coneris, iacet exiguus cum ramice nervus*   205
> *et, quamvis tota palpetur nocte, iacebit.*

[For sex has now been long forgotten – or should you try, your small penis with its swollen veins lies slack, and though it be stroked all night long, will lie there still.]

Again this is not simple parody. The spreading of the words 'iacet ... et ... iacebit' over nearly two lines, and still more the rhetorical force of the delaying clause 'quamvis ... nocte', a more expansive equivalent of Virgil's 'aeternumque', give the sentence an amplitude that affects or should affect the reader's response. The theme is undignified, but Juvenal's tone suggests a kind of majestic, bitter pity for one of the most shabby and humiliating facts of the human condition. Such an interpretation may sound altogether too high-falutin', and certainly the harshness of the gibe cannot be ignored; but it is combined with an *element* of something more, so that the tone is ambivalent and the emotional effect complex.

Undoubtedly there were other places where Juvenal was prepared to study from Virgil the art of exciting pathos. *Georgics* 4 contains a famous simile:

> *qualis populea maerens philomela sub umbra*
> *amissos queritur fetus, quos durus arator*
> *observans nido implumis detraxit; at illa*
> *flet noctem, ramoque sedens miserabile carmen*
> *integrat, et maestis late loca questibus implet.*   515

[Even as the nightingale, mourning in the shade of a poplar, laments the loss of her young, which a pitiless ploughman has spied and torn unfledged from the nest; but she weeps all night, and sitting on a bough renews her piteous song, and fills the place far round with her sorrowful plaint.]

The sudden 'at illa' at the end of line 513 heightens the contrast between the unfeeling ploughman and the pathetic lamentation of the nightingale. In *Satire* 3 Juvenal describes the bustle of preparation for the return of a man who, unknown to his household, has been killed in a traffic accident:[26]

---

[26] No doubt he also recalled Homer's scene of Andromache preparing the bath for Hector, not knowing that he is already dead.

haec inter pueros varie properantur, at ille
iam sedet in ripa taetrumque novicius horret   265
porthmea nec sperat caenosi gurgitis alnum
infelix nec habet quem porrigat ore trientem.

[The servants hasten about these various tasks, but he is already sitting
on the bank, a new arrival, and shuddering at the hideous ferryman; he
has no hope of a passage over the muddy waters, unhappy man, nor has
he a coin in his mouth to offer.]

Juvenal's 'at ille', marking a dramatic shift from one mood to another,
borrows from Virgil's technique in a very specific way, while his picture of the underworld owes a general debt to the sixth book of the
Aeneid.

The rhetorical splendours of the lines in *Satire* 10 where Juvenal
speaks of Priam – the reverberant m's, n's, r's and s's, the elevated
proper nouns – are immediately plain:

incolumi Troia Priamus venisset ad umbras
Assaraci magnis sollemnibus Hectore funus
portante ac reliquis fratrum cervicibus inter   260
Iliadum lacrimas, ut primos edere planctus
Cassandra inciperet scissaque Polyxena palla . . .

[Priam would have gone to join the shade of Assaracus with Troy still
unharmed and with solemn pomp, with Hector and his brothers bearing
the corpse upon their shoulders, while the women of Ilium wept; Cassandra and Polyxena with robe torn would have led the lamentation . . .]

Virgil had used a metrical trick at *Aeneid* 5.481; Entellus kills an ox
with a blow of his fist, and the animal's sudden collapse is conveyed
by a monosyllable at the end of the line: 'sternitur exanimisque tre-
mens procumbit humi bos' ('prostrate and lifeless, the ox falls trembling to the ground'). Juvenal imitates this in describing Priam's death
(10.265–70):

longa dies igitur quid contulit? omnia vidit   265
eversa et flammis Asiam ferroque cadentem.
tunc miles tremulus posita tulit arma tiara
et ruit ante aram summi Iovis ut vetulus bos,
qui domini cultris tenue et miserabile collum
praebet ab ingrato iam fastiditus aratro.   270

[What advantage then did long life bring him? He saw everything over-
thrown, and Asia crumbling in flames before the sword. Putting aside his
headdress, he picked up his arms, a tremulous soldier, and fell before the
altar of supreme Jupiter like a poor old ox that, scorned now by the
ungrateful plough, offers its scrawny, pitiable neck to its master's knife.]

A device which Virgil employed to excite a thrill of violence, Juvenal intends for pathetic effect – obviously so; indeed the emotionalism of the adjectives in line 269f. is overdone and rather coarse. As in the description of old men's sexual impotence, so here satire and high rhetoric go hand in hand; but whereas in the former case readers are liable to miss the pathos, here it is the satire that can easily be overlooked. The probing question of line 265 (with that fourth-foot dactyl again) somewhat undercuts the declamatory force of the previous sentence; the comparison of the king to an old animal fit only for the knacker has a touch of derision in it. The diminutive 'vetulus' may be, as well as pitying, a little scornful; the notion of scorn appears again in the word 'fastiditus'. There may be more pathos and less satire here than in (say) the depiction of the poet in *Satire* 7, but in neither case are the proportions exactly definable; here as elsewhere the reader is allowed an area within which he may move. It is, however, of vital importance that the satirist's voice is not *altogether* stilled; Juvenal's sentences on Priam have faults, but they gain in vigour and honesty from the thin steely thread of harshness that runs through them.

In *Satire* 6 Juvenal mocks the passion of well-to-do women for horoscopes and fortune-tellers; then he turns to their social inferiors with an epigram (588), 'plebeium in circo positum est et in aggere fatum' ('plebeian destinies are determined in the Circus or on the Embankment'). Next he adds,

quae nudis longum ostendit cervicibus aurum
consulit ante falas delphinorumque columnas   590
an saga vendenti nubat caupone relicto.

[The woman who wears a long gold chain on her neck enquires in front of the towers and the dolphin columns whether she should leave the tavern-keeper and marry the man who sells old clothes.]

This tailpiece serves to sharpen his satire against the rich. The vanity of human desires is the more painfully exposed by the picture of a poor woman, in unconscious mimicry of her social betters, bothering about a paltry disloyalty: shall she throw over one indigent man for another (with his love of the particular Juvenal details their professions)? The setting of the scene – a humble figure, with the massive towers and columns of the circus for a backdrop – strengthens both the vividness and the satiric force of the passage. That the modern reader is right to be touched by this picture of pathetic, trivial folly is confirmed by the next paragraph, in which Juvenal launches a ferocious attack on abortion, 'murdering human beings in the belly' ('homines in ventre necandos', line 596). The moral squalor of the abortionist's prosperous clients is summed up in a brilliantly callous phrase, 'vexare uterum pueris salientibus' ('to bother one's womb with jumping babies', line 599), and contrasted with the decent sufferings of the poor, who have no choice but to bear children and nurse them. There is obviously a danger, when one is describing a passage such as this, of appearing to sentimentalise an ungentle poet, but this danger is one more for the critic than for the common reader. If we look to the text itself, we shall not be likely to miss the impetus of Juvenal's satiric drive; the pathos is not so overt, but it is not the less effective – perhaps it is even more effective – for being held within a framework of contemptuous invective.

There are of course other places where tenderness is not in the least concealed, for example the account of poor Cordus losing his possessions in a fire (3.203–11):

> *lectus erat Cordo Procula minor, urceoli sex*
> *ornamentum abaci, nec non et parvulus infra*
> *cantharus et recubans sub eodem marmore Chiron,*   205
> *iamque vetus Graecos servabat cista libellos*
> *et divina opici rodebant carmina mures.*
> *nil habuit Cordus, quis enim negat? et tamen illud*
> *perdidit infelix totum nihil. ultimus autem*
> *aerumnae cumulus, quod nudum et frusta rogantem*   210
> *nemo cibo, nemo hospitio tectoque iuvabit.*

[Cordus had a bed too small for Procula, six pitchers to adorn his sideboard, a small cup too underneath and a Chiron reclining below that same slab of marble. An old chest held his Greek books and the uneducated mice gnawed at the divine poesy. Cordus had nothing, who denies it? And yet, poor man, he lost all his nothing. And to complete his heap of misery, when he goes naked begging for a crumb, no one will help him with food or the shelter of a roof.]

By the end of the passage the mood has tipped over into sentimentality, but lines 208–9 are saved from this by the simplicity of their language and the wryness of the paradox 'totum nihil'. And once more the satirical note is helpfully astringent, though this time the satire is witty and affectionate rather than harsh. Juvenal's description of the monolingual mice has a tone that finds an echo in Elizabeth Bowen's novel, *The Death of the Heart* (pt. 6, ch. 2): 'The twitch of the coral ball did not disturb the apathy of the library cat – this furious mouser had been introduced when mice began to get at the *belles lettres*, but he only worked by night.' Juvenal was capable, when he wanted, of a humorous charm.

Though sometimes ruthlessly uncompassionate, he knew also how to be tender and cruel at the same time. Indeed the complexity of tone, leaving us uncertain exactly how to take what he is saying, is of high poetic value; it gives a solidity to the satire, showing us an artist who is neither blind to the nastiness of the world nor dependent on the glibness of a universal cynicism. This emerges especially from his treatment of children. There is an amplitude to the lines in which a noble is invited to celebrate the birth of his – or rather his wife's – child (6.78–81):

> *longa per angustos figamus pulpita vicos,*
> *ornentur postes et grandi ianua lauro,*
> *ut testudineo tibi, Lentule, conopeo*   80
> *nobilis Euryalum murmillonem exprimat infans.*

[Let us erect long platforms in the narrow streets, let the door and door-posts be decorated with noble laurel, that your highborn baby, Lentulus, may display to you from its tortoiseshell cradle the features of Euryalus or a gladiator.]

The third line with its lavish long words and spondaic fifth foot has a wealthy, aristocratic flavour. The little child in its exotically opulent cradle is in itself a charming idea; its analogue in visual art would be something like the enchanting cradle tomb of the Princess Sophia in Westminster Abbey: the baby so small – and so richly housed. The shape of the sentence invites us to follow the proud father as he bends over the crib and then to receive with him the sudden shock of horror: there, looking up at him, is an infant gladiator. There is a bitter force in that last word 'infans': even a tiny child displays the (by implication coarse) features of the adult Euryalus. So we have been deceived, thinking that we were to have a touch of sentiment and finding that even the baby is ugly; and yet not wholly deceived. The last line is splendid in sound and construction; there is a kind of nobility or elevation that cannot quite be eliminated from the effect that it leaves on us, despite the ugliness of what it says. Nor perhaps can we completely forget the pretty scene of babyhood that for a moment we seemed on the point of observing, even though in the event it has been snatched away from us.

Later in the same satire the nightmarish phantasmagoria that is Juvenal's picture of nocturnal Rome turns for a few lines into fantasy in the strongest sense; by a great leap of imagination he springs out of the satirist's natural milieu into an allegorical vision worthy of Virgil. 'Stat Fortuna' – the scene is monumental (6.605–9):

>   *stat Fortuna inproba noctu*   605
> *adridens nudis infantibus: hos fovet omni*
> *involvitque sinu, domibus tunc porrigit altis*
> *secretumque sibi mimum parat; hos amat, his se*
> *ingerit utque suos semper producit alumnos.*

[Malicious Fortune stands by night smiling upon the naked babes. She cuddles them and wraps them close to her bosom, then presents them to great houses, devising for herself a secret comedy; them she loves, on them she presses her gifts, and always helps them on as her own fosterlings.]

The naked babes, Fortune smiling upon them, fondling, cuddling, loving them – the language suggests the charm and pathos of motherhood, but in fact Fortune is acting a terrible parody of maternal affection: her laughter is mocking and she wraps the infants in her bosom to conceal her deceit.

In this second passage the tenderness which we naturally feel towards children and parental love seems to be a bait to trap us: Juvenal excites the sentiment in us in order to stamp upon it; the tenderness and the ferocity do not mix. But in *Satire* 5 bitterness and humane feeling concerning children seem to be fused into one complex but indivisible emotion.

> dominus tamen et domini rex
> si vis tunc fieri, nullus tibi parvolus aula
> luserit Aeneas nec filia dulcior illo.   140
> sed tua nunc Mycale pariat licet et pueros tres
> in gremium patris fundat semel, ipse loquaci
> gaudebit nido, viridem thoraca iubebit
> adferri minimasque nuces assemque rogatum,
> ad mensam quotiens parasitus venerit infans.   145

[However, if you wish to become a great man and a great man's master, let there be no little Aeneas playing in your halls, nor a daughter more charming than he. But as it is, though your Mycale give birth and pour forth three boys at once into their father's lap, Virro will delight in the chattering nestlings; he will order a green tunic to be brought and tiny nuts and a coin if it is asked for, whenever the parasite child comes to his table.]

A characteristic allusion to Dido's longing for a 'parvulus Aeneas', (*Aen.* 4.328f.), reminding us of a grand, heroic world, a yardstick against which the modern world is to be measured and found wanting, introduces the subject; then we have a gay, almost rococo picture of Mycale ('*your* Mycale' – a coaxing touch) pouring children into their father's lap. Next comes Virro, and for two lines we have what seems to be a sentimentally appealing picture of an otherwise odious personage ('loquaci . . . nido' is especially pretty). The last line is brusquely disillusioning: Virro corrupts not just Trebius himself but his very children. And yet Juvenal is not merely arousing sentimental feelings in us in order to squash them, or to expose their mushiness (though this is one element in a highly complex effect). As in *Satire* 6, the final 'infans' carries an intense charge. The very phrase 'parasitus . . . infans' has the smell of oxymoron about it: a corrupted child seems more unnatural and repulsive than a corrupted adult. But why is this? Surely because children are, to Juvenal as to us, the most lovable and (at least apparently) innocent of human creatures. To the end we are left uncertain whether Virro's indulgence to them constitutes his one redeeming feature or his most sinister baseness, and this uncertainty is impressive, because it reflects the complexity of real life: commonly, the kindness of adults to children is like their kindness to pets, at once affectionate and ruthlessly self-gratifying.

This picture of Juvenal's attitude to children receives support from *Satire* 14 (a poem which admittedly dates from a later stage in his career, when he was in the habit of rather self-consciously obtruding a note of high morality into his work). His famous adage, 'maxima debetur puero reverentia', is more strongly and startlingly paradoxical than is commonly realised. It deserves to be seen in context (14.45–9):

> procul, a procul inde puellae   45
> lenonum et cantus pernoctantis parasiti.
> maxima debetur puero reverentia, si quid
> turpe paras, nec tu pueri contempseris annos,
> sed peccaturo obstet tibi filius infans.

[Away, you procurers' women; away, songs of that night creature, the parasite. The greatest reverence is due to a child, if you are planning something disgraceful; do not despise a child's few years, but let your infant son stand in your way when you are about to sin.]

As in *Satire* 5 there is an ironic echo of Virgil ('procul o procul este profani', *Aen.* 6.258), and again the effect is complex: the tone is serious, even solemn, and yet parodistic at the same time. In an age which thought little about children, or saw them as miniature adults merely, Juvenal, with that extraordinary power of concrete imagination, has an unusual sense of the child's *presence*. The little boy stands in the path of the great big adult (note the monumental spondees of 'peccaturo'), and the adult recoils in awe (for that, after all, is what 'reverentia' means). A later age would have been tempted to turn Juvenal's sharp metaphor into a bogus actuality, with an angelic infant beseeching the big bad man to 'sell no more drink to father'. But Juvenal is not sentimental; whereas the Victorian angel-child is a vulgar fantasy purporting to correspond to reality, Juvenal's child is the reverse: a simulacrum created by the conscience, but so vividly conceived that it seems momentarily to have a concrete, physical presence. His image is plain and economical. There are no decorative epithets; every word is working.

This same capacity to give a physical presence to an abstract idea reappears later in the poem (14.215f.):

parcendum est teneris; nondum implevere medullas   215
maturae mala nequitiae.

[The young should be gently treated; the evils of a ripened wickedness have not yet infected their marrow.]

Juvenal breathes life into the simple 'teneris' by picking it up with 'medullas'. This word, so unexpected and yet brilliantly apt, serves at one and the same time to conjure up a grotesque fantasy – the flesh-creeping picture of wickedness ripening within the bones and spreading through the bone-marrow – and to set the soft, brittle bodies of real children vividly before us, giving to the bald injunction to 'spare the tender' a compelling force and pathos.

In the third line of the satire Juvenal announces its subject: the importance of parental example. This theme, trite in itself, is immediately restated in the form of a particular instance: if the old man is a gambler, the child plays at gaming and shakes a toy dice-box. Humour and horror are combined. Juvenal shows unusual insight into the way children behave through his accurate and affectionate observation of their passion for imitation; and yet the picture of childhood already blighted is painful. The reader is torn: is this an almost charming scene of a boy innocently mimicking his elders, or is this innocence already corrupted? In keeping with this mood is the superb scene of the good mother vulture bringing home chunks of dead dogs and crucified criminals to her young, thus teaching them to do the same when they are grown up (77ff.). As with *Satire* 5, the ghastliness and the pathos depend on each other. These passages are so short and economical that it may seem laboured to expound them, but they are merely a few examples among dozens of Juvenal's power of imaging his ideas. The text prickles with detail.

4

Juvenal is often considered to be a notably dirty writer, but this is true, if at all, only in a specialised sense. What he can be is a very shocking writer, which is not at all the same thing; indeed the shock may depend on his avoiding the easier forms of obscenity. *Satires* 2 and 9 have been ignored in the past by many commentators because their theme is homosexuality; but unless the subject be considered wholly impermissible, it must be granted that Juvenal's way of handling his topic is, in the modern cant phrase, 'artistically necessary'.[27] Macaulay derided Croker for maintaining that 'there are none of Juvenal's satires to which the same objection may be made as to one of Horace's, that it is *altogether* gross and licentious'; but Croker was more or less right.[28] Outside *Satire* 6 there are few places where he takes up obscene themes with the insouciance of a Martial, and even in *Satire* 6 the 'medical dictionary' language is largely restricted to the lines preserved in the Oxford manuscript; the use of words like 'colocyntha' and 'chelidon' is exceptional in Juvenal's work (6.O 6). He is not scatological; whereas Catullus splashes excremental jokes freely across his verses, Juvenal refers to excretion only once, in a passage of especial intensity. 'Mentula' and 'arrigere', favourite words of Martial, are not part of his vocabulary, and indeed the purpose of the two poets is radically different. Martial justifies his *grivoiseries* by explaining that his poems are 'lusus' and 'nequitiae'. His poetry is sportive ('lascivus'); the readers for whom he writes are urbane.[29] 'Hic totus volo rideat libellus' (10. 15. 3) ('I want this whole book to smile'); Juvenal borrowed certain themes from his predecessor, and yet it should be obvious that Martial's joking is a long way from the satirist's vehemence and anger. Martial says that he will excite sexual desire in his readers (11.16.4); Juvenal's characteristic attitude to sexual activity is one of disgust or pity. Martial resorts to oral sex to keep his readers titillated; it is in the cold dissection of normal sexuality that Juvenal is most powerfully disillusioning.[30] He is shocking because, unlike Catullus or Martial, in such cases he composes still with his eye on the object. For example, in *Satire* 3.109ff. he complains that neither girl, boy nor matron is safe from the lust of a Greek (with his instinct for the concrete and the physical he writes 'inguen' for 'lust'); then comes the punchline: 'horum si nihil est, aviam resupinat amici' ('if none of these is available, he tips his friend's grandmother on her

---

[27] For the most part he is not a moralist in the modern sense (the chief exceptions coming in his later work); although he deals with theft, fraud, murder and other gross crimes, the burden of his attack is commonly to expose people and institutions not as 'wicked' or 'sinful' but as disgusting, squalid, vulgar or ridiculous. From the true moralist we demand a higher degree of sincerity than from other kinds of writer; but it is not in an important sense an imputation on Juvenal's sincerity that he enjoys denouncing degradation with a wealth of loving detail. (None the less, I cannot help feeling that *Sat.* 9 suffers from its subject-matter: the complicated perversion chosen for assault is too easy a target and (I suspect) was rare even in imperial Rome. The bitter coolness of his technique resembles that of Swift's *Modest Proposal*, but for all Juvenal's brilliance here, the later work has far more *satiric* power, because it deals with much greater issues.)

[28] Macaulay's essay on Boswell's Life of Johnson.

[29] Martial 11. 16. 7; 1. 4. 8; 11. 16. 2.

[30] When Juvenal mentions oral sex at the start of *Sat.* 9 (line 3f.), it is for special effect. The poem's texture is blandly conversational; the sudden and apparently irrelevant obscenity, thrown away in a subordinate clause, hints briefly at the horrors which the urbanity will prove to conceal.

back'). The economy of this is brilliant.[31] There is a new and unexpected twist of the knife in both 'aviam' and 'amici'; 'aviam', indeed, does in a single word what Horace twice took a whole elaborately nasty epode to do. But the disillusionment is above all in 'resupinat'. This terse, accurate verb conveys the speed and efficiency with which the business-like Greek sates his appetite; but at the same time its drab exactitude points to the banality or futility of all coition. Juvenal has already used this cruel literalism a little earlier in the same satire; commenting on the efficacy with which a Greek can act a female role, he adds (3.96f.), 'vacua et plana omnia dicas/infra ventriculum et tenui distantia rima'. What is the great difference between men and women? Juvenal's last three words give a vivid answer, exact, and destructive of all romantic sentiment.

In *Satire* 10. 223f. he remarks that the diseases of the old are so numerous that he could more readily tell 'quot longa viros exorbeat uno/Maura die, quot discipulos inclinet Hamillus' ('how many men tall Maura drains in a day, or how many pupils Hamillus bends'). Here too he works through the factual correctness of the verbs. 'Inclinet' is similar to 'resupinat' in *Satire* 3; 'exorbeat' is still more bleakly truthful. In similar mood he had written in *Satire* 3. 132–4,

> *alter enim quantum in legione tribuni*
> *accipiunt donat Calvinae vel Catienae,*
> *ut semel aut iterum super illam palpitet; at tu . . .*

[Another man gives to Calvina or Catiena as much as tribunes in a legion get for the sake of jerking above her once or twice; but you . . .]

The concessive tone of 'aut iterum' (once, maybe even twice!) is a fine satiric touch, and the 'truthful' verb 'palpitet' is admirably placed: the dactylic scansion, the snappy consonants p and t, the brusque pause so near the end of the line all augment the sense of scorn.[32] However vehement his sentiments, the language remains clear; at times appallingly clear. What does Maura's frenetic activity amount to? The passage of a little moisture from one body to another. What is this thing for which men will sacrifice so much? A few pulsations, that is all.

A similar disenchantment breathes from a poem traditionally attributed to Petronius:

> *foeda est in coitu et brevis voluptas*
> *et taedet Veneris statim peractae.*

---

[31] 'Nihil' for 'nemo' is a harsh detail: the Greek treats people as objects.

[32] The effect is similar to that of Juvenal's favourite pause after a fourth-foot dactyl. After 'palpitet' the declamatory voice presses on to the end of the line with two stabbing monosyllables, 'at tu'.

[Doing, a filthy pleasure is, and short;
And done, we straight repent us of the sport. (tr. Ben Jonson)]

But whereas this poem offers a refined and subtly worldly alternative
to 'doing' – nothing but kisses, an eternity of half-satisfied desire –,
Juvenal is wholly bleak. He has to put to his readers a view which, in
even the most wearily sophisticated of ages, a majority of them will
not share; and so we can see why for him a conventionally smutty
vocabulary will not do. He has to break through convention to expose
the dull reality. His method is at once 'poetic', in its pursuit of vivid
imagination, and satiric: a means of argument and persuasion.

These passages are very brief, mere sideswipes in the midst of other
satiric material, but it would be wrong to regard them either as
insignificant or as irrelevances stuffed in to satisfy the prurience of
author or audience. It is characteristic of Juvenal to be firing at more
than one target at once; in the programmatic first satire he depicts
himself as almost overwhelmed by the confusion and quantity of his
impressions, and he commonly aims at verse of a dense texture which
at its worst risks tumbling into incoherence, at its best has an energy
and muscularity unsurpassed in Latin poetry. Besides, his terseness
is itself expressive: sexual passion is a subject to be swatted aside with
a word or two of devastating contempt, and the force of that contempt
could only be less if it were spelled out more explicitly. It is in any
case a constant habit of his to flash a picture before us and to pass
rapidly onwards; if the reader is alert, the picture is the more sharp
for being momentary.

Very different in this respect is Juvenal's one excursion into scatol-
ogy, which exhibits another of his techniques, a fixing of the attention
upon some physical particular. In *Satire* 9 Naevolus explains the
disadvantages of his profession:

> *an facile et pronum est agere intra viscera penem*
> *legitimum atque illic hesternae occurrere cenae?*
> *servus erit minus ille miser qui foderit agrum*   45
> *quam dominum.*

[Is it simple and easy to thrust a decent-sized prick into a man's guts and
meet yesterday's dinner there? The slave who digs a field will prove less
wretched than the one who digs into his master.]

The memory is so nasty that at first Naevolus cannot get away from
it. 'I'm no better off than a slave' is his thought in line 45, but the
detail in 'qui foderit agrum', with 'agrum' placed, like 'cenae' immediately above, as the last word in the line, keeps us down in the
dirt for a little longer, forcing us to face what Naevolus is saying.
Juvenal's mind is fully concentrated on his theme, whereas when

Catullus writes something like 'pedicabo ego vos et irrumabo', he is only half aware of the literal sense of what he is saying.

If we are tempted to think that the 'poetic' part of Juvenal's imagination is somehow separate from the satiric part, and confined to a few softer passages, Naevolus should enlighten us. *Satire* 16 affords another fine example of Juvenal's use of visual fixation, equally tough, though not this time obscene. With bitter irony he describes the advantages of a soldier's life. In the first place, you can beat up a civilian and he will never dare to complain; or if he does, the tribunal hearing his complaint will be formed of a centurion and his cronies. This tribunal is described entirely in terms of its legs (16.13f.):[33]

> *Bardaicus iudex datur haec punire volenti*
> *calceus et grandes magna ad subsellia surae . . .*

[The man who seeks redress for this is given as judge a soldier's boot and great calves drawn up to big benches]

The writing is empathetic: we imagine the complainant obsessed by those legs and boots, and reasonably enough: he has had the boot put into him already, teeth knocked in, an eye gouged out. At the same time we realize that the poor man is not daring to look the judges in the face: his line of vision is fixed on the benches and below. Even without the empathetic element, we have a remarkably telling picture: what other Latin poet would have noticed the planks of wood and the brawny calves in their relation to each other, and put them solidly before our eyes? Ten lines later he is still haunted by legs:

> *dignum erit ergo*
> *declamatoris mulino corde Vagelli,*
> *cum duo crura habeas, offendere tot caligas, tot*
> *milia clavorum.*   25

[Since you have two legs, you would have to have a mulish spirit worthy of the declaimer Vagellius to offend so many jackboots, so many thousand hobnails.]

You would be crazy to offend so many – not people, as we expect him to say, but hobnails. The contrast between the two legs of the civilian and, with the vagueness and exaggeration of horror, the thousands of nails on the soldiers' boots is perversely vivid: the eye is still fixed fearfully on the prospect of mutilation.

It may be objected that Juvenal's picture of human sexuality is both narrow and false; that to represent copulation as nothing but a more or less undignified physical act is wilfully to ignore a great part of

---

[33] Perhaps Juvenal recalled the 'varicosos centuriones' of Persius 5. 189.

human experience. The objection is of course just; how far, if at all, it is damaging is another and more difficult question. What Juvenal does is not to tell the whole truth – a task in which he is not at all interested – but to express brilliantly a view which comparatively few people have felt all the time but which many, perhaps, have felt some of the time. If he errs, he errs in company with Timon and Lear, neither of whom, admittedly, is the whole of the play to which he gives his name; but for that matter Juvenal too has something more to tell us about relations between the sexes. Much of *Satire* 6 is extravagant and fanciful; but it also contains brief glimpses of the married state which reveal a kind of insight that we find in no other Latin poet. Would you not do better, he asks Postumus, to sleep with a boy rather than a wife?

> *pusio, qui noctu non litigat, exigit a te*   35
> *nulla iacens illic munuscula, nec queritur quod*
> *et lateri parcas nec quantum iussit anheles.*

[. . . a boy, who would not litigate with you at night or ask you for little presents as he lies by you or complain because you give your flanks a rest and do not puff away as much as he has told you to.]

The climax of the sentence is another of his harshly factual verbs: sex is just so much puffing and blowing.[34] But before we reach this final taunt, we have a dreadfully convincing picture of conversation in the marriage bed, with the wife first arguing, then wheedling (the diminutive 'munuscula' mimics her tone: 'just a *little* favour'), then getting her own back by complaining of the husband's shortage of sexual vigour – all this in three lines. 'Litigat' is a brilliant verb, hinting in one word at a whole history of weary bickerings; it is also splendidly comic. We might suspect it of having inspired Alice, were there the smallest reason to believe that Alice had read Juvenal:

> 'In my youth,' said his father, 'I took to the law,
>   And argued each case with my wife;
> And the muscular strength, which it gave to my jaw,
>   Has lasted the rest of my life.'

Lines 161–74 are in a lighter vein:

> *'nullane de tantis gregibus tibi digna videtur?'*
> *sit formonsa, decens, dives, fecunda, vetustos*
> *porticibus disponat avos, intactior omni*
> *crinibus effusis bellum dirimente Sabina,*
> *rara avis in terris nigroque simillima cycno,*   165

[34] Compare, at 6. 21f., his description of adultery as 'alienum . . . lectum concutere'. The phrase is typical of him both in its seizure of a concrete detail and in its belittling of the act: a matter of creaking beds.

quis feret uxorem cui constant omnia? malo,
malo Venustinam quam te, Cornelia, mater
Gracchorum, si cum magnis virtutibus adfers
grande supercilium et numeras in dote triumphos.
tolle tuum, precor, Hannibalem victumque Syphacem   170
in castris et cum tota Carthagine migra.
'parce, precor, Paean, et tu, dea, pone sagittas;
nil pueri faciunt, ipsam configite matrem'
Amphion clamat, sed Paean contrahit arcum.

['Does no wife from all these crowds seem to you acceptable? Suppose she is pretty, elegant, rich and fecund; suppose she arranges her old ancestors in the colonnade and is chaster than any of those Sabine women with streaming locks who stopped the war, a bird so rare upon this earth as to be just like a black swan, who will put up with a wife who is perfect in every way? I would rather have Venustina to wife, I really would, than you, Cornelia, mother of the Gracchi, if with your great virtues you bring a proud brow and number military glories in your dowry. Take away your Hannibal, I beg, and your Syphax defeated in his camp; be off, and all Carthage with you. 'Be merciful, Apollo, I pray, and thou, goddess, put aside thy arrows: the children do no wrong, shoot their mother herself,' Amphion cries, but Apollo draws back his bow.]

The comic paraprosdokian in the last line indicates the mood: we expect the appeal to Apollo to come heroically from Niobe, but it turns out to come from her long-suffering husband instead. The amused cynicism with which the poet declares that a woman with every perfection would be intolerable aims to persuade us through laughter; certainly, the suggestion that marriage to the virtuous Cornelia would be a dog's life carries ready conviction. And amid the comedy there are phrases which, as in the passage examined before, give us sudden glimpses, funny and horrid, into the married state. 'Vetustos/porticibus disponat avos' – through the dynamic verb 'disponat' we see the bossy wife in action, filling the house with *her* family busts, arranging the decor to her own satisfaction as she commands the slaves to place her ancestors here, here and here. '*Numeras ...* triumphos', '*tuum ...* Hannibalem' – with the lightest of touches Juvenal gives us a vision of the women nattering endlessly on about the eminence of her family. We can see that 'grande supercilium' crushing the husband down; and the phrase also seems to give this virago unattractively heavy features.

Earlier (143–8) Juvenal has been fiercer:

si verum excutias, facies non uxor amatur.
tres rugae subeant et se cutis arida laxet,
fiant obscuri dentes oculique minores,   145
'collige sarcinulas' dicet libertus 'et exi.
iam gravis es nobis et saepe emungeris. exi
ocius et propera. sicco venit altera naso.'

[If you shake out the truth, he loves his wife's face, not herself. Suppose three wrinkles appear, her skin goes dry and slack, her teeth get discoloured and her eyes contract; the freedman will say, 'Collect your baggage and get out. You're an utter nuisance to us, and you keep blowing your nose. Get out quickly; hurry. Another woman is coming, with a dry nose.']

The description in line 145 is vague and poor, but the next lines show his craft at its best. The contemptuous diminutive 'sarcinulas' signals the change to colloquial tone and a more rapid pace; the unexpected 'libertus' slips in a further humiliation (the husband does not even bother to dismiss the wife himself); the freedman's 'nobis' is peculiarly offensive. The repeated 'exi' gives the man's peremptory manner (the words are skilfully positioned so as to be even more emphatic on repetition); and the last four words are the crowning insult. The scene is cruel, but we are permitted to pity the woman; the fine epigram, 'facies non uxor amatur', consistent with Juvenal's view that sexual attraction is simply a matter of externals, carries with it the implication that human relations ought to be something more. It may be said that the wife's dismissal, as he imagines it, is improbable; and yet there is a verity behind it. 'Quaedam parva quidem, sed non toleranda maritis,' he tells us later (184) ('Some faults are small and yet unbearable to married men'); and many married couples have testified to this effect. What could be more maddening than a wife whose nose is always running? It is depressing to think that so small a thing could destroy love, but we may well hesitate to say that it is untrue. Juvenal's view of love, sex and marriage is an unfriendly one, but it is not merely glib or preposterous. His quick apprehension of scenes of domestic life (caricatured of course) displays what in a later writer we might call the novelist's eye.

He has indeed been compared to Dickens by several writers. Like other analogies, this one is to be used only so far as it is useful, and then put aside, but it may in fact help us to see how he operates both as a satirist and as a poet. Here, from *Our Mutual Friend* (ch. 17), is Dickens in characteristic vein:

Mr. Twemlow's little rooms . . . would be bare of mere ornament were it not for a full-length engraving of the sublime Snigsworth over the chimney-piece, snorting at a Corinthian column, with an enormous roll of paper at his feet, and a heavy curtain going to tumble down on his head, these accessories being understood to represent the noble Lord as somehow in the act of saving his country.

The satiric thrust comes from the writer's literalism: he refuses to acknowledge the customary convention and describes exactly what is there. Dickens is forever depicting paintings, statues, dinner-tables, theatrical entertainments in this fashion; and Juvenal was no less

addicted to the technique. Indeed, just how engrained a habit of mind
it was with him can be seen from a passage where he is writing rather
badly. The merchant who risks the dangers of seafaring must be crazy,
he suggests (14.290f.),

cum sit causa mali tanti et discriminis huius 290
concisum argentum in titulos faciesque minutas.

[Since the reason for all this misery and danger is silver cut into tiny
inscriptions and images.]

This sarcasm would be effective against a coin-collector; applied to a
businessman it is feeble. To pretend that the end of money-making is
the acquisition of small round objects is mere silliness; money is valu-
able for what can be done with it, and the disadvantages of poverty
are a subject upon which Juvenal waxes eloquent enough in other
places. The significance of the passage for us is the evidence that this
manner of satiric attack was so bred into Juvenal's bones that he uses
it even when it is inappropriate. And even here we find an impressive
liveliness of imagination, especially if we take these lines with the
two that precede:

curatoris eget qui navem mercibus implet
ad summum latus et tabula distinguitur unda . . .

[the man who loads his ship with merchandise right up to the gunwale
and is separated from the water by just a plank needs a keeper]

The contrast between the ship's load of merchandise and the tiny
coins, the sense of the futility of human grandeur given by the idea of
'miniature titles' (we have seen coins all our lives; why did *we* never ·
think of their inscriptions like that?), the dynamism that depicts process not state (the merchant *filling* his ship, the silver cut *into* faces),
the precise vision that both clarifies the picture (the ship filled right
up the gunwale) and reveals the safest sea travel for what is really is
(one plank's thickness between you and the water) – all these are
signs of the poet's eye and mind alive to the world about him.
    Literalism may sound to be the very opposite of poetry, but in reality
this is not so, for to exhibit a clear eye and an undeceived perception
of things as they really are is one of the poet's possible functions. In
Juvenal literalism, which is, after all, closely related to the vivid
depiction of scenes and situations, can be a central theme throughout
a whole poem. 'Stemmata quid faciunt?' The vigour with which the
eighth Satire opens derives not just from the briskness of the question
and the way in which the subject of the whole poem is summed up in
the very first word. The verbs too are working: not 'what's the point

of family trees?' but 'what do they *do*?' – and then the declaimer's voice, insistent and argumentative, presses on with a vocative and a second question: 'What *gain* is there, Ponticus . . .?'

> *quid prodest, Pontice, longo*
> *sanguine censeri, pictos ostendere vultus*
> *maiorum et stantis in curribus Aemilianos*
> *et Curios iam dimidios umeroque minorem*
> *Corvinum et Galbam auriculis nasoque carentem,*
> *si coram Lepidis male vivitur? effigies quo*
> *tot bellatorum, si luditur alea pernox*
> *ante Numantinos . . . ?*

[What is the advantage, Ponticus, of being valued for your ancient blood, of displaying painted faces of ancestors, Aemiliani standing in chariots, Curii half crumbled away, a Corvinus short of a shoulder or a Galba missing his ears and nose, if you live dissolutely in the presence of the Lepidi? To what purpose all those effigies of warriors, if you play with the rapid die in front of the Numantini . . .?]

At once Juvenal follows up the announcement of his theme with a series of pictures. What are ancestors after all? painted faces, battered busts with pieces chipped off them. The attitude is robustly practical (a hostile critic might say philistine or unimaginative). And yet in the next lines the dead ancestors acquire, unrealistically, a threatening life. The degenerate descendant misbehaves 'in the presence of the Lepidi', the gambler 'in front of the Numantini'; it is as though they are watching his every action and passing judgment.

Throughout this impressively unified satire Juvenal plays with variations on two motifs which he has introduced right at the beginning: first, names and how they fail to make a simple connection with reality; second, statues and images. These variations are presented not just as ideas but as scenes or pictures. In line 19f. we see the *imagines* on the walls of the gentleman's house: mere wax, mere decoration ('exornent . . . cerae'). In the next lines we are assured that moral ancestry is the only ancestry that counts, and this notion is dramatically enacted: we are to fancy the nobleman processing through the streets with the effigies not of his ancestors but of those great Romans whom he resembles in character – a scene more arresting, and perhaps more shocking, to Juvenal's first readers than it can be to ourselves. We name a dwarf Atlas and a negro Swan, he tells us a little later (31f.); we *see* the grotesqueness, so that we are persuaded when he declares (37f.), 'ergo cavebis/et metues ne tu sic Creticus aut Camerinus' ('so you must take care and fear that it is not in that way that you are a Creticus or a Camerinus'). We suddenly realise that the possession of a great name can be not merely meaningless, but something worse, a dreadful parody of greatness; and it is Juvenal's pictorical way of thinking that has shown this to us.

Statues and images return at line 52f.: 'at tu/nil nisi Cecropides truncoque simillimus Hermae' ('but you are nothing but a Cecropid, and just like a limbless Herm'). 'Nil nisi Cecropides' is an ironic echo of Rubellius' boast at line 41, 'ast ego Cecropides'; we hear the satirist's mocking, rhetorical voice. Then comes the pictorial demonstration: 'You are merely a Herm' – that is, just a head and a set of genitals. This is an excellent joke, too good for elaborate explication, which hits its victim in two or three places at once; at the same time it is a vivid and surprising image, at once simple and bizarre.

The satirist follows up quickly with another thrust:

nullo quippe alio vincis discrimine quam quod
illi marmoreum caput est, tua vivit imago.   55

[By no single criterion are you superior to a Herm, except that its head is marble, while you are an effigy that lives.]

The last word is *para prosdokian*; we expect the contrast to be between stone image and living reality, but Rubellius turns out to be a mere 'image' himself. And the language manages to suggest that of the two images the marble head is the more solid and substantial.[35] Juvenal exploits the monumentality of marble again later (8.227–30):

maiorum effigies habeant insignia vocis,
ante pedes Domiti longum tu pone Thyestae
syrma vel Antigones seu personam Melanippes,
et de marmoreo citharam suspende colosso.   230

[Let the images of your ancestors receive the emblems of your perform-ances: before the feet of Domitius lay the long robe of Thyestes or Antigone or the mask of Melanippe, and hang your lyre on a marble colossus.]

Nothing can persuade modern readers, even those acquainted with small children who are learning the violin, that playing stringed instruments is a crime of the deepest dye; but the idea could hardly be better represented than in this superb image of the lyre – the thin wires against massive marble – hanging from the giant ancestral effigy. Like the spewed wine on the Spartan marble in *Satire* 11, the picture has an almost symbolic force; the visual imagination and the satiric thrust are wholly unified.

Later still in the satire Juvenal turns to praise the great Romans of modest birth; and he declares,

---

[35] The construction of this passage is worth noting: lines 52 and 54 both end with a pair of monosyllables, drawing our attention to the way that the big phrases in lines 53 and 55 fall, like *sententiae*, into a complete hexameter.

plebeiae Deciorum animae, plebeia fuerunt
nomina; ...   255

[Plebeian were the spirits of the Decii, plebeian were their names]

Since so much of the poem has been about names, the heavy emphasis
given to 'nomina' does not seem merely a metrical trick or convenience
but the proper response of poetic rhetoric. Juvenal says that names
are empty; but he is, perhaps inconsistently, conscious of their past.
The lines just quoted are followed by such words as Virgil used to
evoke the deepest, darkest roots of the Roman people in the soil of
ancient, ancestral Italy: 'pubes Latina', 'di inferni', 'Terra parens',
'trabea', 'Quirinus'. A more remarkable passage is line 100ff.; at one
time, Juvenal says, Rome's allies had not been despoiled:

plena domus tunc omnis, et ingens stabat acervos   100
nummorum, Spartana chlamys, conchylia Coa,
et cum Parrhasii tabulis signisque Myronis
Phidiacum vivebat ebur, nec non Polycliti
multus ubique labor, rarae sine Mentore mensae.
inde †Dolabella atque hinc† Antonius, inde   105
sacrilegus Verres referebant navibus altis
occulta spolia et plures de pace triumphos.

[Then every house was full: great heaps of coins lay there, Spartan cloaks,
Coan purple, the pictures of Parrhasius, the statues of Myron and Phidias'
living ivory; there were many works of Polyclitus everywhere and few
tables without a Mentor. Then Dolabella and Antonius, then sacrilegious
Verres brought back in the holds of their ships secret spoils and more
triumphs won from peace than from war.]

In *Satire* 3 the Greeks were the objects of an itchy contempt; in *Satire*
11. 138–40 indigestible Greek words will be cleverly employed to make
elaborate cookery sound unappealing –

sumine cum magno lepus atque aper et pygargus
et Scythicae volucres et phoenicopterus ingens
et Gaetulus oryx   140

[a big sow's belly, hare, boar, antelope, pheasants, a huge flamingo and
a Gaetulian gazelle]

– but here in *Satire* 8 the Greek names are used, as Virgil might have
used them, to suggest the splendours of a high culture (indeed the
phrase about Phidias' living ivory here is surely inspired by the 'spi-
rantia mollius aera' of Anchises' speech in Elysium). When the Roman
names enter, they bring devastation with them – a humiliating reversal of Juvenal's commoner contrast between decadent Greece and
the dignity of the Roman past, the more effective in that the humili-

ation is wrought by implication only, through the use of associative language. Finally he twists the knife in the wound with a taut epigram describing the perversion of a deeply cherished institution. 'Plures de pace triumphos': no word was more profoundly emotive to the Roman mind than the word with which he ends.[36]

5

The finest achievement of Juvenal's literalism comes in *Satire* 10, when he exposes the nature of military glory; with remorseless accuracy he sees through the fog of convention to what is truly there.

> *bellorum exuviae, truncis adfixa tropaeis*
> *lorica et fracta de casside buccula pendens*
> *et curtum temone iugum victaeque triremis*   135
> *aplustre et summo tristis captivos in arcu*
> *humanis maiora bonis creduntur.*

[The spoils of war, a corslet fastened to a stump as a trophy, a cheek-piece hanging from a broken helmet, a yoke shorn of its pole, the flagstaff of a captured trireme and a sad prisoner at the top of an arch are believed to be blessings more than human.]

What are the insignia of victory? A *damaged* helmet, a *broken* yoke, the statue of an *unhappy* prisoner. How can such things be thought so good? The note of harsh pity for the captive is just right; terse and unsentimental. There is no windy moralising; we are simply shown the facts with the utmost clarity, and forced to draw the conclusion *ourselves*; seldom does Juvenal seem so persuasive.

>   *patriam tamen obruit olim*
> *gloria paucorum et laudis titulique cupido*
> *haesuri saxis cinerum custodibus, ad quae*
> *discutienda valent sterilis mala robora fici,*   145
> *quandoquidem data sunt ipsis quoque fata sepulcris.*

[Yet again and again a nation has been destroyed by the ambition of a few and by their lust for glory and a title that shall cling to the stones that guard their ashes, stones which the rough strength of a barren fig-tree has the force to rend asunder, since the very tombs too have their fates assigned them.]

What is a title? Just words clinging to the stone of a tomb. But then Juvenal, without relaxing his satiric intensity, adds one of those

---

[36] Horace appropriately ends his Cleopatra ode with it (*Carm.* 1. 37). Juvenal himself maintains that had Marius died on the day of his triumph he would have enjoyed a supreme blessing (10. 278ff.); this in a satire exposing the vanity of military conquest.

strange, vivid pictures that prevent his 'realism' from becoming monotonous, the roots of the fig-tree cracking the sarcophagus open. Hannibal is anatomised with the same harsh exactitude:

> *expende Hannibalem: quot libras in duce summo*
> *invenies? hic est quem non capit Africa Mauro*
> *percussa oceano Niloque admota tepenti*
> *rursus ad Aethiopum populos aliosque elephantos.*   150
> *additur imperiis Hispania, Pyrenaeum*
> *transilit. opposuit natura Alpemque nivemque:*
> *diducit scopulos et montem rumpit aceto.*
> *iam tenet Italiam, tamen ultra pergere tendit.*
> *'acti' inquit 'nihil est, nisi Poeno milite portas*   155
> *frangimus et media vexillum pono Subura.'*
> *o qualis facies et quali digna tabella,*
> *cum Gaetula ducem portaret belua luscum!*
> *exitus ergo quis est? o gloria! vincitur idem*
> *nempe et in exilium praeceps fugit atque ibi magnus*   160
> *mirandusque cliens sedet ad praetoria regis,*
> *donec Bithyno libeat vigilare tyranno.*
> *finem animae, quae res humanas miscuit olim,*
> *non gladii, non saxa dabunt nec tela, sed ille*
> *Cannarum vindex et tanti sanguinis ultor*   165
> *anulus. i, demens, et saevas curre per Alpes*
> *ut pueris placeas et declamatio fias.*

[Weigh Hannibal; how many pounds will you find in that greatest of generals? This is he whom Africa could not contain, Africa pounded by the Moorish sea and stretching to the warm Nile and then down to the Ethiopian tribes and further elephants. He adds Spain to his empire, he leaps over the Pyrenees. Nature has put the Alps and their snow in his way; he sunders rocks and bursts the mountain with vinegar. Now he holds Italy, but still he strives to press onward. 'Nothing is achieved,' he says, 'unless with my Carthaginian soldiery I break down the gates and plant my standard in the midst of the Subura.' When the Gaetulian monster carried the one-eyed commander, what a sight it was, what a picture it would make! What then is his end? O glory! He is indeed conquered, flees headlong into exile, and there sits, a great, amazing suppliant, by the palace of a king, until it pleases the Bithynian monarch to awake. Not swords, not stones or spears shall put an end to the life of this man who once threw human affairs into confusion, but that punisher for Cannae and avenger of so much blood, a little ring. Go madman, run over the savage Alps, to please children and become a subject for declamation.]

So Hannibal is the 'greatest' of commanders? What does he now *weigh* exactly? How many *pounds* 'greatness'? Then the literalism fades away for a little and we hear of romantic lands and peoples – Africa, the Nile, the Ethiops – before the sentence culminates in the notoriously baroque paraprosdokian of 'aliosque elephantos'. The vigorous

asyndeta of lines 151–4 convey Hannibal's speed and energy ('transi-
lit', rapid and emphatic, is splendidly thrown away: 'the Pyrenees – a
mere nothing!'). The fantastic language – the leaping and breaking of
mountains – is an admirable foil to the literalism that returns in the
next line. What is Hannibal's ultimate goal? To plant a pole in, of all
places, the Subura (a fine bathos at the end of the sentence; the Subura
was not Rome's most salubrious quarter). And what, truly, was his
appearance? 'Quali digna tabella' – Juvenal 'photographs' the occasion, as it were, to show us exactly what it *looked* like: a one-eyed man
perched on a grotesque monster.[37] Another scene quickly follows, a
parody almost of the Roman client system, with the defeated commander waiting not for a great gentleman in a civilised city but for
an oriental monarch. Then come the celebrated lines on Hannibal's
death, rhetoric at its best, but with the little ring, as we have seen,
forming one small nugget of hard reality in the midst of the declamation. And we leave Hannibal with two lines equally famous. Here
the movement of ideas in lines 151–8 is compressed into a mere thir-
teen words; the foolishness of ambition is brought out linguistically
by the contrast between the splashy exaggeration with which Hannibal's achievements are described – 'running over the Alps' – and the
plain reality of the boys at school. The twenty-one lines on Hannibal
are full of variety and invention, but throughout the controlling impulse is a refusal to accept anything other than the hard facts of the
case.

Alexander is handled in the same spirit, but more briefly.

unus Pellaeo iuveni non sufficit orbis,
aestuat infelix angusto limite mundi
ut Gyarae clausus scopulis parvaque Seripho;   170
cum tamen a figulis munitam intraverit urbem,
sarcophago contentus erit. mors sola fatetur
quantula sint hominum corpuscula.

[One globe is not enough for the youth of Pella: he seethes unhappily
within the narrow bounds of the world as though confined by the cliffs of
Gyara or little Seriphus. But when he enters the city which was fortified
by potters, he will be content with a sarcophagus. Death alone reveals
just what size our little bodies are.]

The elder Seneca recalls someone saying of Alexander, 'orbis illum
suus non capit' ('the world that is his cannot contain him', *Suas* 1.5).
The first of Juvenal's lines takes over (and improves) this idea, but at
once he is building upon it, giving it body and solidity. The ordinary
word 'orbis' is picked up by the next line, and its full physical, literal

[37] For the grotesque overtones of 'Gaetulus' compare 11.140 ('Gaetulus oryx') and
especially the sneering oxymoron at 5. 59, 'Gaetulum Ganymedem'.

meaning explored. 'Orbis' is a circle; Alexander is encircled, enclosed, imprisoned by the world, a fantastic notion which receives paradoxically vivid, concrete expression ('limes' is another firm, definite word). At the same time the verb 'aestuat' suggests that he is like the Ocean itself encircling the world. But as with Hannibal, Alexander's deluded sense of his own size and power is to be corrected. So the world seems narrow? But just how big is Alexander literally? Juvenal employs diminutives sparingly but usually with great effect, and the two in line 173 are superbly placed. After the solemn tolling of 'mors sola fatetur' the little sounds that follow, culminating in another of those fourth-foot dactyls, are admirably scornful, but the diminutives impress above all by the way in which they focus our attention on the precise size of men's small bodies; a sarcophagus is a snug fit. Imagine some other word in place of 'sarcophagus' – 'bustum' or 'tumulus' – and Juvenal's energetic concentration on the object is dissipated at once.

Juvenal's literalism, it is plain, cannot be considered simply on its own. It is intimately connected with his fancy – the capacity to find unexpected comparisons and strange similitudes –; and fancy in its turn is connected with fantasy, and even shades into it. The comparison with Dickens may still be serviceable. The strength of Dickens's fancy is well known; John Carey remarks of him, 'He fills his novels with objects that vividly loom – locks, graveyards, cages – intensely themselves, not signs for something else'; and a little later he writes, 'The exuberance of the similes is equalled only by their precision. "It is my infirmity," wrote Dickens, "to fancy or perceive relations in things which are not apparent generally." The infirmity indispensable to poets.'[38] These observations may help us to see the similarity between some of Juvenal's and Dickens's procedures, the link between literalism and fancy, and the relation of both to the poetic imagination.

As an example of Dickens's fantasy we may take the Veneering dinner table, from the same novel that gave us the sublime Snigsworth:

> Everything said boastfully, 'Here you have as much of me in my ugliness as if I were only lead; but I am so many ounces of precious metal worth so much an ounce ...' A corpulent straddling epergne, blotched all over as if it had broken out in an eruption rather than been ornamented, delivered this address from an unsightly silver platform in the centre of the table. Four silver wine-coolers, each furnished with four staring eyes, each head obtrusively carrying a big silver ring in each of its ears, conveyed the sentiment up and down the table.... All the big silver spoons and forks widened the mouths of the company expressly for the purpose of thrusting the sentiment down their throats ... (*Our Mutual Friend*, ch. 11)

[38] John Carey, p. 130.

Dickens satirises Twemlow's engraving by stating precisely what is there, no more, and he satirises Veneering's table by describing much more than is there; but we should not conclude that he is a mere opportunist, assailing his victims from contradictory positions, as suits his convenience. The undeceived eye that sees with clarity what is really there is the same as the curious eye that finds out odd resemblances; and that curious eye is alive and exploratory because it is fired and directed by an imagination which is impelled to attribute life to inanimate objects and in other ways to go beyond the literal truth not because it is deceived but because it observes and enquires with an alertness that requires it to add in an element of fantasy if it is to do full justice to its experience. That coarse complacent epergne and those mouth-widening spoons and forks are not objects that Dickens has failed to see but objects that he has seen with an unusual intensity. Sometimes, indeed, literalism and fantasy are hardly to be distinguished, as here (ch. 2): 'The Herald's College found out a Crusading ancestor for Veneering who bore a camel on his shield . . . and a caravan of camels take charge of the fruits and flowers and candles, and kneel down to be loaded with the salt.' Literal-mindedness finds camels on a dinner-table absurd; but at the same time fantasy animates them and sees them bending in the act of genuflection.

The same principles can be applied to Juvenal; in particular, he too tends to treat inanimate objects as though they were alive, and in such a way as to make their physical appearance the more vivid. Often this impulse comes out in small details, modest in themselves, but contributing to the texture of the poetry. Thus he imagines the eagles on top of the standards keeping an eye on the defeated Dutch: 'domitique Batavi/*custodes* aquilas' (8.15f.) ('the eagles that guard the conquered Batavi'). The Roman night has a thousand eyes: 'adeo tot fata, quot illa/nocte patent vigiles te praetereunte fenestrae' (3.274f.) ('as many deaths await you as there are watchful windows open that night as you go past'). This is a particularly fine stroke, picturing the many patches of flickering candlelight against the blackness, and at the same time getting us inside the skin of the jumpy pedestrian; momentarily Rome seems to become a savage forest, with the eyes of beasts winking in the dark. To Juvenal a purse is not just a purse but a devouring maw. We have seen how early in *Satire* 11 he uses metre and word-order to fix our attention on the purse as an object. A little later he comes back to this motif:

> *quis enim te* deficiente crumina
> *et* crescente gula *manet exitus, aere paterno*
> *ac rebus* mersis in ventrem *fenoris atque*   40
> *argenti* gravis *et pecorum agrorumque* capacem?

[For what end awaits you if your purse fails as your gullet expands, if your inherited money and possessions have sunk into a belly that can hold income, solid silver, cattle and land?]

The gormandising spendthrift's mouth gapes wider as his purse contracts; the parallelism between the two ablatives absolute impels us to see the purse, like the man, as a hungry, gaping creature. Conversely, the man turns into a sort of purse devouring bronze and heavy silver, even flocks and fields. On one level this is an exuberant, preposterous exaggeration; on another, the concentration on mouths and bellies is apt, because the man is spending his substance on food. The ludicrous picture of the greedy brute stuffing himself with coin and land actually makes us see his gormandising more physically; the odd resemblance between gaping purse and gaping man presents both of them as objects for us to look at.

Juvenal plays a similar game in *Satire* 14. 138: 'pleno cum turget sacculus ore' ('while the purse swells with its mouth stuffed full'). This is a sharp, witty picture. The purse – more precisely a little purse, for here is another well judged diminutive – is too small to hold that cash; the leather is swollen, and its mouth is crammed like a man who has taken too large a spoonful; the personification is pressed upon us by the noun 'ore'. Later in the satire (281–3) he writes,

grande operae pretium est, ut tenso folle reverti
inde domum possis tumidaque superbus aluta,
Oceani monstra et iuvenes vidisse marinos.

[It is well worth while to have seen sea monsters and young mermen, in order that you may come home with purse stuffed tight, puffed up with your swollen money-bags.]

The thought of the sentence is simple, even trite: money is not worth the effort and danger that people undergo in acquiring it. But as usual Juvenal thinks visually. 'Tenso folle' gives us an immediate picture, but the juxtaposition of 'tumidus' and 'superbus' gives it another dimension: the purse's swelling seems to express its pride, the man's pride seems to swell out physically.

These purses, pressing, swelling, gaping, seem to have a tense activity of their own; it is a part of Juvenal's energy that even his personifications are dynamic. In *Satire* 12 it is not enough for him to personify breakwaters as 'arms'; they must seem to be in motion, *stretching* forth, *running* out into the sea, *leaving* the land far behind:

tandem intrat positas inclusa per aequora moles   75
Tyrrhenamque pharon porrectaque bracchia rursum
quae pelago occurrunt medio longeque relincunt
Italiam

[At last the ship passes within the moles laid there to enclose the sea, and goes past the Tyrrhenian lighthouse and the arms which stretch round, come together again out at sea and leave Italy far behind.]

It is in keeping with this active, energetic spirit, and perhaps especially appropriate in a satirist, that he likes to imagine objects watching, spying, and passing judgment. We have already seen the guardian eagles, the watchful windows, and the oppressive presence of the *imagines* in *Satire* 8; sometimes the idea is more extended. In *Satire* 7 (127f.) there is the equestrian statue that threatens with its spear and meditates battle with its one eye. The device of animating a work of art was a favourite with Dickens too; in *Bleak House*, for example, there are the painted Dedlocks watching from the walls of Chesney Wold and the mythological Roman pointing from the ceiling of Mr Tulkinghorn's chambers. In *Satire* 9 the rich man is told that he cannot hope to have any secrets: even if the slaves keep quiet, the beasts of burden will talk, the dog, the door-posts, the very marble. Juvenal proceeds along an ascending scale of dumbness, so to speak: from men to brutes, and from brutes to matter, and yet more solid matter. As with the lines from *Satire* 3, we get inside the victim's mind, while his neurotic fears are still further brought out by a series of imperatives – shut the windows, close the doors, remove that light – after which the poet's voice cuts in with a cooler, smoother sentence, assuring the evil liver that his precautions are vain. Metre, sentence structure and fantasy all work together.

Juvenal's animation of the inanimate is perhaps at its most brilliant in *Satire* 5, and here especially the technique benefits from being seen in context as one among a number of resources working towards this poet's characteristic combination of precision and fantasy. The satire is in the form of a dissuasion addressed to one Trebius, urging him not to go and dine as a client or parasite with the mean and sadistic Virro. For example, there will be squalid brawls (26f.):

iurgia proludunt, sed mox et pocula torques
saucius et rubra deterges vulnera mappa . . .

[Abuse is the prelude, but soon you are drunkenly hurling cups and wiping your wounds with a red napkin.]

'Saucius' means both 'drunk' and 'wounded'. At first we take it in the former sense, but with the word 'vulnera' Juvenal picks up the second meaning and plays with it.[39] Why is the napkin red? Stained with wine or blood? In a fantastic way he has conflated the two.

[39] 'Saucius' is syntactically ambiguous, and could be taken either as the last word of the previous clause or as the first word of the new one. Duff comments that to take it with the following clause (in the sense 'wounded') is flat and tautological; this is true, but not the whole truth. In the first instance we must take 'saucius' with the previous clause; the force of 'vulnera' is that it reveals a *fresh* meaning in the adjective and a *new* syntactical possibility.

The name of the host, Virro, is delayed until line 39; delayed, too, in its position within the sentence, so that it comes suddenly, emphatically at the beginning of the line, while the heroic names of the martyrs for liberty – Brutus, Cassius, Thrasea Paetus and Helvidius Priscus – are still reverberating in our memories (33, 36–45):

cras bibet Albanis aliquid de montibus . . .
quale coronati Thrasea Helvidiusque bibebant
Brutorum et Cassi natalibus. ipse capaces
Heliadum crustas et inaequales berullo
Virro tenet phialas: tibi non committitur aurum,
vel, si quando datur, custos adfixus ibidem,   40
qui numeret gemmas, ungues observet acutos.
da veniam: praeclara illi laudatur iaspis.
nam Virro, ut multi, gemmas ad pocula transfert
a digitis, quas in vaginae fronte solebat
ponere zelotypo iuvenis praelatus Iarbae.   45

[Tomorrow he will drink a wine from the Alban Hills . . . such as Thrasea and Helvidius used to drink, garlanded, on the birthdays of Cassius and the Bruti. Virro himself holds large cups overlaid with amber, goblets rough with beryl; to you no gold is entrusted, or if it is given, a guard is attached to it to count the jewels and watch your sharp fingernails. For Virro, like many, transfers from fingers to cups jewels such as the hero preferred to jealous Iarbas used to put on the face of his scabbard.]

Juvenal used the name Virro again in *Satire* 9; it is perhaps one of those names, like Stiggins or Carruthers, that is meant to be instantly recognisable as carrying a satiric charge, or at least Juvenal's manipulation of the verse gives it that effect. To the abstract contrast between heroic and contemptible names is added another implied contrast brought about by visual description, between republican simplicity and vulgar modern luxury. Virro's cup is encrusted with amber and beryl. The heaviness of this encrustation (and also, we may infer, its tastelessness) is brought home to us by the dragging rhythm of 'inaequales berullo'; this is the only line in Juvenal to end with three successive spondees. Our eye has been drawn to the cup, to Virro holding it; and now Juvenal plays with the idea of fingers and fingernails. Virro transfers jewels from fingers to cups; the larcenous guest, in a different sense, tries to transfer the jewels from the cup to his fingers. A watcher keeps his eye on those sharp fingernails; the precise detail of 'ungues acutos' is functional, because the would-be thief needs his nails to get behind the gems and prise them off.[40] The passing

[40] LaFleur wishes at the end of line 41 to read 'amicos' (which is found in a few mss). But 'acutos' is not 'relatively uninteresting', as he supposes (p. 232); and his claim that his reading 'clearly represents the lectio difficilior' (p. 235) seems out of place, since some form of the noun 'amicus' concludes six and perhaps seven other lines of *Sat.* 5, including the last one.

reference to the *Aeneid* is characteristic of Juvenal: it works in two ways, contrasting heroic poetry with mean reality, and yet at the same time tweaking Virgil's nose by presenting Aeneas as though he were the victor in an unseemly struggle for the favours of, as it were, a Lesbia or a Cynthia.

A litttle later Juvenal introduces a new theme:

> *non eadem vobis poni modo vina querebar?*
> *vos aliam potatis aquam. tibi pocula cursor*
> *Gaetulus dabit aut nigri manus ossea Mauri*
> *et cui per mediam nolis occurrere noctem,*
> *clivosae veheris dum per monumenta Latinae.*   55
> *flos Asiae ante ipsum, pretio maiore paratus*
> *quam fuit et Tulli census pugnacis et Anci*
> *et, ne te teneam, Romanorum omnia regum*
> *frivola. quod cum ita sit, tu Gaetulum Ganymedem*
> *respice, cum sities. nescit tot milibus emptus*   60
> *pauperibus miscere puer, sed forma, sed aetas*
> *digna supercilio.*

[Was I complaining that the same wines are not set before you? You drink different water. You will get your cup from a Gaetulian coachman or from the bony hands of a black Moor, a man you would not care to run into at midnight while driving past the monuments on the hilly Latin Way. Before Virro himself stands the flower of Asia, a youth bought for a price greater than the wealth of pugnacious Tullus and Ancus, greater, in short, than all the bits and pieces owned by the Roman kings. This being so, look to your African Ganymede, when you are thirsty. A boy bought for so many thousands does not know how to mix wine for poor men, but his youth and beauty justify his disdainful eyebrow.]

The implication that the water is dirty and unhygienic makes a natural transition to the fierce frisson of racial disgust that follows. Trebius will receive his cup from a black man – 'Gaetulus' is forceful at the beginning of the line –, the sort of fellow that one would not care to bump into on a dark night. From the Gaetulian or Moor our eye then moves to the lovely oriental boy, 'flos Asiae'; there is an ironic *double entendre* in these words, because a phrase like 'flos Italiae', the flower of Italy, would be nobly resonant, but here the hint of effeminacy in 'flos' is inescapable. Soft Asia, indeed, is contrasted with Tullus and Ancus, symbols of the virile unluxurious Roman past. From this elegant youth we move back to Trebius' own attendant, and recalling that the Ganymede of myth was himself Asian, we realize that 'Gaetulum Ganymedem' is an oxymoron, designed to produce a shudder of repulsion in the sexually charged atmosphere. Then we pass back to the eastern boy – the repeated shift of gaze from the one to the other is telling –, so young, so pretty that he can afford to raise his eyebrow at the parasitic guest. 'Supercilio', in place of some abstract noun like 'contemptus', is an effective physical detail; since the boy's beauty is so insisted upon, we *see* that charming eyebrow, disdainfully curved.

At line 80 the lobster is brought in:

> *aspice quam longo distinguat pectore lancem*   80
> *quae fertur domino squilla, et quibus undique saepta*
> *asparagis qua despiciat convivia cauda,*
> *dum venit excelsi manibus sublata ministri.*

[See how the lobster which is being brought to the host marks out the dish with its long breast; see how, encircled on all sides by asparagus, it looks down on the feast with its tail, when it enters borne aloft by the hands of an attendant.]

'Aspice', Juvenal says, but fantasy is to supplement what the eye beholds. The dead lobster is animated, and described as though it were a great man. On all sides it is 'saeptus' by asparagus, as a Roman notable is 'saeptus' by his clients or his bodyguards; and it is borne aloft by an attendant, as though carried in a litter. The verb 'despiciat' is both physical and abstract: the lobster looks down upon the guests, and it despises them. Indeed, it despises them with its tail, a brilliantly imaginative phrase suggesting that the curving tail plays the part of a lip curled or an eyebrow raised. The picture of the lobster looking coldly down upon the assembly has something in common with the scene in George Eliot's *Daniel Deronda* (ch. 48), where Gwendolen Grandcourt is trying to avoid her husband's lizard-like expression – one of the passages that most clearly illustrate this novelist's debt to Dickens: 'She turned her eyes away from his, and lifting a prawn before her, looked at the boiled ingenuousness of its eyes as preferable to the lizard's.' Juvenal animates the food again when the boar is brought in (115f.): 'flavi dignus ferro Meleagri/spumat aper' ('a boar foams, worthy of yellow-haired Meleager's weapon'). 'Spumat' is literal, because the meat is piping hot; but at the same time, since we have just been told that the boar is worthy of Meleager's spear, we think of a living animal, foaming with heroic indignation.

The final course is very different:

> *Virro sibi et reliquis Virronibus illa iubebit*
> *poma dari, quorum solo pascaris odore,*   150
> *qualia perpetuus Phaeacum autumnus habebat,*
> *credere quae possis subrepta sororibus Afris:*
> *tu scabie frueris mali . . .*

[Virro will command that to him and the rest of his family be served fruits on the mere scent of which you might feed, such as the perpetual autumn of the Phaeacians knew, or which you could believe had been abstracted from the African sisters; you will enjoy a rotten fruit . . .]

The three superlative lines describing Virro's fruit might have come from the most highly finished of neoteric poems. There is a lovely assonance of o and r in the first of them, of p, t, u and m in the second, of r and s in the third. And this romantic elegance matches the content, for the fruits belong to a world of legend: they are so delicious that one might feed off the mere smell of them, they belong to the magical world of Odysseus' Phaeacians, or they might have been abstracted from the Afric sisters – and there is no harsh word for the larceny here, but the soft subtle 'subrepta'. It is a remarkable picture; no less remarkable is the way that Juvenal, having conjured up this evocative mood, harshly destroys it: 'tu scabie frueris mali . . .' If we now look back to the first line about the fruit, we find that it has acquired a new and ironical meaning: it is just as well that one could feed upon the smell alone, for the smell is as much of the fruit as Trebius will get. And we suddenly realise that the line could have meant all along, 'fruit which you are *permitted* merely to smell'. This is a striking example of poetic eloquence – poetic in the slushiest sense of the word – being harnessed to the service of bitter denunciation. Here, once more, as constantly throughout this poem, observation, imagination and satire combine.

6

This examination of Juvenal has ignored certain large aspects of his poetry, and passed lightly by some teasing problems; it is perhaps a tribute to him that so much has had to be left out. The principal theme has been his capacity for what one might call, for want of better words, perception and penetration; these are not the whole of Juvenal's art, but they are qualities of high literary value in themselves, qualities moreover in which he far surpasses the other writers of satura. To say that Horace never exhibits such powers would be to say too much; for example, there is Philippus' first sight of the auctioneer Vulteius Mena in *Epistle* 1.7:

> *conspexit, ut aiunt,*
> *adrasum quendam vacua tonsoris in umbra*   50
> *cultello proprios purgantem leniter unguis.*

[He caught sight, as they relate, of a man newly shaved, calmly cleaning his own fingernails in the shade of the barber's empty booth.]

This is perfect of its kind: the first of the two lines devoted to Vulteius sets the scene – the heat, the shade, the leisure – and the second discovers its significance. The crisp, prissy consonants, the adverb 'leniter', the focusing detail of 'cultello' – the *little* knife poking neatly into the crevices – and above all the superb adjective 'proprios' ('his personal fingernails') give us with economy and complete authority

the man's utter absorption in his delicate and inelegant occupation.[41]
Horace does not merely depict this vividly, but penetrates to its essence; we enter into Vulteius' world, and the cleansing of his nails is
indeed his entire world at this moment. But to recognise a penetrative
power here is to realise also how rare it is in Horace, whose large
virtues in satire and epistle belong mostly to a different order of
poetry; in Juvenal, on the other hand, we find it again and again.

The satirist commonly has a tendency to generalisation, to using
particular cases as examples, or means towards an end. Juvenal lacks
this tendency. In a formal sense he argues by means of 'exempla', but
his constant impulse is towards realising the particular for its own
sake. This is perhaps the same point that E. J. Kenney is making, in
livelier language and from a less favourable point of view, when he
writes of Juvenal's 'simple inability to see beyond the end of his nose
– up to that point his vision has hardly ever been equalled except by
a few such as Hogarth and Dickens.'[42]

Juvenal's specific quality can be seen from a comparison between
him and his great imitator, Johnson. Charles XII of Sweden in *The
Vanity of Human Wishes* is a generalised representative of the restless,
warlike spirit, a descendant of those seventeenth-century 'characters'
modelled on Theophrastus; Juvenal sees Hannibal in his uniqueness
as an individual, with his one eye and his elephant. Charles's march
on Moscow has an abstract grandeur:

> The march begins in military state   205
> And nations on his eye suspended wait;
> Stern Famine guards the solitary coast,
> And Winter barricades the realms of Frost . . .

Juvenal could never have written in such terms; he would have shown
us not 'stern Famine' but men's starving eyes and faces, not 'the
realms of Frost' but ice congealing on the standards. Charles's ultimate fate is universal (221f.):

> He left the name, at which the world grew pale,
> To point a moral, or adorn a tale.

Hannibal crossed the Alps, a uniquely venturesome act, and he is put

---

[41] Fraenkel describes the scene as 'The enviable and blissful leisure of the Roman
popolano, who, after a morning's strenuous work, in the hot hour after lunch-time, is
loitering in the shade of a barber's shop and . . . is manicuring himself into a *signore*'
(p. 337). This seems to me misleading, even when we have discounted the German
Schwärmerei for the south. There is no suggestion of social pretension; indeed, the tone
may even be closer to (for example) J. R. Ackerley's picture of his father's habit, 'while
reading his newspaper in his armchair, of picking his nose abstractedly and rolling the
little bit of snot between his thumb and forefinger' (*My Father and Myself*, ch. 9).

[42] Kenney (1963), p. 715.

to a specific humiliation: little boys in school declaim virtuously about him. If Juvenal did indeed write the famous lines in *Satire* 1 –

quidquid agunt homines, votum, timor, ira, voluptas,   85
gaudia, discursus, nostri farrago libelli est

[Whatever men have been doing, their prayers, fear, anger, pleasures, joys, goings to and fro – these make up the hodge-podge of my book]

– he misled his readers not only in claiming a breadth of interest that his verse does not justify, but also because his subjects are not really fear, anger and pleasure, but frightened men, an angry woman or a pleasured pervert.

It is not necessary to argue that Juvenal's type of satire is inherently superior to any other type; indeed, some may feel that a more generalised form of satire allows a nobility of judgment which they especially admire.[43] But it is certainly true that the particularising tendency has often been regarded as peculiarly poetical. 'As there can be no stronger sign,' Macaulay wrote, 'of a mind destitute of the poetical faculty than that tendency which was so common among the writers of the French school to turn images into abstractions, Venus, for example, into Love, Minerva into Wisdom, Mars into War, and Bacchus into Festivity, so there can be no stronger sign of a mind truly poetical than a disposition to reverse this abstracting process, and to make individuals out of generalities.'[44]

We have seen Juvenal's disposition to make individuals out of generalities; conversely, we have seen Johnson turning images into abstractions; Macaulay's assertion, indeed, exemplifies the reaction of the nineteenth century against the eighteenth. The romantic or post-romantic conception, with much truth in it, nevertheless does not encompass the whole of poetry; but it has had an enduring influence, and to some degree it is with us still. Garrod unquestionably showed himself the inheritor of romantic presuppositions when he dismissed satire from his *Oxford Book*. We have found reasons for thinking that his view of poetry was too narrow; more revealing is the discovery that in regard to Juvenal at least he was profoundly mistaken within his own terms. By any definition of poetry, Roman literature acquired, when Juvenal took up his pen, a poetic mind more original, imaginative and penetrative than any it had known since Virgil ceased to breathe.

[43] The moral question is one of those vexing problems that I have largely evaded. Its trickiness may be estimated from the fact that it entangles even Kenney. He spends pp. 713–14 of his article (1963) arguing that Juvenal's moral character is irrelevant to his poetry, but on p. 716 he writes that Horace wrote better satire than Juvenal 'because he was a bigger man and a better artist'. If there is not a moral judgment concealed in 'bigger man' I am much deceived.
[44] Essay on Bunyan.

APPENDIXES

1. Sappho, fr. 31

Fr. 31 does not immediately appear to be a difficult poem; yet scholars have found more problems in it than in any other of Sappho's fragments. Of several such problems it is claimed that the solution may affect our interpretation of the whole piece. To avoid sticking in a slough of polemical argument I have passed lightly over these in my analysis, but I offer some further account of the principal cruces here. For the most part my conclusions agree with those of Guido Bonelli, whose admirable survey of the controversies around this poem cuts through much nonsense, besides containing observations on method that have a bearing not just on Sappho but on the study of ancient poetry generally.

1. What is the function of the indefinite relative *ottis* in line 2? Page offers three elucidations of the opening lines, which can be given in his own words. (*a*) '*That* man is fortunate, inasmuch as he sits opposite you (and so would anyone else be who did the same).' (*b*) '*Any* man who sits opposite you is fortunate.' (*c*) '*That* man, whatever his name may be, who is sitting opposite you, is fortunate.' Most scholars are aggreed in rejecting (*b*): *kēnos* and *ōnēr* (i.e. *ho anēr*) together suggest a specific man, while a general statement seems less effective, and less in Sappho's manner, than a particular instance. I would add that the whole tenor of the poem seems to me to require us to imagine what West calls a 'knock-out blow' and Dover a 'shock wave' hitting the speaker on one particular occasion; but some would say that this was begging the question. If (*b*) can be set aside, it does not seem to me important whether we choose (*a*) or (*c*). A fourth possibility, discounted by Page, is that *ottis* is no different in meaning here from the definite relative *os*; this view is upheld by Rydbeck (p. 164), who maintains that 'the difference, in Attic usage, between *hostis* and *hos* cannot be discerned in early non-Attic dialects'.

2. What is the meaning of *isos theoisin* in line 2, 'as fortunate as the gods' or 'as strong as the gods'? Scholars have debated this a good deal, but the question is misconceived. There is no doubt about the *meaning* of *isos theoisin*, which is 'equal to the gods'; the only question is what implications this meaning carries. Nor is there necessarily any simple answer to this further question; such answer as can be given is to be found through a sympathetic appreciation of the phrase in its context. My own analysis represents *isos theoisin* as a suggestive expression, in which the idea of good fortune plays a large but not an exclusive part.

I take the careful and detailed article of M. Marcovich as representative of those scholars who seek to deny that jealousy or anxiety about the relationship between the man and the girl enters into the poem. Part of his case is the claim that *isos theoisin* is equivalent to 'as strong as the gods'. I have no hesitation in rejecting this theory, despite its eminent proponents, for the following reasons: (*a*) 'Strong as the gods' must in this context be equivalent to 'as resistant to passion as the gods'. The gods were not notorious for their resistance to passion. (*b*) The firm contrast required by this interpretation – '*He* is strong, but *I* am weak' – is not to be found in the structure of Sappho's sentence. The supposedly emphatic 'I' is represented by the unemphatic *moi*, an enclitic; and if Sappho intended a contrast between clauses, she could hardly have chosen a less suitable connective than *to*. We know how fond the Greeks were of *men* and *de*; not only are these absent, but there is no other conjunction equivalent to English 'but' or 'whereas'. (*c*) If Sappho wished to stress the man's cool collectedness, it is surprising that she made him so attentive: *upakouei*. According to Marcovich (p. 21) the man is 'apparently unimpressed', which suits his case, but is clean contrary to the indication of the text. (*d*) What positive reason is there to accept the interpretation? The main argument put forward is that, in Marcovich's words (p. 23), 'The most likely meaning of the Homeric "godlike" in the formulae *isotheos phōs* (14 times); *epessuto daimoni isos* (7 times), or only *daimoni isos* (3 times) is "*strong* or powerful as a god".' Let us set aside the confusion between meaning and what I have called implication. The argument remains in effect this: because in Homer 'equal to a god' is *commonly* a way of praising someone's *physical* strength, it is immediately perspicuous to Sappho's audience that she means to praise a type of *mental* self-control in the man that the gods themselves frequently failed to display. This is not a strong argument. In any case, Sappho says 'equal to the gods', and in Homer, if such parallels are really important, the conspicuous characteristic of gods in the plural is not strength but happiness and freedom from care. (*e*) Although Marcovich's assertion can be met on its own terms, it must finally be emphasised, once again, that those terms are misconceived. To insist upon one single connotation of a phrase to the exclusion of all others is to deny to poetry the suggestiveness that is fundamental to its nature.

3. What is the signification of the aorist tense of *eptoaisen* in line 6? Dover disposes briskly of this much debated question (p. 178): ' "Set my heart ..." is in the aorist tense in accordance with a common Greek idiom: the speaker communicates the fact that he is in an emotional state by saying that it came upon him, *sc.* a moment before speaking.' I have little doubt that this is right: it is the simplest explanation, and in keeping with the poem's vigorous directness. Two other possibilities, at least in theory, are gnomic aorist ('habitually flutters my heart') and ingressive aorist ('first fluttered my heart (and continues to do so)', i.e. 'first made me fall in love with you'). This last interpretation, favoured by Marcovich, seems to me difficult to understand in the context without any word for 'first'.

4. Is the antecedent of *to* in line 5 *gelaisas* or the whole clause from *ottis* to *imeroen*? If *eptoaisen* were an ingressive or gnomic aorist, the antecedent would have to be *gelaisas*.[1] If, as I believe, *eptoaisen* simply describes an immediate reaction, there is no clear way of settling the matter; but as I imply in my analysis, I do not see that we are forced to make a choice. Alternatively,

---

[1] This would not necessarily follow in the case of a gnomic aorist if Page's interpretation (b) of the relative *ottis* were accepted.

the matter may be put like this: the whole situation is disturbing to the poet, but the girl's laughter above all; the shape of the poem imposes this thought upon us, and once it is grasped, the precise syntactical function of *to* ceases to have an aesthetic importance.

Marcovich is in fact gravely embarrassed here, as Bonelli shows (p. 488f.). In order to exclude jealousy from the poem, it is vital for him that the reference of *to* be strictly confined to *gelaisas*, and Bonelli justly exclaims against the absurdity of resting an interpretation of the entire piece upon so tiny a syntactical nicety. The reader will not consent to be so confined: he will interpret unforcedly, in accordance with the context, and that context includes a man whose presence has been prominently indicated.

5. What is the nature of the speaker's emotion – envy, anxiety, jealousy, love? I am sure, again, that to put the question in this form is a mistake. Sappho conveys emotion, she does not analyse it; and though her account is amply suggestive, we should not expect to be able to give a clear-cut, one-word answer to the question 'Why does she have these symptoms?' any more than she could herself.[2] No account of the poem will be satisfactory which does not link the situation in the opening lines to the confession that follows. It is the emotion felt by Sappho at the sight of the girl conversing with a man that prompts her outburst. Does jealousy or envy play some part in creating the feeling of distress? A knowledge of human nature demands the answer yes; but the symptoms which follow are those of love as well. Horace, who may be supposed to have read Sappho with particular care and sympathy, understood her passion as one of mingled love and jealousy, as may be seen from his adaptation in *Cum tu, Lydia, Telephi*.[3]

6. The subjunctive of *idō* is iterative. Therefore, Marcovich argues, Sappho suffers the sensations described every time that she sees the girl, whether the man is there or not; therefore jealousy, anxiety or envy inspired by seeing the man and the girl together can play no part whatsoever in causing her symptoms. This is Marcovich's strongest point, and it deserves consideration, although his interpretation must be rejected on other grounds. Line 17, however, presents an objection to his argument: if Sappho collapses and feels close to death *every* time she sees the girl, it is odd of her to continue, 'But all can be endured . . . ' What we need is a single occasion from which she may hope to recover. This difficulty would make Marcovich's view suspect even if no alternative could be found to it.

Marcovich's argument can be met in either of two ways. The first is very simple, and I have little doubt that it is correct. Dover, however, adopts it only with hesitation; and in case that hesitation is shared, I add a second solution.

The first solution is that the iteration is limited to one occasion. 'Whenever I look at you' means not 'whenever I look at you at any time' but 'whenever I look at you now, while you and the man are together'. Here, as throughout the poem, our attention is concentrated on a specific incident; and there is, I

---

[2] It is of course legitimate for psychologists, historians and anthropologists to ask and answer this question, but what they are engaged upon is something quite different from aesthetic appreciation. Equally, the restrictions that psychoanalysts may wish for their own purposes to put upon such words as 'anxiety' and 'jealousy' are irrelevant here.

[3] *Carm.* 1. 13. Presumably Lucretius thought the same: he imitates Sappho's lines in order to describe the symptoms of fear (3. 154ff.).

suspect, an implicit contrast between Sappho's short, distracted glances at the girl and couple's continuous sitting and conversing.

The second solution is less clear cut. We might say that the sight of man and girl together prompt the poet's *confession* of her symptoms, and Marcovich's argument does not combat this claim. However, I would go further and maintain, against Marcovich, that we feel the effect of the man on the *nature* of the symptoms as well. After all, the iteration in *idō* is not stressed; to translate *ōs* by 'whenever' is to give the word an emphasis that it lacks in the Greek. If Sappho was disturbed on other occasions when she saw the girl, she was disturbed *par excellence* on the occasion when she saw her in company with the man. And we must allow that Sappho gets carried away by her own emotion: though she begins with feelings that she had at other times, by the end she is describing sensations that are probably meant to be unique in their violence. Certainly, the increasing intensity of her sensations is paralleled by a temporal movement from past to present, and in the third and fourth stanzas our attention is concentrated on the immediate moment of experience. This makes good poetry, even though it may not be altogether good logic. Besides, Sappho's sensations, though they are symptoms of love, are not symptoms of a happy and successful love. They are sensations of a kind found in first love or guilty love or unrequited love or when the lover is unsure whether he will be successful.[4] Timidity, anxiety and fear or jealousy of rivals usually, perhaps necessarily, form a part of such emotions. Lovers have traditionally claimed to be jealous of all who share the company of the beloved, including parents, relations and friends who cannot realistically be regarded as rivals; they even express envy of the inanimate objects with which the beloved comes into contact. The presence of a man does not change the nature of Sappho's emotion; it intensifies an element that is already present in it.

2. Sappho, fr. 105

Hermann Fränkel (p. 172n.) suggests that the similes in frs. 105a and 105c are meant to stand in contrast to each other, and that the latter describes an 'untended' girl who has lost her virginity before her marriage, unlike the bride in whose honour the epithalamium is written. I consider this interpretation unlikely for three reasons.

1. It is poetically inferior. The simile of the flower, on this account, ministers by force of contrast to the greater glory of the virgin bride; it thus loses the pathos which I would like to see in it, and the emotional tension created by the infusion of an element of regret into a poem of rejoicing.

2. Catullus is aware of no such contrast. At 62. 39ff. he uses the simile of the destruction of a flower to represent the bride on her wedding night; note especially the harshness of line 46 ('cum castum amisit polluto corpore florem'), crueller than anything in Sappho's fragment, and yet applied to the bride herself. (Compare too the very tender quality of his flower simile at lines 22–4.)

3. In fr. 114 Sappho herself treats the loss of virginity by a bride with the same feeling of regret that I attribute to her in fr. 105c, and which is certainly

---

[4] Cf. the anecdote in Plutarch *Demetr.* 38. Antiochus fell in love with his father's wife, and tried to suppress or conceal his passion, but a physician discovered the truth by observing in him the signs described by Sappho.

to be found in Catullus 61 and 62. The poem represented to us by fr. 104a may well have continued in a similar vein ('Evening, you bring the child back to her mother, but this girl you will never bring to her mother again . . .'). There is no parallel in the fragments to Fränkel's interpretation.

3. Catullus 64 and Virgil's Shield of Aeneas

Any account of a work of pictorial art is liable to go beyond rigidly literal description to what strictly can only be inferred: the movements and intentions of the people depicted, the sounds of voices or musical instruments, and so on. This tendency is already apparent in Homer's account of the Shield of Achilles and in the Shield of Heracles traditionally attributed to Hesiod. Where Catullus differs is in emphasising the illogicality and exploiting it for poetic ends; but in this too he may have had precedent of a kind of Theocritus' first Idyll. The goatherd begins explaining the scenes carved on his cup thus: 'And within *is wrought* a woman, such a thing as the gods might fashion, bedecked with cloak and circlet. And by her two men with long fair locks contend either side in *alternate speech*. Yet these things touch not her heart, but *now* she looks on one and smiles, and *now* to the other she *shifts* her thought . . .' (32–7, tr. A. S. F. Gow). Theocritus gives us what no single picture can give, a succession of actions; if this description came in the middle of his account, it would be less noticeable, but coming as it does immediately after words telling us that the woman is merely part of an artefact, it seems to draw attention to itself. The two other scenes are also full of animation and movement; they are like Catullus' picture, *short* spaces of time, caught and frozen. The fox is waiting to make a quick grab at the boy's wallet while his attention is distracted; the fisherman is just about to make his throw: 'The old man gathers up a great net for a cast as one that labours mightily. Thou wouldst say that he was fishing with all the strength of his limbs, so do the sinews stand out all about his neck' (40–3). The stress on extreme realism in a work of art is conventional enough; but by preceding it with the woman and her suitors, Theocritus may have meant to accentuate the paradox.

If Catullus learnt from Theocritus, he went far beyond his model; and we might expect his use of this motif to have made an impression on the most perceptive of his successors. I believe that it indeed did so. Commentators have tended to suppose that when Virgil came to describe the Shield of Aeneas (*Aen.* 8.626–728), he allowed himself to lose sight of the fact that he was dealing with a piece of metalwork, and used the opportunity to create a series of scenes from Roman history without troubling to reconcile them with the limitations of plastic art; but on close inspection this theory starts to look very implausible.

Again and again Virgil seems to go out of his way to remind us that the images on the shield are not reality. Like Catullus ('parte ex alia', line 251), he notes the positioning of the various scenes: 'nec procul hinc' (635), 'haud procul inde' (642), 'in summo (652), 'hic' (655), 'hic' (663), 'hinc procul' (666), 'haec inter' (671), 'in medio' (675), 'hinc' (678), 'parte alia' (682), 'hinc' (685), 'contra' (711), 'hic . . . hic . . .' (724f.). He also makes occasional references to the maker of the shield: 'fecerat ignipotens' (628), 'fecerat' (630), 'addiderat' (637), 'extuderat' (665), 'addit' (666), 'fecerat ignipotens' (710), 'finxerat' (726). Phrases of the form 'you might see', and other expressions of similar character, remind us that the images are not reality: 'indignanti *similem similemque* minanti/*aspiceres*' (649f.), 'ibat imago' (671), 'cernere erat' (676), 'videres' (676), 'credas' (691), 'videbatur' (707). Several times we are invited to note the material of the shield. Like the shields of Achilles and Heracles, it is evidently made of various metals: 'auratis volitans argenteus anser/porticibus' (655f.), 'aurea caesaries ollis atque aurea vestis' (659), 'imago/aurea' (671f.), 'argento clari delphines' (673), 'classis aeratas' (675), 'Mavors/caelatus ferro' (700f.). These details show us that the other references to colour, texture or gleaming light in the text are not casual (660f., 672, 677, 684, 695, 703, 709, 713, 720). Some of these descriptions, it is true, fit reality much more naturally than they fit the image, and are difficult to image in metal (for instance, the milk-white necks of the Gauls in line 660 or the blue sea flecked with white foam in line 672), but coming as they do so close to what are obviously descriptions of metalwork (the gold clothing of the Gauls at line 659, the golden sea of 671f.), it is clear that these oddities are deliberate on Virgil's part.

Faced with this battery of evidence, we may feel it paradoxical that P. T. Eden should write (on line 634) that 'Virgil was not at pains to describe the shield as a material object'. The passage which inspired this judgment deserves a closer examination.

fecerat et viridi fetam Mavortis in antro   630
procubuisse lupam, geminos huic ubera circum
ludere pendentis pueros et lambere matrem
impavidos, illam tereti cervice reflexa
mulcere alternos et corpora fingere lingua.

[He had represented the wolf as having laid herself down, after giving birth, in the green cave of Mars; hanging about her teats, twin boys were playing, and licking the mother without fear; she, with smooth neck bent back, was caressing them alternately and shaping their bodies with her tongue.]

Of course a relief cannot literally show the wolf licking first the one child and then the other; but if we think back to the goatherd's words in Theocritus, we may doubt whether a poet as thoroughly soaked in Hellenistic poetry as Virgil allowed the illogicality through mere indifference to the material object.[5] A small detail confirms this impression: why is the wolf's neck 'teres', smoothly rounded, when we would naturally expect it to be rough and hairy? The answer is surely that this is a metal wolf. Vulcan has caught the transitional moment at which the wolf turns *back* from one baby to the other (the compound in 'reflexam' is a fine, exact detail), and that is why our notice is drawn to the *curve* of her neck; what we are shown is clearly a *pose*. Virgil has chosen to say not 'the mother was licking them alternately', but '[Vulcan] fashioned the mother licking them alternately', and we should take him seriously. Like Catullus, Virgil enjoys the paradox; the maker has wrought the static object with such skill that he seems to the viewer's imagination to have represented successive actions.

---

[5] Virgil used this part of *Idyll* 1 as the basis for Menalcas' description of the wooden cup at *Ecl.* 3. 37ff.; so he would have known it well. The idea of alternation is prominent both in Theocritus and in *Aen.* 8.

Eden (loc. cit.) notes two other passages which are 'difficult to visualise in terms of static art'.

1. In line 695 the sea grows red with blood. The illogicality is less obtrusive here than in the earlier passage and most readers will probably not notice it; those who do can apply the same principle as with the wolf. The redness is in the metal (compare the blood-red sword at line 622); the process of reddening is supplied by the spectator's eager imagination. This line comes, perhaps significantly, in one of the passages where Virgil affects to be most excited by his theme.

2. At line 707f., 'The queen herself . . . was seen setting sail and on the very point of ['iam iamque'] letting the sheets run out loose' (Eden's translation). Why Eden finds 'iam iamque' inappropriate to static art I do not understand. On the contrary, by pinning down the precise moment that the artist had captured, the phrase emphasises that the scene is motionless.

Virgil has followed Catullus in imagining an artefact which struggles to escape from art into reality; everything, or almost everything, that he mentions is *formally* compatible with visual representation, but at some moments we will think more naturally of metalwork, at others of the actual events. The straining of the picture against its frame imparts life and energy to the whole, but at the same time Virgil also uses this idea as a structural principle, as a means of shaping his climaxes. For the greater part of the *ekphrasis* Virgil uses imperfect tenses to show that he is writing about frozen action (compare Catullus at line 251ff.); but in two places he bursts into the more vivid present. In both cases it is Augustus who inspires this enthusiasm. We see him first at the battle of Actium (line 678ff.); the present participles without a main verb make the transition from past to present tense almost imperceptible. The present tenses are maintained through the high excitement of the battle scene; then in line 704 our eyes are directed up to the figure of Apollo, the serene avenger, aiming his bow from above, and Virgil returns to the imperfect tense. At line 714 he moves on to the scenes of Augustus' triumph, and at line 720f., as we focus on the great man himself ('ipse'), the present tenses return.

The description of the shield is almost exactly divided between Augustus and the rest of Roman history. In one sense the pace is much faster in the first half, as we flash rapidly through a number of varied scenes; but Virgil counterbalances this by increasing the emotional pace in the second half. The Battle of Actium is the centrepiece of the shield, and the dramatic heart of Virgil's *ekphrasis*; and yet he continues to remind us throughout it that he is describing an image. The triumph of Augustus forms a climax of a different kind; the mood is less frenetic than in the account of Actium, but it is here if anywhere that the scenes escape from art into life. As in Catullus, there is a stress upon noise: the din of applause in the streets, choruses of women in all the temples (this is indeed difficult to visualise; how many temples are on the shield? and how do we see inside them?). In this passage the words indicating that the scenes are static representations disappear; the words 'hic . . . hic . . .' in line 724f. are in themselves perfectly compatible with reality, and it is only with the emphatic 'finxerat' at the beginning of line 726 before a heavy pause that we are jerked back to the remembrance of Vulcan's artistry.

Virgil's shield, like Catullus' tapestry, is a source of wonderment ('mira . . . arte', Cat. 64.51; 'miratur', *Aen.* 8.619 and 730). In both cases we are not given a precise description of the masterpiece, but a notion of it: Virgil closes his *ekphrasis* with the word 'talia' ('such things'), just as Catullus had written 'talibus ... figuris' at the corresponding point of his poem.[6] Virgil follows Catullus again in straining the possibilities of visual representation to their limits at the end of the *ekphrasis*. Where he differs is in making the jerk back to reality *just before* the very end; the last three lines, listing subjected peoples and rivers, conclude the description on a note of slight anticlimax.[7] Catullus had brought off the *coup de théâtre* at the end of his own *ekphrasis* with such mastery that Virgil would seem feebly derivative unless he made some variation, and in any case it is Virgil's habitual practice when imitating to imitate with a difference; but he may have had a more specific reason for what may seem momentarily an uninspired conclusion to the account of the shield. Virgil does not want simply to shatter the mood he has created as Catullus does; whereas Catullus shows us that Bacchus and Ariadne are merely embroidered symbols, the shield of Aeneas is symbol and reality in one. In the magnificent last line of the book the hero hoists upon his shoulder the fame and fate of his descendants; the shield is both literally a heavy weight of engraved and beaten metal and metaphorically the burden of Rome's destiny that Aeneas carries with him into the war against the Italians. The strife between art and reality acquires a new and profound meaning.

If this interpretation is accepted, it can hardly be doubted that Virgil learnt, here as elsewhere, from *Peleus and Thetis*, and the interpretation that I have offered of Catullus' poem is confirmed.

[6] A full description would be impossible, Virgil tells us: 'clipei non enarrabile textum', line 625.

[7] In ending with rivers at the far bounds of the civilised world, Euphrates, Rhine and Araxes, Virgil surely recalled that Homer ends the shield of Achilles with 'the river of Ocean'.

BIBLIOGRAPHY
Some works consulted

This list makes no claim to balance or completeness. It includes those works to which I have made more than a passing allusion in the text, together with a number of others from which I am conscious of having learned.

Bagg, Robert, 'Love, ceremony and daydream in Sappho's lyrics', *Arion* 3 no. 3 (1964), 44–82.

Bate, W. Jackson, *The Burden of the Past and the English Poet* (London, 1971)

Boissier, Gaston, *Tacite* (Paris, 1903)

Bonelli, Guido, 'Saffo, 2 Diehl = 31 Lobel-Page', *AC* 46 (1977), 453–94

Boucher, J.-P., 'A propos du Carmen 64 de Catulle', *RÉL* 34 (1956), 190–202

Bowra, C. M., *Greek Lyric Poetry: from Alcman to Simonides* (2nd edn, Oxford, 1961)

Bramble, J. C., 'Structure and ambiguity in Catullus LXIV', *PCPhS* 16 (1970), 22–41

Bremer, J. M., 'The meadow of love and two passages in Euripides' *Hippolytus*', *Mnem* 4th.s. 28 (1975), 268–80

Burnett, Anne, 'Desire and Memory (Sappho frag. 94)', *CP* 74 (1979), 16–27

Cairns, Francis, *Generic Composition in Greek and Roman Poetry* (Edinburgh, 1972)

Cameron, A., 'Sappho's prayer to Aphrodite', *HThR* 32 (1939), 1–17

Cameron, A., 'Sappho and Aphrodite again', *HThR* 57 (1964), 237–9

Carey, C., 'Sappho fr. 96 LP', *CQ* n.s. 28 (1978), 366–71

Carey, John, *The Violent Effigy: a study of Dickens' imagination* (London, 1973)

Castle, Warren, 'Observations on Sappho's *To Aphrodite*', *TAPhA* 89 (1958), 66–76

Chantraine, P., 'Grec *meilichios*', *Mélanges Boisacq* I (Brussels, 1937), 169–74

Clay, Diskin, 'Fragmentum Adespotum 976', *TAPhA* 101 (1970), 119–29

Coffey, Michael, *Roman Satire* (London, 1976)

Couat, Auguste, *Étude sur Catulle* (Paris, 1875)

Curran, Leo C., 'Catullus 64 and the heroic age', *YCS* 21 (1969), 169–92

Daniels, Marion L., ' "The Song of the Fates" in Catullus 64: epithalamium or dirge?', *CJ* 68 (1972), 95–101

De Decker, Josué, *Juvenalis declamans: étude sur la rhétorique déclamatoire dans les satires de Juvénal* (Ghent, 1913)

Devereux, George, 'The nature of Sappho's seizure in fr. 31 LP as evidence of her inversion', *CQ* n.s. 20 (1970), 17–31

Dover, K. J., *Greek Homosexuality* (London, 1978)

Du Bois, Page, 'Sappho and Helen', *Arethusa* 11 (1978), 89–99

Duff, J. D., *D. Iunii Iuvenalis saturae XIV* (new edn, with introduction by Michael Coffey, Cambridge, 1970)

Eden, P. T., *A commentary on Virgil: Aeneid VIII* (Leiden, 1975)

Elliger, Winfried, *Die Darstellung der Landschaft in der griechischen Dichtung* (Berlin and New York, 1975)

Ellis, Robinson, *A commentary on Catullus* (2nd edn, Oxford, 1889)

Fordyce, C. J. (ed.), *Catullus* (Oxford, 1961)

Fränkel, Hermann, *Early Greek Poetry and Philosophy*, tr. Moses Hadas and James Willis (Oxford, 1975)

Fraenkel, Eduard, *Horace* (Oxford, 1957)

Friedländer, Paul, *Johannes von Gaza und Paulus Silentiarius* (Leipzig and Berlin, 1912)

Galiano, Manuel F., *Safo* (Madrid, 1958)

Gehlen, J., *De Iuvenale Vergilii imitatore* (Göttingen, 1886)

Gentili, Bruno, 'La veneranda Saffo', *QUCC* 1.2 (1966), 37–62

Gerber, Douglas E., 'Studies in Greek Lyric Poetry: 1967–75', *CW* 70 (1976), 65–157

Giangrande, Giuseppe, 'Das Epyllion Catulls im Lichte des hellenistischen Epik', *AC* 41 (1972), 123–47

Gomme, A. W., 'Interpretations of some poems of Alkaios and Sappho', *JHS* 77 (1957), 255–66

Granarolo, Jean, *L'oeuvre de Catulle* (Paris, 1967)

Griffin, Jasper, 'Augustan poetry and the life of luxury', *JRS* 66 (1976), 87–105

Harmon, D. P., 'Nostalgia for the age of heroes in Catullus 64', *Latomus* 32 (1973), 311–31

Havelock, E. A., *The Lyric Genius of Catullus* (Oxford, 1939)

Highet, Gilbert, *Juvenal the Satirist* (Oxford, 1954)

Hoffmann-Loss, H., 'Die Bedeutung von ōra in Deduke men a selanna', *Mnem.* 21 (1968), 347–56

Hooker, J. T., *The Language and Text of the Lesbian Poets* (Innsbruck, 1977)

Howie, J. G., 'Sappho fr. 16 (LP): self-consolation and encomium', *Papers of the Liverpool Latin seminar 1976*, ed. Francis Cairns (Liverpool, 1977), 207–35

Howie, J. G., 'Sappho fr. 94 (LP): farewell, consolation and help in a new life', *Papers of the Liverpool Latin seminar second volume 1979*, ed. Francis Cairns (Liverpool, 1979), 299–342

Irwin, Eleanor, *Colour terms in Greek Poetry* (Toronto, 1974)

Kenney, E. J., 'The first Satire of Juvenal', *PCPhS* n.s. 8 (1962); 29–40

Kenney, E. J., 'Juvenal: Satirist or Rhetorician?', *Latomus* 22 (1963), 704–20

Kinsey, T. E., 'Irony and structure in Catullus 64', *Latomus* 24 (1965), 911–31

Kirkwood, G. M., *Early Greek Monody: the history of a poetic type* (Ithaca and London, 1974)

Klingner, Friedrich, *Catulls Peleus-Epos* (Munich, 1956)

Koniaris, George L., 'On Sappho, fr. 1 (Lobel-Page)', *Philologus* 109 (1964), 30–8

Koniaris, George L., 'On Sappho, fr. 16 (L.P.)', *Hermes* 95 (1967), 257–68

Koniaris, George L., 'On Sappho, fr. 31 (L.P.)', *Philologus* 112 (1968), 173–86

Konstan, David, *Catullus' Indictment of Rome: the meaning of Catullus 64* (Amsterdam, 1977)

Krischer, Tilman, 'Sapphos Ode an Aphrodite', *Hermes* 96 (1968), 1–14

Kroll, Wilhelm (ed.), *C. Valerius Catullus* (3rd edn, Stuttgart, 1959)

LaFleur, Richard A., 'Juvenal's "Friendly Fingernails"', *WS* n.s. 9 (1975), 230–5

Lanata, Giuliana, 'Sul linguaggio amoroso di Saffo', *QUCC* 1.2 (1966), 63–79

Lavagnini, Bruno, *Nuova antologia dei frammenti della lirica greca* (Turin, 1932)

Lefkowitz, Mary R., 'Critical Stereotypes and the Poetry of Sappho', *GRBS* 14 (1973), 113–23 (reprinted in *Heroines and Hysterics*, London, 1981)

Lenchantin de Gubernatis, M. (ed.), *Il libro di Catullo* (Turin, 1953)

Lesky, Albin, *A History of Greek Literature*, tr. James Willis and Cornelis de Heer (London, 1966)

Lobel, Edgar (ed.), *Sapphous melē: the fragments of the lyrical poems of Sappho* (Oxford, 1925)

Lobel, Edgar and Page, Denys (ed.), *Poetarum Lesbiorum Fragmenta* (Oxford, 1955)

Longo, Vincenzo, 'Aristofane e un'interpretazione di Saffo', *Maia* 6 (1953), 220–3.

Maas, Paul, 'Zum griechischen Wortschatz', *Mélanges Émile Boisacq* II (Brussels, 1938), 129–32.

McEvilley, Thomas, 'Sappho, fragment ninety-four', *Phoenix* 25 (1971), 1–11

McEvilley, Thomas, 'Sappho, fragment two', *Phoenix* 26 (1972), 323–33

McEvilley, Thomas, 'Sapphic imagery and fragment 96', *Hermes* 101 (1973), 257–78

McEvilley, Thomas, 'Sappho, fragment thirty-one: the face behind the mask', *Phoenix* 32 (1978), 1–18

Macleod, C. W., 'Two comparisons in Sappho', *ZPE* 15 (1974), 217–20

Marcovich, M., 'Sappho fr. 31: anxiety attack or love declaration?', *CQ* n.s. 22 (1972), 19–32

Marmorale, Enzo V., *Giovenale* (2nd edn, Bari, 1950)

Marry, John D., 'Sappho and the heroic ideal: *erōtos aretē*', *Arethusa* 12 (1979), 71–92

Marzullo, Benedetto, *Studi di poesia eolica* (Florence, 1958)

Mason, H. A., 'Is Juvenal a classic?', *Critical Essays on Roman Literature: Satire*, ed. J. P. Sullivan (London, 1963), 93–176

Merkelbach, Reinhold, 'Sappho und ihr Kreis', *Philologus* 101 (1957), 1–29

Mora, Édith, *Sappho: histoire d'un poète* (Paris, 1966)

Nisbet, R. G. M., 'Notes on the text of Catullus', *PCPhS* n.s. 24 (1978), 92–115

Otis, Brooks, *Virgil: a study in civilized poetry* (Oxford, 1964)

Page, Denys, *Sappho and Alcaeus: an introduction to the study of ancient Lesbian poetry* (Oxford, 1955)

Page, Denys, '*Deduke men ha selana*' [with a reply by A. W. Gomme], *JHS* 78 (1958), 84–6

Parry, Adam, 'Landscape in Greek poetry', *YCS* 15 (1957), 1–29

Pasquali, Giorgio, 'Il carme 64 di Catullo', *SIFC* n.s. 1 (1920), 1–23

Perrotta, Gennaro, *Saffo e Pindaro: due saggi critici* (Bari, 1935)

Privitera, G. Aurelio, *La Rete di Afrodite: studi su Saffo* (Palermo, 1974)

Putnam, Michael C. J., 'The art of Catullus 64', *HSPh* 65 (1961), 165–205 (reprinted in *Approaches to Catullus*, ed. K. Quinn (Cambridge and New York, 1972), 225–65)

Quinn, Kenneth, *Catullus: an interpretation* (London, 1972)

Quinn, Kenneth, *Catullus: the poems* (2nd edn, Basingstoke and London, 1973)

Reeve, M. D., review of D. F. S. Thomson (ed.), *Catullus: a critical edition* (Chapel Hill, 1978), *Phoenix* 34 (1980), 179–84

Robinson, David M., *Sappho and Her Influence* (London, 1925)

Rudd, Niall, *Lines of Enquiry: studies in Latin poetry* (Cambridge, 1976)

Rydbeck, Lars, 'Sappho's *Phainetai moi kēnos*', *Hermes* 97 (1969), 161–6

Saake, Helmut, *Zur Kunst Sapphos* (Paderborn, 1971)

Saake, Helmut, *Sappho-Studien* (Paderborn, 1972)

Schadewaldt, Wolfgang, *Sappho: Welt und Dichtung Dasein in der Liebe* (Potsdam, 1950)

Scott, Inez G., *The Grand Style in the Satires of Juvenal* (Northampton, Mass., 1927)

Serafini, Augusto, *Studio sulla satira di Giovenale* (Florence, 1957)

Silk, M. S., *Interaction in Poetic Imagery with Special Reference to Early Greek Poetry* (Cambridge, 1974)

Stanley, Keith, 'The Role of Aphrodite in Sappho Fr. 1', *GRBS* 17 (1976), 305–21

Treu, Max, *Sappho* (new edn, Munich, 1954)

Tsagarakis, Odysseus, *Self-expression in Early Greek Lyric, Elegiac and Iambic Poetry* (Wiesbaden, 1977)

Voigt, Eva-Maria (ed.), *Sappho et Alcaeus* (Amsterdam, 1971)

West, D. A., *The Imagery and Poetry of Lucretius* (Edinburgh, 1969)

West, M. L., 'Burning Sappho', *Maia* 22 (1970), 307–30

Wilamowitz-Moellendorff, Ulrich von, *Sappho und Simonides: Untersuchungen über griechische Lyriker* (Berlin, 1913)

Wilamowitz-Moellendorff, Ulrich von, *Hellenistische Dichtung in der Zeit des Callimachos* (2 vols, Berlin, 1924)

Wills, Garry, 'The Sapphic "Umwertung aller Werte" ', *AJPh* 88 (1967), 434–43

Wills, Garry, 'Sappho 31 and Catullus 51', *GRBS* 8 (1967), 167–97

Wiseman, T. P., *Catullan Questions* (Leicester, 1969)

Index of Passages Discussed

General Index